T. P Grinsted

Last Homes of Departed Genius

T. P Grinsted

Last Homes of Departed Genius

ISBN/EAN: 9783337029838

Printed in Europe, USA, Canada, Australia, Japan

Cover: Foto ©ninafisch / pixelio.de

More available books at **www.hansebooks.com**

RELICS OF GENIUS.

PREFACE.

PILGRIMAGES to the birthplaces and last homes of men of genius have ever been sources of refined interest, as well to the general wayfarer as to the visitor of a more reflective turn of mind. This feeling has, doubtless, its degrees of intensity; but there is no being within the pale of civilisation who is insensible to the delights of Poetry, Painting, and the Dramatic Art,* or indifferent to the fates and fortunes of their professors. They contribute more largely to our just appreciation of the better things of life than its mere enjoyment; their lives are full of vicissitudes, and are "constant in nothing but perpetual change;" and the recital of the salient points of their histories, it is reasonable to infer, must prove attractive to a large portion of readers.

The passion for visiting the burial-places of eminent persons has distinguished all ages. Our school-day

---

* The notices in this volume are mostly confined to Poets, Painters, and Players; but incidentally are mentioned other distinguished dead near whom they lie sleeping.

reminiscences carry us back to Cicero finding the tomb of Archimedes, in Sicily, covered with weeds; and our reading of yesterday tells us how the ruler of the Russian empire paid homage to the remains of the discoverer of the art of curing herrings, by commanding a monument to be erected over his grave. In like manner we venture to predict that all who are moved by a Poem, a Picture, or a Play, will feel interested in the contents of the present volume; and, should our vaticination be correct, a very numerous class of patrons will be the result.

Of the general interest of its subjects there can be no doubt, more especially as it relates, almost exclusively, to the genius of our own country. The object of our pilgrimage is to persuade the reader to accompany us to the depositories of the distinguished dead, commencing with the hallowed and stately Abbey and Cathedral of our metropolis; next to such of its churches or cemeteries as hold these venerated remains; and then ranging into the provinces, and far away to the picturesque abbey ruins, amid which sleeps the great master-mind of Scotland. Our plan is, first, to sketch the edifice or locality; then, standing by the tombs or graves, to glance at the busy lives of those who there lie sleeping, and thus to present to the reader their *first and last*:—

> " O Death, all eloquent! you only prove
> What dust we dote on."

In the several biographical sketches, impartiality has been aimed at, and not the indiscriminate encomium which is sought to be enjoined in the old maxim, *De mortuis nil nisi bonum.* Whilst the excellencies of the dead have been fairly estimated, the author has felt that the lessons of their lives would be incomplete were their failings omitted; for "our virtues would be proud if our faults whipped them not." Meanwhile, the latter have been leniently dealt with.

The tone of the following pages has little or none of the melancholy of either of the classes whose celebrities it seeks to commemorate. Their births, and the leading events of their lives, are here told as well as their resting-places, where, rather than seek to overwhelm the reader with gloom, we would enliven him with the brightness of hope. The feelings over these several "Relics" may be various, like the chequerwork of their existence; but honour is, in some degree, due to all; and

> "Praising what is lost,
> Makes the remembrance dear."

LIST OF ILLUSTRATIONS.

	PAGE
PART OF POETS' CORNER, WESTMINSTER ABBEY (*Frontispiece*).	
THE PAINTERS' GRAVES IN THE CRYPT OF ST. PAUL'S CATHEDRAL	69
TABLET TO EDMUND KEAN, RICHMOND CHURCH, SURREY	180
TOMB OF THE POET ROGERS, HORNSEY CHURCHYARD	196
MAUSOLEUM OF BURNS, DUMFRIES	260
TOMB OF SIR WALTER SCOTT, DRYBURGH ABBEY	272

CONTENTS.

	PAGE
WESTMINSTER ABBEY	1
Geoffrey Chaucer	4
Edmund Spenser	7
Francis Beaumont	8
Michael Drayton	9
Ben Jonson	10
Abraham Cowley	12
John Dryden	13
Sir John Denham	15
The Earl of Roscommon	16
James Macpherson	17
Nicholas Rowe	17
Joseph Addison	18
Matthew Prior	19
John Gay	21
Sir William Davenant	22
Samuel Johnson	23
David Garrick	25
John Henderson	26
Richard Brinsley Sheridan	27
Thomas Campbell	29
Richard Cumberland	31
G. F. Handel — Sir William Chambers — William Gifford	31

	PAGE
WESTMINSTER ABBEY continued—	
Adam, the architect— Old Parr	32
William Congreve	32
Thomas Betterton	34
Mrs. Anna Oldfield	35
Mrs. Bracegirdle	36
Mrs. Cibber	38
Mrs. Aphra Behn	38
Mrs. Barry	41
Spranger Barry	41
Samuel Foote	42
Mrs. Pope	44
Monuments to Butler, Shakspeare, John Kemble, Isaac Watts, Newton, Purcell, Kneller, Thomson, Goldsmith, Gray, Cowper, Mrs. Siddons, Mason, Southey, Wordsworth	46—48
Distant Graves of Pope, Swift, Cowper, Parnell, Waller, Collins,	

CONTENTS.

	PAGE
Young, Crabbe, Blair, Keats, Shelley, Burns, Allan Ramsay, Hogg, Scott	48, 49
ST. MARGARET'S, WESTMINSTER	49
William Caxton	50
Sir Walter Raleigh	51
John Skelton	53
Thomas May	54
Thomas Hull	55
Mrs. Bland	56
ST. MARY OVERIE	57
John Gower	60
John Fletcher	61
Edmund Shakspeare	62
Philip Massinger	63
CITY CHURCHES—Allhallows Barking, and the Poet Lord Surrey; St. Andrew Undershaft, and the Chronicler Stow; St. Catharine Cree, and the painter Holbein	64
ST. GILES, CRIPPLEGATE	65
Speed, the Chronicler—John Fox, the Martyrologist	66
John Milton	66
ST. PAUL'S CATHEDRAL	69
Sir Philip Sydney	72
John Donne	73
Sir Anthony Vandyck	76

	PAGE
ST. PAUL'S CATHEDRAL continued—	
Sir Joshua Reynolds	79
Benjamin West	80
James Barry	82
John Opie	83
Henry Fuseli	85
Sir Thomas Lawrence	85
J. M. W. Turner	86
Richard Suett	88
ST. BRIDE'S, FLEET-STREET	89
Wynkyn de Worde—Sackville, Earl of Dorset—Sir Richard Baker—Richard Lovelace	89
J. Ogilby—T. Flatman	90
Samuel Richardson	90
ST. ANDREW'S, HOLBORN	91
John Webster	92
Henry Neele	92
Thomas Chatterton	93
John Emery	95
PORTUGAL-STREET BURYING-GROUND	97
"Joe Miller"	97
TEMPLE CHURCH	99
Oliver Goldsmith	101
ST. CLEMENT DANES	104
John Lowen	105
Thomas Otway	106
Nathaniel Lee	107
William Oxberry	109
Dr. Kitchiner	111

CONTENTS.

	PAGE		PAGE
ST. PAUL'S, COVENT GARDEN	111	ST. GILES-IN-THE-FIELDS	133
		George Chapman	133
Samuel Butler	112	James Shirley	134
William Wycherley	114	Andrew Marvell	135
Thomas Southern	114	John Flaxman	137
Sir Peter Lely	115	ST. LEONARD'S, SHOREDITCH	138
Charles Macklin	115		
John Edwin	116	Richard Burbage	138
John Wolcot (Peter Pindar)	117	Richard Tarlton	139
		ST. LUKE'S, CHELSEA	139
"Joe Haines"	119	Sir Thomas More	139
Robert Wilkes	119	Thomas Shadwell	140
Edward Shuter	119	Henry Mossop	141
Robert Baddely	120	HOLY TRINITY, BROMPTON	141
William Farren	120	John Reeve	141
Thomas King	120	KENSINGTON CHURCH	143
Alexander Rae	121	George Colman the Elder	143
Michael Kelly	121		
Mrs. Davenport	121	George Colman the Younger	144
Grinling Gibbons	122		
Edward Kynaston	122	Mrs. Inchbald	144
ST. MARTIN'S-IN-THE-FIELDS	123	ST. MARY'S, PADDINGTON	145
		Mrs. Siddons	145
Nell Gwynne	123	B. R. Haydon	147
George Farquhar	125	William Collins	148
Mrs. Centlivre	125	ST. GEORGE'S, BLOOMSBURY	149
Charles Bannister	126	Richard Wroughton	149
John Bannister	127	Mrs. Glover	149
Robert Palmer	128	ST. JOHN'S, WATERLOO ROAD	150
Louis Francis Roubiliac	129		
ST. JAMES'S, PICCADILLY	130	Robert William Elliston	150
Mark Akenside	130	CAMDEN TOWN	151
Tom D'Urfey	131	Charles Dibdin	151
David Ross	132	ST. JAMES'S CHAPEL, PENTONVILLE HILL	151
ST. PETER'S, PIMLICO	132		
Richard Jones	132	Joseph Grimaldi	151

CONTENTS.

	PAGE
OLD ST. PANCRAS	152
Samuel Cooper	153
MARYLEBONE CEMETERY, FINCHLEY	154
Sir H. R. Bishop	154
BUNHILL FIELDS, CITY ROAD	155
Isaac Watts	155
John Bunyan—Daniel Defoe	156
Thomas Stothard—William Blake	157
KENSALL GREEN CEMETERY	158
Sydney Smith—Thomas Barnes	159
Allan Cunningham	160
Dr. Valpy — Andrew Ducrow—Sir A. Calcott—W. R. Daniell—Winthrop M. Praed—George Dyer—Thomas Hood — Mrs. Mountain — Thomas Cooke—Mrs. Fitzwilliam	162
John Liston — Charles Kemble	163
John Pritt Harley	164
NORWOOD CEMETERY	165
Davidge and Osbaldiston—Mrs. Waylett—Alexander Lee	165
Sir Thomas Noon Talfourd	167
Douglas Jerrold	167

	PAGE
DISTANT GRAVES	168
DULWICH	169
Edward Alleyn	169
CHISWICK	171
William Hogarth	171
De Loutherbourg — Kent—Sir John Chardin—Ugo Foscolo—Charles Holland	173
KEW	174
Thomas Gainsborough	174
Johnan Zoffanij	175
Jeremiah Meyer	177
RICHMOND	177
James Thomson	178
Edmund Kean	180
TWICKENHAM	183
Alexander Pope	184
Sir Godfrey Kneller	187
Mrs. Clive	188
TEDDINGTON	189
Mrs. Woffington	189
Paul Whitehead	190
HIGHGATE	191
Samuel Taylor Coleridge	191
EDMONTON	194
Charles Lamb	194
HORNSEY	196
Samuel Rogers	197
CROSTHWAITE	199
Robert Southey	200
RYDAL MOUNT	204
William Wordsworth	205
STRATFORD-UPON-AVON	207
William Shakspeare	208

CONTENTS.

	PAGE
DEPTFORD	215
Christopher Marlowe	215
DOVER	216
Charles Churchill	217
BEACONSFIELD	218
Edmund Waller	218
Edmund Burke	220
STOKE	221
Thomas Gray	221
WELWYN	225
Edward Young	225
EAST DEREHAM	228
William Cowper	228
HALES OWEN	231
William Shenstone	231
CHICHESTER CATHEDRAL	234
William Collins	235
HUCKNALL	238
George Gordon Byron	238
BROMHAM	244
Thomas Moore	244
TROWBRIDGE	249
George Crabbe	249
BATH ABBEY CHURCH	253
James Quin	255
GREYFRIARS, EDINBURGH	257
George Buchanan	258
Allan Ramsay	259
CANONGATE, EDINBURGH	259
Robert Fergusson	259
DUMFRIES	260
Robert Burns	260
ETTRICK	266
James Hogg	266
DRYBURGH	272
Sir Walter Scott	273
ADDENDA—	
ST. JAMES'S CHAPEL, HAMPSTEAD ROAD	281
George Morland	281
John Hoppner	284
ST. JAMES'S CHURCH, PICCADILLY	285
George Henry Harlowe	285
ST. JOHN'S WOOD CHAPEL, MARYLEBONE	286
Daniel Terry	287
John Jackson	287
KENSALL GREEN	289
John Braham	289
Madame Vestris	290
Madame Soyer	291
SOUTHWICK, NEAR BRIGHTON	291
Charles Mayne Young	292
ST. LEONARD'S-ON-SEA	293
Mrs. Nisbett	293
ALL SAINTS' CHURCH, CAMBRIDGE	295
Henry Kirke White	295
THE CONCLUSION AND THE FAREWELL	295

RELICS OF GENIUS.

WASHINGTON IRVING has truly said: "There is a voice from the tomb sweeter than song; there is a remembrance of the dead to which we turn even from the charms of the living." In contemplating the burial-places of those who have rendered themselves objects of regard, the mind is elevated and refined, and the memento raised is calculated to produce a train of thought tending to good. There are such graves—graves of goodness and of genius—to be pointed out even in a limited walk. Some may be unmarked; but the occupants, though slumbering under a nameless tomb, are not forgotten. The prostrate column and the fallen arch are crumbled by the footsteps of Time, and the very art by which they are raised is forgotten; but a great name is written in characters of more enduring vitality. The beautiful and the true pass from before our sight, but they do not wholly die away:

> "Die away? No! not all dead,
>   Seeds are there of light and truth;
> Not in vain the book outspread
>   Has been read by age and youth."

The warriors of old, on whichever side they were engaged, united after the struggle to do honour to the illustrious dead. In like manner we would wish, in our proposed visits, to add a tribute to those who have fought for the world's good, but have been vanquished by death. Such we esteem to be our poets, whose effusions have been described as streams which have kept the mental world green, and rendered it fruitful. To them has been awarded the corona of genius, and their graves are invested with peculiar interest.

However simple the memorial raised above the poet, it will attract more grateful attention than the costlier tomb by which it may be surrounded. Though the pedigree of the minstrel have no historic charm, the "cold curiosity" excited by the rich mausoleum will give place to warm and genial feeling at the shrine of the bard, whose stores of wisdom, clothed with the richness of language, were bequeathed to us as an inheritance; and we linger around his tomb as though it were that of one we had known and loved. The grave may long since have closed upon his lineaments, but his voice is still heard, and the intercourse between him and posterity will be ever new.

London—in which our earliest visits will be paid—is in itself a little world, and a volume is unfolded in the contemplation of its "map of busy life." In our present mission, however, we will turn from the crowded thoroughfares to the shrines around which Religion spreads a mystic sanctity, breathing of purity, of peace, and hope. We may there "tread the winding avenues of the past, pausing at many a forsaken niche."

Our first visit shall be to

WESTMINSTER ABBEY.

The site of this venerable structure was originally a most desolate spot, known as Thorney Island, being overgrown with brambles, and surrounded by water.

Tradition gives to the site a Temple of Apollo, destroyed by an earthquake in the fifth century. Sebert, King of the East Saxons, about 616, founded here a church, which was consecrated, according to a Romish legend, by St. Peter and a host of angels! About the same period, St. Paul's Church was founded by this King Sebert, and was known as the East, and St. Peter's as the West, Minster —the present name of the Abbey and its surrounding district. The western church having been nearly destroyed by the Danes, it was restored by Edgar in 958. Edward the Confessor pulled down this structure, which was probably of wood, and rebuilt the Abbey of stone with much magnificence, completing the same in 1066. One hundred and seventy-nine years subsequently, Henry III. conceived the idea of outdoing his predecessor, the pious Edward. For this purpose the Abbey was again pulled down, and reconstructed with a richer endowment. The work was continued by succeeding sovereigns, and Henry VII. finally added to it the beautiful chapel in which he sleeps.

In the Abbey thus commenced by the third Henry, what stores of wealth are to be found! Each step is hallowed with association, for slumbering around lie those whom England delights to honour—her best, her greatest men. Kings have walked through these aisles to receive a crown, and have again returned to mingle "dust to dust," even as the fifth Harry came after his long pilgrimage, bringing back the battered casque he wore at Agincourt. Here are the monuments of Editha and her husband the Confessor; the benevolent Matilda; the cherished Eleanor and her warlike Edward; the haughty Elizabeth, with her persecuted cousin, whose beauteous neck felt the blade at Fotheringay. No party contests are decided in these sacred precincts, and Chatham, Pitt, Fox, Canning, Wilberforce, Sheridan, Grattan, lie peacefully within a short distance of each other. But our present mission relates to "Poets, Painters, and Players." We therefore seek the chosen "Corner" with which our sons of song are so dearly allied:

> "Come, I'm counsel for the poets, enter ye the Court of Fame;
> Chaucer, Shakspeare, Milton, Dryden, answer each one to your name;
> Ye, that with unfailing genius bade humanity advance,
> With dominion in your voices, and with empire in your glance;
> Ye, that with heroic daring sought the people in distress,
> Seeking to o'erbridge the chasm 'tween their hopes and their success.
> Humanism more expansive, 'twas for *this* your genius strove,
> Equal justice for the lowest, equal laws, and federal love."

On entering the south transept of the Abbey, known as "Poets' Corner," we turn to the right, and the eye rests on one of the most interesting memorials on this renowned spot. The fine old piece of Gothic sculpture before which we stand is the tomb of the first poet buried in the Abbey,—

GEOFFREY CHAUCER.

This minstrel, who combined in himself qualities which rarely belong to one individual, stands out as one of the master-spirits of his age. To him we award the title of the "Father of English Poetry," ascribing to his genius the rise of the graceful art in this country. Chaucer was born in London, and in the reign of Richard II., or in the first year of that of his successor, was clerk of the king's works at Charing—the site of the present National Gallery, and once occupied by mews, which, from a very early period, were used for the reception of the royal falcons. Our poet was a frequent guest at the Palace of the Savoy, when possessed by John of Gaunt. Here were passed some of his happiest days, and here were composed some of his finest poems. But Chaucer had his troubles. He was connected with the struggle which arose between the sovereign and the city of London, having reference to the city's election of its own chief officer. But little is known of the details of this contest; but Chaucer was prominent amidst the popular party in the city, and for a time thought it wise to absent himself. In 1386 he ventured to return to London, and approval of his conduct was marked by his being returned to Parliament for Kent. Only think of a poet being returned as a county member! but this was in the fourteenth century. By this popular feeling, however, in favour of Chaucer, the ire of the government was roused against him, and he was, in consequence, deprived of his office of comptroller of the customs in the port of London, and was likewise arrested and sent to the Tower. Here he remained in confinement for three years, and touching are some of his lamentations: —"For riches, now I have poverty; for dignity, now am I imprisoned; instead of power, wretchedness I suffer; and, for glory of renown, I am now despised and fully hated." Chaucer regained his liberty in 1389, and was restored to his office. He was at one time clerk of the works at Windsor Castle, to which appointment Campbell thus makes reference :—

"But should thy towers in ivied ruin rot,
  There's one—thy inmate once—whose strain renown'd
Would interdict thy name to be forgot,
  For Chaucer loved thy bowers, and trod this very spot.
Chaucer—our Helicon's first mountain stream,
  Our morning star of song—that led the way
To herald the long-after coming beam
  Of Spenser's light and Shakspeare's coming day."

Chaucer died in 1400, but he left behind him (in his "House of Fame") a prophecy of the palace of glass in Hyde Park, in which the nations assembled in 1851. Three years later and its successor was reared at Sydenham, in which thousands have gazed upon the sculptured effigy of Geoffrey Chaucer.

The borough of Southwark possesses a relic of Chaucer. In the High-street is a gateway opening into the yard of the Tabard, which time has degenerated into the Talbot Inn. Here is still preserved somewhat of its ancient character, and the quaint wooden balcony, the grey walls, and the dingy balustrades speak of the ancient hostelrie at which the poet informs us he lay, nearly five hundred years since,—

"Redy to wenden on my pilgrimage
  To Canterbury with devout courage."

The Tabard of the fourteenth century stood upon this spot; and, although the buildings must have been frequently repaired, their general character has remained unaltered, whilst no proof exists of the inn ever having been pulled down. There are reasons, then, for supposing that, along portions of that gallery, Chaucer himself may have walked!

To return to Westminster Abbey. The second poet

buried here, on the other side of the entrance, is a worthy successor to the first—

EDMUND SPENSER,

the author of the "Faërie Queen," whose monument has the following short but beautiful inscription:—" Here lies, expecting the second coming of our Saviour Christ Jesus, the body of Edmund Spenser, the prince of poets in his time, whose divine spirit needs no other witness than the works which he left behind him." Spenser, like his great predecessor, was born in London about 1553. It is probable that his parents were in humble circumstances, though he was connected with the noble family of the Spensers of Althorp, in Northamptonshire. Gibbon exhorted this distinguished family to "consider the 'Faërie Queen' as the most precious jewel in their coronet." It would seem to be so considered, for in the library at Althorp there is a portrait of Spenser with the following inscription:—

"The glorie of the noble house."

Chaucer has been designated the "day starre" and Spenser the "sunrise" of English poetry. The latter, whilst at Cambridge, gave evidence of poetic genius. Quitting the University, he became for some time a tutor in the family of a relative, and married an accomplished lady, to which circumstance we owe many of his sweetest poems. It was in Ireland that he wrote his "Faërie Queen," which "became at once the delight of every accomplished gentleman, the model of every poet, the solace of every scholar." From Ireland the poet escaped with difficulty the flames lighted by an infuriated mob, and in which one of his children perished. Returning to England, he closed his days in King-street, Westminster. Ben Jonson says he " died for lake of bread," refusing " twenty pieces sent to him by my Lord of Essex, adding, ' he was sorry he had no time to spend them.' "

Spenser had many patrons—Sir Philip Sydney, Raleigh, Leicester, and Essex being among the number. Let us, therefore, encourage the hope that Jonson had been misinformed, and that the last hour of the poet was less darkened than his fearful statement would infer. The expense of Spenser's funeral was defrayed by his patron Essex, his hearse being attended, says Camden, " by poets and mournful elegies and poems, with the pens that wrote them, thrown into his tomb : "

> " What though pale penury may haunt the spot
> That genius hallows with its earliest flame,
> Correggio lives while princes are forgot—
> The canvas speaks when kingdoms lose their name."

FRANCIS BEAUMONT

became the third tenant of " Poets' Corner." Descended from an ancient family in Leicestershire, and completing his education at Cambridge, he was entered as a student in the Inner Temple, but forsook the law to enter the service of the Muses. Associated with him in friendship and in literature was John Fletcher, with whom he flourished as a dramatist in the seventeenth century. They resided on the Bankside, the same house and the same clothes serving the purpose of both. The grave of Fletcher, who sleeps apart from his friend, will be visited " anon, anon, sir." It was on the 9th of March, 1615, that Francis

Beaumont was interred in the sacred spot around which we linger. No memorial or inscription points out his resting-place, which is before the entrance of St. Benedict's Chapel, immediately behind the monument of Chaucer. Calling to mind a friendship at once touching and beautiful, we cannot but regret that the ashes of Fletcher are not beneath the pavement on which we stand.

Beaumont was followed to the " Corner " by

MICHAEL DRAYTON,

who was born in Warwickshire, in 1563, and studied at Oxford. But little is known of his after-career. He lived for some time in the family of the Earl of Dorset, the lord chamberlain of his sovereign. Drayton's " Pollyollion," though full of fine poetry, is now but little read. His monument was erected by the Countess of Dorset, who likewise raised the tablet which perpetuates the memory of Spenser. Drayton's tomb has a beautiful inscription, though Time, in defacing the same, has denied to the marble the fulfilment of the pious wish expressed. Gossiping John Aubrey informs us that Marshall, the stonecutter, told him the inscription was supplied by Quarles; but it would appear to have been written by Ben Jonson, being generally inserted in his collected works. The now almost obliterated lines are as follow:—

> " Do, pious marble, let thy readers know
> What they and what their children owe
> To Drayton's name, whose sacred dust
> We recommend unto thy trust.
> Protect his memory and preserve his story,
> Remain a lasting monument of his glory.

> And when thy ruins shall disclaim
> To be the treasury of his name,
> His name, that cannot fade, shall be
> An everlasting monument to thee."

Drayton died in 1631, and, six years later, a funeral train was seen approaching the Abbey with the remains of

"O RARE BEN JONSON!"

Such is the quaint epitaph to be seen beneath a tablet, with a head in relief of the poet, on entering "Poets' Corner." It is in the north aisle of the nave, however, near to the monument of Killigrew, that Jonson sleeps. He is supposed to have been born at Charing Cross, near to where Craig's Court now stands. At all events, he resided there when very young. Fuller says: "I cannot, with all my industry, trace him to his cradle, but I can fetch him from his long coats. When a little child he lived in Hartshorn Lane, Charing Cross, where his mother married a bricklayer for her second husband. He was first bred in a private school in St. Martin's Lane, and then in Westminster School." To the latter he was removed by Camden (the antiquary, and master of the school), who not only became his instructor, but his friend. His next advancement was to Cambridge, where he drank deep of the learning for which he had thirsted when at the more humble school in St. Martin's Lane. Returning to London, he doubtless followed for a time the calling of his second father, and which drew upon him in after years the "lime-and-mortar" reproach. But genius triumphed over these opposing circumstances, and "Young Ben" ultimately became the companion of Shakspeare, Camden (whose effigy is looking down upon us from the opposite wall), Selden, Raleigh, Beaumont and Fletcher, Donne, and the master-minds of the age of "Eliza and our James." When the last-named sovereign was on the throne Jonson was imprisoned, with Chapman and Marston, for an alleged libel against the Scots in their play of *Eastward Ho!* From this incarceration, however, Jonson was soon released, and subsequently received the appointment of poet laureate. Disease and penury ultimately overtook him, and in his later days he appears to have resided in an alley, if we may judge from his answer to Charles I., who had sent him but a small sum after much delay. " I suppose he sends me this," said Jonson, " because I live in an alley. Tell him his soul lives in an alley." Jonson's literary life extended over forty years, and in the main was a successful one. From Aubrey we gather the precise place of our poet's sepulture. " He lies buried in the north aisle, in the path of square stone (the rest is lozenge), opposite to the scutcheon of Robertus de Bos, with this inscription only on him, in a pavement square, blue marble, about fourteen inches square : ' O rare Ben Jonson !' which was done at the charge of Jack Young (afterwards knighted), who, walking there when the grave was covering, gave the fellow eighteenpence to cut it." At the late relaying of the pavement, this stone was unfortunately removed.

Leaving Jonson to ruminate upon the "wit combats" once maintained by him with his less classical but great rival, Shakspeare, we turn to a tomb near to Chaucer and Spenser, and read the name of

ABRAHAM COWLEY.

This learned poet was born in London, in 1618, his father being an engrosser and law-stationer in Fleet-street. Westminster School witnessed some of his boyhood gambols, and Cambridge his maturer studies. At the University he acquired much literary distinction, and subsequently entered the field of contention, engaging himself in the royal cause. From this circumstance his earlier career was considerably chequered, and there was likewise an absence of steadiness in his purpose, which occasionally led him into difficulties, even with those who distinguished themselves by their devotion to the cause of the Stuarts. At the Restoration he returned to this country, after a residence in France, and eventually took up his abode at Chertsey, in Surrey; and here, in 1667,

"The last accents flowed from Cowley's tongue."

At one time his name was placed with the most eminent of the poets, but his writings are now held in much less estimation. According to Johnson, " he contented himself with a deciduous laurel, of which the verdure in its spring was bright and gay, but which time has been continually stealing from his brows." Evelyn attended the funeral of this poet, which is thus described by him :—" Went to Mr. Cowley's funeral, whose corpse lay at Wallingford House, and was thence conveyed to Westminster Abbey in a hearse with six horses and all funeral decency, near a hundred coaches of noblemen and persons of quality following—among these all the wits of the town, divers bishops and clergymen. He was interred next Geoffrey

Chaucer, and near Spenser. A goodly monument since erected to his memory." The Latin inscription on this monument, which was raised by George, Duke of Buckingham, declares the poet to have been the Pindar, Horace, and Virgil of England. From this friendly eulogy the eye turns to a noble bust, beneath which is inscribed the simple inscription,—

"J. DRYDEN."

Yes! this is the grave of "Glorious John," to which, after a life of much neglect, he was accompanied by mourners on horseback, twenty mourning coaches (each drawn by six horses), a multitude of other equipages—an ode of Horace being sung, with an accompaniment of trumpets, hautboys, and other instruments! The Athenians of old were reproached for the indifference they exhibited to their great men while living, and for the profuse adulation they bestowed on their memories when dead. England has occasionally committed the same sin, forgetting her poet when living, but seeking to atone for the neglect by posthumous honours. "It is strange," said Thomas Moore, writing home to his mother on his earliest introduction to London, "that people who value the *silk* so much should not feed the poor *worm* who wastes himself in spinning it out to them."

Dryden was born at Aldwinkle, in Northamptonshire, in August, 1631. He received his rudimentary education at Westminster School, under Dr. Busby, and was elected (1650) to a Westminster scholarship at Cambridge. On the death of Cromwell, Dryden became a candidate for public fame by publishing some heroic stanzas. These appeared in 1659, and three years later he produced his first play, *The Wild Gallant*. On the death of Davenant, Dryden received the appointment of poet laureate—his rising popularity gaining him the envy of the profligate Rochester, and the lion's share of the satire contained in the Duke of Buckingham's "Rehearsal." Becoming a convert to the Church of Rome, on the accession of the second James, Dryden was disqualified for the laureateship, and abuse of a most violent and personal nature was continually heaped upon him. His subsequent life was passed in writing for the means of support. He lived for some years in Gerrard-street, Soho,* a street in which Burke resided some seventy years afterwards. The poet was accustomed to visit Will's coffee-house, in Bow-street, at that time the great resort of wits and critics. Pope, when a boy, was taken there to see Dryden, for whom he conceived admiration, which was encouraged by him during the remainder of his life. Upon any literary dispute, appeal would be made to Dryden, and the young wits of the day deemed it a great honour to take a pinch of snuff from his box. Dryden died on the 1st of May, 1700, leaving behind him twenty-six plays and innumerable other productions.

Conflicting judgments have been pronounced upon the

* Leigh Hunt, speaking of some literary localities in the metropolis, says: " I once had duties to perform which kept me out late at night, and severely taxed my health and spirits. My path lay through a neighbourhood in which Dryden lived; and though nothing could be more common-place, and I used to be tired to the heart and soul of me, I never hesitated to go a little out of the way, purely that I might pass through Gerrard-street, and so give myself the shadow of a pleasant thought."

rank to be assigned to Dryden as a poet; but a very general verdict has awarded him a high place, even above all his contemporaries, to which position he has been principally elevated from his strength of thought and diction. Johnson says of him : "Perhaps no nation ever produced a writer that enriched his language with such variety of models. To him we owe the improvement, perhaps the completion, of our metre ; the refinement of our language, and much of the correctness of our sentiments." Though severely lampooned in his day, he appears to have been a man possessing much kindliness of heart. "He was," says Congreve, "of a nature exceedingly humane and compassionate, ready to forgive injuries, and capable of a sincere reconciliation with those who had offended him." Dryden's monument was erected, twenty years after his death, by Sheffield, Duke of Buckingham. The mention of the poet's friend and patron brings to remembrance Pope's couplet,—

"This Sheffield raised: the sacred dust below
Was Dryden's once; the rest who does not know?"

Beneath the pavement, in front of Dryden's monument, lies the author of " Cooper's Hill,"—

SIR JOHN DENHAM,

who was born at Dublin in 1615, and was educated at Trinity College, Oxford ; being there, it is said, " given more to cards and dice than study." Removing to Lincoln's Inn, he divided his attention between law and poetry. In 1642 he attracted notice by the publication of " The Sophy," upon which Waller remarked " that he broke out like the Irish Rebellion, threescore thousand strong, when nobody was aware, or in the least suspected it." During the Civil Wars he was engaged in several employments on behalf of the royal family, and for a time resided in France with the exiled king. The Restoration placed in his hands some rewards for his services; but domestic affairs brought upon his later years much disquiet. Denham died on the 19th of March, 1668, his remains being placed here seven days subsequently beneath a nameless stone. The old gossip Aubrey says: " He was of the tallest, but a little incurvetting at his shoulders, not very robust. His hair was but thin and flaxen, with a moist colour. His gait was slow, and was rather a stalking (he had long legges). His eye was a kind of light goose gray, not big, but it had a strange piercingness." In better taste is it written :

"On Cooper's Hill eternal wreaths shall grow,
While lasts the mountain, or while Thames shall flow!
Here his first lay majestic Denham sung."

A few years later, Westminster Abbey received another poet familiar with the court, and who, like Denham, was born in Dublin. This was

THE EARL OF ROSCOMMON,

whose uncle and godfather was the unfortunate Strafford. Having passed some time in Normandy and Italy, Roscommon returned to England at the Restoration, and became master of the horse to the Duchess of York, and "busied his mind with literary projects." He was interred here on the 21st of January, 1684, some sixteen days before the death of Charles II. Pope has celebrated Roscommon as the only moral writer in the reign of that sovereign. His greatest work is his " Essay on Translated Verse." Johnson says : " He improved taste if he did not enlarge knowledge, and may be numbered among the benefactors to English literature."

> " Such was Roscommon, not more learn'd than good,
> With manners generous as his noble blood :
> To him the wit of Greece and Rome was known,
> And every author's merit but his own."

Not far from Denham, under a plain blue stone, nearer the centre of the transept, lie the remains of Macpherson, to whom is now generally awarded the authorship of the poems given to the world as the productions of Ossian.

Memorials of our poets are still numerous around us. In the corner behind the screen, which faces the door, we find one raised to

NICHOLAS ROWE.

Like Jonson, Cowley, and Dryden, from whose tombs we have just passed, this writer was a Westminster scholar. Born in Bedfordshire, his education was commenced at Highgate, from whence he was removed to the school located near the place of his final rest. He was entered of the Middle Temple, became under-secretary of state and poet laureate to George I. He died on the 6th of November, 1718, at the age of forty-five, leaving behind him eight plays, and gaining from Pope the following epitaph :—

> " Thy reliques, Rowe, to this sad shrine we trust,
> And near thy Shakspeare place thy honour'd bust.
> Oh, next him skill'd to draw the tender tear,
> For never heart felt passion more sincere ;

With nobler sentiments to fire the brave,
For never Briton more disdain'd a slave!
Peace to thy gentle shade, and endless rest,
Blest in thy genius, in thy love, too, blest;
And blest that timely from our scene removed,
Thy soul enjoys that liberty it loved."

A few months after the burial of Rowe the Abbey received the remains of

JOSEPH ADDISON,

an ornament to polite literature, who was born in Wiltshire, in 1672, and held various offices under government. He is most justly regarded as a man of high literary attainments; and his chaste imagination, correct sentiment, and graphic power are displayed in the " Spectator " and its kindred paper " The Tatler." Who has not heard of and admired Sir Roger de Coverley, who, " when he was in town, lived in Soho Square ?" The portrait of this fine old English gentleman is to be found in thirty of the " Spectator's " papers, of which number twenty are ascribed to Addison, two to Budgell, and eight to Steele (the schoolfellow of Addison at the Charter House), Addison exercising a rigid and harmonising vigilance over the entire. Sir Roger accompanied the Spectator to the Abbey, in which our thoughts are now centred, and recorded this reflection : " When I see kings lying by those who deposed them—when I consider rival wits placed side by side, or the holy men that divided the world with their contests and disputes—I reflect with sorrow and astonishment on the little competitions, factions, and debates of mankind."

During Addison's last illness he sent for the poet Gay, who had not visited him for some time previously, and told him that he (Addison) had injured him, but that if he recovered he would make him full amends. What this injury was he did not explain, nor did Gay himself ever know. Addison did not recover; but in Gay's kindliness of heart we have an assurance that his friend was forgiven. The rival wits sleep peacefully beneath the same roof:

> "The passions which inspirit youthful hearts,
> And spread a beauty o'er the spring of life,
> And bid the hopes of young ambition bound,
> Decay and cool as further down the vale
> Of darkling years we wend; until at length
> The time-worn spirit muses on the tomb
> With elevating sadness, and the shades
> Of death dissolve amid those cheering rays
> Which revelation sheds from heaven."

Addison died at Holland House on the 17th of June, 1719, having previously sent for his dissolute son-in-law (Lord Warwick), that "he might see how a Christian could die." He lies buried in the north aisle of Henry VII.'s Chapel; a full-length statue by Westmacott, on a circular pedestal, is to be found in the " Corner."

Two years after the interment of Addison, there was brought to this transept all that was mortal of

MATTHEW PRIOR.

Another Westminster boy! not trained, however, by Ben Jonson's kind preceptor, Camden, but by the venerated Dr. Busby, whose beautifully-sculptured monument is to be found to the right, as you cross to the screen of the choir.

Losing his father at an early age, Prior was transferred to the care of an uncle, who then kept the Rummer Tavern, the site of which is in the rear of No. 14, Charing Cross. By this uncle was Matthew sent to Westminster School. Returning to his uncle's abode, he was one day discovered by the Earl of Dorset reading Horace at the window of the Rummer Tavern; and by this nobleman's kindness he was enabled to study four years at Cambridge. Matthew Prior subsequently rose to distinction both as a poet and as a diplomatist. He became a member of the senate—appending to his own name his own initials—and was likewise employed as an ambassador; but after narrowly escaping an impeachment, these honours flew away, leaving him to begin the world afresh, with an exchequer minus the cost of a dinner! He had now reached the age of fifty-three, but abilities and friends were still his own. Milton sold his divine epic for a few pounds; but Prior, from a publication of his own poems, realised £4000. Fortunate poet! A similar sum to that produced by his compositions was presented him by the Earl of Oxford, which enabled him to purchase an estate in Essex, where he passed the remainder of his days. Prior left £500 for a monument, which few can fail to perceive on entering "Poets' Corner."

Prior at one time resided in Duke Street, Westminster, where he was frequently visited by Swift. In the poet's "Extempore Invitation to Lord Oxford," he says,—

> "Our wealthy friends to-morrow meet
> At Matthew Prior's, in Duke Street,
> To try, for once, if they can dine
> On bacon, ham, and mutton chine."

Returning to Rowe's monument behind the screen facing the doorway, we discover adjoining it a memorial to the poet who, in point of time, followed Prior to his resting-place. It is the grave of

JOHN GAY,

to which he was borne in 1732, at the early age of forty-four. Descended from an ancient family in Devonshire, he was early in life placed in the shop of a mercer in the Strand, which he quitted for the study of literature. On the death of Queen Anne he returned to England, after a residence in Hanover; read his manuscript play of *The Captive* to Queen Caroline; and dedicated his " Fables," by permission, to the Duke of Cumberland. Gay's *Beggar's Opera* subsequently brought him more substantial compliments. He failed to make a fortune, like Prior, but led a comfortable life with his noble patrons, the Duke and Duchess of Queensbury, at whose mansion he died on the 17th of December, 1732. Gay's kindliness and good humour gained him the love of all, and he is characterised

"Of manners gentle, of affections mild,
In wit a man, simplicity a child."

He was the favourite correspondent of Pope and Swift; and when the news of his death was conveyed to the latter he was afraid to open the letter containing the information (having a presentiment of its contents), and carried it about with him for some days!

We have tarried thus long amid the monuments of

"The poets, who on earth have made us heirs
Of truth and pure delight in deathless lays;"

and now turn for a few moments from their sculptured effigies to gaze upon the pavement beneath us.

Who is it sleeping there? Could the grave give back its answer, we should incline our ear to the hallowed stone, and from its deep recesses would come a gentle voice whispering of Davenant, Johnson, Garrick, Henderson, Sheridan, Cumberland, Campbell. The " Poets and the Players" are, indeed, here together.

The first-named in the response which the grave, could it speak, would give us,

SIR WILLIAM DAVENANT,

was born at Oxford in 1605, and early in life showed promise of a lively genius. In 1629 he produced a tragedy, and on the death of Ben Jonson the poet-laureateship was conferred upon him. In 1641, however, he was arrested on a charge of seducing the army from its adherence to parliamentary authority, but, obtaining bail, he withdrew to France. Returning at length to England, he signalised himself at the siege of Gloucester, and was knighted by the king. During the disastrous period which followed, Sir William was constantly involved in difficulties, being at one time a prisoner in the castle at Cowes, from whence he was removed to the Tower of London. When the storm partly subsided, Davenant was found making an attempt to revive the drama, which had met serious rivals in the ranks of fanaticism. At the Restoration he obtained a patent for the representation of dramatic pieces, and the theatre again looked out upon cheering days. He continued at the head of his comedians until his death, in 1668, and left behind him twenty-six plays. As a man he was much beloved; and his remains, upon interment in the Abbey, were covered by a stone, on which was inscribed, in imitation of the epitaph on Ben Jonson, " O rare Sir William Davenant ! "

We must still loiter upon such a pavement as the one on which we stand; and, though no Boswell is of the party, our next gossip shall be of

SAMUEL JOHNSON.

The 18th of September, 1709, witnessed the birth of this giant of literature, who was the son of a country bookseller, and was born at Lichfield, where he received the preliminaries of an education completed at Oxford. From the misfortune which befell his parent, he quitted Pembroke College without a degree, and became for a time the usher of a school. He subsequently opened an academy near to his native city, but with Garrick, his pupil—now sleeping by his side—he ultimately came to London :

> " Here come two
> Less feverish, less exalted, soon to part—
> A Garrick and a Johnson : wealth and fame
> Awaiting one, even at the gate; neglect
> And want the other."

Poverty became the companion of Johnson, who, in his earlier day, was ashamed to appear at the dinner-table of his publisher, on account of his threadbare coat, and was content to devour his platter of food behind a screen! Genius, however, will rise superior to circumstances. Men of the highest renown have built their own fame—poverty, want of education, and opposition of every kind disappearing before the human mind, and becoming stepping-stones to fame. It has been said that " Genius has rarely arrived at the Promised Land without first marching through the Red Sea, lingering for awhile in the wilderness, and crossing the Jordan. She has been pursued by the Egyptians, refused hospitality by Edom, and cursed by Balaam; and yet has triumphed in spite of all!" In this way Johnson ultimately triumphed, his success being only obtained after long adversity. He possessed gigantic strength of body and mighty powers of mind, and has left upon posterity a strong and vivid impression. His distinguished career terminated in 1783, when literature was deprived of a successful cultivator, and virtue of a steady supporter. London has many places which retain a recollection of Johnson, his respective residences having exceeded a dozen. We should scarcely expect, however, to encounter memories of him in the brewery of Messrs. Barclay and Perkins. Such, nevertheless, are there to be found. The great moralist was one of the executors of Mr. Thrale, the original possessor of the brewery; and Boswell relates that, " when the sale of Thrale's brewery was going on (which fetched £135,000), Johnson appeared bustling about with an inkhorn and pen in his button-hole like an exciseman; and, on being asked what he really considered to be the value of the property which was to be disposed of, said, ' We are not here to sell a parcel of boilers and vats, but the potentiality of growing rich beyond the dream of avarice.'"

Our thoughts wandered first, as in duty bound, to the tutor; but the pavement on which we loiter was, in point of time, raised first to receive the remains of the pupil,—

DAVID GARRICK.

This celebrated actor was born at Hereford on the 20th of February, 1716, his father having been a captain of the Old Buffs. Whilst at a grammar-school in Lichfield he evinced his predilection for the stage by performing Sergeant Kite in *The Recruiting Officer*. After a visit to Lisbon Garrick returned to Lichfield, and became the pupil of Johnson, with whom he started for London on the 2nd of March, 1736. At first he thought of the law, and became connected with Lincoln's Inn ; other pursuits followed, but all were at length forsaken for the stage. His first trial in London was made at the theatre in Goodman's Fields, on the 19th of October, 1741, in the character of Richard III. After a few nights he became a favourite with the town, and from the distant East he was soon invited to Drury Lane and Covent Garden. He reached the highest step of the dramatic ladder, and ultimately became sole manager of Drury Lane, which he conducted until his retirement from the stage, June 10th, 1776, his farewell performance being Don Felix, in *The Wonder*.

Garrick has been declared the most complete actor that ever trod the British stage. He died at his residence on the Adelphi Terrace, on the 20th of January, 1779, at the age of sixty-three, when the stern moralist, Johnson, remarked that the gaiety of nations was eclipsed. His remains were honoured with a sumptuous funeral, being followed to the Abbey by "troops of ·friends," the list including Samuel Johnson, Sheridan (chief mourner), and Richard Cumberland. These were indeed friends, honouring his remains when they were on their transit to the tomb, and finally lying down by their side. They rest beneath this pavement!

> "If manly sense; if nature link'd with art;
> If thorough knowledge of the human heart;
> If powers of acting, vast and unconfined;
> If fewest faults with greatest beauties join'd;
> If strong expression and strange powers, which lie
> Within the magic circle of the eye;
> If feelings which few hearts like his can know,
> And which no face so well as his can show,
> Deserve the preference—Garrick, take the chair,
> Nor quit it till thou place an equal there."—CHURCHILL.

JOHN HENDERSON,

honoured with interment in the midst of such goodly company, was an actor of great talent, which paled only before the brilliance of Garrick's reputation. Henderson was born in Cheapside in 1746, and his earliest histrionic attempt was made upon the boards of the Bath Theatre in 1772. The "little theatre" in the Haymarket introduced him to the metropolitan playgoers in 1777, the same year marking his *entrée* upon the more lordly stage of Drury Lane. From this period until the time of his death (1785) he continued an honour to the stage and to the society into which he was welcomed. This gifted actor, during Lent, gave readings at Freemasons' Tavern, and frequently amongst the delighted auditory were to be encountered the manly figure of John Kemble, with the graceful form of his incomparable sister, Mrs. Siddons, both of whom the Abbey seeks to perpetuate by statues. Henderson died before he had reached his fortieth summer, and when the partial shade into which he had been cast by the refulgence of Garrick was gradually passing away. George III. once witnessed his performance of Benedick, which afforded him so much pleasure that he forwarded to the favoured actor the message : " If the king were manager of a theatre, Mr. Henderson would perform upon the same boards with Mrs. Siddons."

Garrick, we have said, lies on one side of Johnson. On the other side repose the remains of

RICHARD BRINSLEY SHERIDAN.

This distinguished writer and orator was born in Dublin, but was brought to England at an early age, and was placed at Harrow School. Upon the completion of his studies he was entered at the Middle Temple. The law occupied, however, but little of his attention, and before reaching his twentieth year he assisted in the translation of some epistles from the Greek ; whilst prior to his twenty-fourth birthday, he had produced his first play, *The Rivals*. Sheridan subsequently became a part proprietor of Drury Lane Theatre, and entered a parliament enlightened by the brilliancy of Burke, and which owned the sway of Pitt and Fox. In his first efforts in the Commons, Sheridan was unsuccessful, and was counselled to seek again the more congenial atmosphere of Drury Lane. There was less of bitterness in this reverse than that which fell to the share of some of his gifted compeers : insolence, for example, was once heaped upon Canning, and sneers met the early wisdom of Burke. In the case of Sheridan perseverance ultimately wrought success, and he became, as an orator, finished and varied. Sheridan's wit was eminently brilliant; but, like much of his speaking, it was doubtless prepared. Being unexpectedly called upon to say grace at a public dinner, he replied, "What! no clergyman present? Thank God for all things." The anticipation of this remark may perhaps be found in the observation of Lady Hobart, recorded in the "Merry Passages and Jests of Sir Nicholas L'Estrange:"—" Every one being set at table, and nobody blessing it, but gazing one upon another, in expectation who should be chaplaine—' Well,' sayes my lady, ' I thinke I must say as one did in the like case, God be thanked, nobody will say grace.'" Sheridan continued for some years to give plays to the footlights of the theatre, and eloquence to the senate; but the sad results of improvidence shadowed the later portion of his life, and in July, 1816, the "orator, dramatist, and minstrel," died in poverty, under an arrest for debt—his body being removed from his residence in Saville Row (for prudential reasons) to the house of Mr. Peter Moore, in Great George Street, Westminster. Friendless and forsaken Sheridan died, but his dazzling talents were remembered *then!* An almost regal funeral followed; the pall being borne by the Duke of Bedford, Lord Holland, Earl Mulgrave, Earl of Lauderdale, the Bishop of London, and Lord Spencer; whilst the royal Dukes of York and Sussex attended as mourners:

"Though the bailiffs should seize his last blanket to-day,
His pall may be borne by the nobles to-morrow."

The last poet for whom this favoured pavement was upraised was

THOMAS CAMPBELL,

whose "Pleasures of Hope" were exchanged, in 1844, for the peacefulness of this hallowed retreat. He was born on the 27th of July, 1777, in High street, Glasgow, being one of eleven children, all of whom he survived. At the time of Campbell's birth, misfortune had befallen the home of his parents. He was taught to read by his favourite sister, who was his senior by nineteen years; was then sent to a grammar-school; at the age of eleven he began to compose verses, and two years later he secured prizes for proficiency in Greek translation. Notwithstanding these honours, which might have been the source of jealousies, he won and retained the love of his companions, who once owed a holiday to his rhymed petition. Campbell was now thirteen, and quitted the grammar-school for the University. Delicate in bodily frame, he here almost exhausted his mental efforts in his struggle for acquirements, more especially as, from the scanty income of his parents, he had to give instruction to others, in part compensation for the receival of his own. This incessant labour reacted upon his system when he attained the middle age, and brought with it a serious reluctance to mental exertion. Quitting the University, he became an instructor of pupils in the island of Mull, travelling on foot some thirty miles in one day to reach the scene of his labours. Despite his incessant duties he proceeded with his metrical compositions, and before he had completed his twenty-second year he gave to the world the work with which his name will ever be associated, and the title of which is engraven on his coffin-plate. The "Pleasures of Hope" was received with enthusiasm in Edinburgh, and was as ardently welcomed in England. The public poured its praise upon the young author, who paid a visit to Germany, occasionally forwarding contributions to the *Morning Chronicle*—a journal which, in other cases, has "helped young merit into fame:" witness Hazlitt, Lord Campbell (who commenced his career in London as a reporter for its columns, and in 1810 was its theatrical critic), Charles Dickens, &c. Returning to England, Thomas Campbell entered the metropolis with only a few shillings in his pocket, but was introduced to Lord Holland, Samuel Rogers, John Kemble, Mrs. Siddons, and other celebrities, including Telford, the engineer, who gave him shelter when he was "flung upon a great city without a home." Campbell subsequently published a splendid edition of his "Pleasures of Hope," which produced him £600: his entire profits upon that poem, which contains eleven hundred lines, were about £900.

The scene before our poet now looked bright. In 1803 he married his cousin, Matilda Sinclair, and in the following year he quitted Upper Eaton-street for Sydenham. During his residence here Crabbe, Rogers, and Moore once dined with him : there had been a similar gathering before in London (at the house of the poet-banker), when Byron, Rogers, Moore, and Campbell dined together. Who would not wish to have been the fifth guest at such an intellectual repast? In a later day, her present Majesty accepted from Campbell the presentation of his works, and did him the honour to forward her portrait in return.

Campbell was ever found engaged on the side of freedom, and took up with much warmth the cause of Poland :
"Come but the day when Poland's battle 's won,
And on my gravestone shine the morrow's sun."

In 1826 Campbell was elected Lord Rector of Glasgow, and in the following year dined with the Sanatus Academicus, in the room where he had never been but once before in his life, and that was when a youth, on a charge of breaking the windows of the college church! He became a wanderer after the death of his wife, when he so plaintively remarked, "My son is mad, my wife dead, and my harp unstrung;" and it was whilst residing at Boulogne, in June, 1844, that he closed his mortal career. His remains were brought to England for interment in the Abbey, and were attended to their resting-place by the most distinguished in rank and literature.

As previously remarked, this favoured pavement covers the grave of Richard Cumberland, whose pen was employed in various departments of literature : his principal dramatic pieces were *The West Indian*, *The Jew*, and *The Wheel of Fortune*. In his own day Cumberland's was a name of high note; but time has allowed it to sink in popular estimation. As we turn to leave this celebrated transept, we may remark that beneath the pavement over which we have so long paused are others who enjoy the honourable companionship of the poets. Here lie the musician Handel, whose monument, by Roubiliac, is above our heads; Sir William Chambers, the architect of Somerset House; William Gifford, at one time a poor shoemaker's apprentice, and subsequently the editor of the potent "Quarterly Review;" Adam, one of the architects of the Adelphi; and, in addition to musician, architect, and critic, here is entombed the veritable "Old Parr," whose great age has been reduced to a mythical celebrity through the researches of the Registrar-General.

Quitting at length the celebrated "Coin des Poètes," we seek in the cloisters of the Abbey for the graves of the players, some of whom lie in strange juxtaposition with the earliest abbots of the monastery. In our first search, however, we alight upon the tomb of a poet, who should have slumbered with his compeers in the renowned transept. As, however, his principal effusions were devoted to the theatre, we may here point to the monumental bust, in high relief, of

WILLIAM CONGREVE.

He is sculptured in the full-bottomed wig of his time; and the inscription beneath acquaints us that the poet lies near this place, and that the memorial was raised by Henrietta, Duchess of Marlborough, as "a mark how dearly she remembered the happiness she enjoyed in the sincere friendship of so worthy and honest a man." Congreve bequeathed to the duchess the whole of his property, some £10,000. This is the second instance we have given of a poet possessing wealth. Congreve was descended from an ancient family, and completed his education at Dublin University. Returning to England shortly after the Revolution, he was entered of the Middle Temple. The law, however, but ill-accorded with his sprightly and volatile genius: he produced a novel at the age of seventeen, and next directed his attention to the drama. His first play, *The Old Bachelor*, was brought out at Drury Lane in 1693; he had not then reached his twentieth year, yet was he hailed as "a prop to the declining stage, and a rising genius in dramatic poetry." Six other plays followed; but from the indifferent patronage awarded to the last, and the long contest in which its author was engaged with Jeremy Collier—who published some severe invectives against the acting of plays—Congreve determined to write no more for the theatre. It was then remarked that he "quitted the stage early, and that Comedy left it with him." He was subsequently appointed to a post in the Customs, and passed his latter years in ease and retirement.

Congreve died in 1729, and his body lay in state in the Jerusalem Chamber, whence it was removed with great pomp, noblemen bearing the pall. The Jerusalem Chamber is built against the northern corner of the base of the west front of the Abbey. It was to this apartment that Henry IV., on falling sick in the church, desired to be carried, saying,—

> "It hath been prophesied to me many years,
> I should not die but in Jerusalem,
> Which vainly I supposed the Holy Land;
> But bear me to that church, and there I'll lie—
> In that Jerusalem shall Harry die."

We have already stood over the grave of Garrick. We now approach the resting-place of his great predecessor,

THOMAS BETTERTON,

who "ought to be recorded with the same respect as Roscius among the Romans," and may be termed the first actor who in his art was a perfect model of theatrical action and dramatic execution. Cibber says that he was born alone to speak what Shakspeare only knew to write, and this eulogy is to a great extent confirmed by Betterton's contemporaries. He was born in Westminster, and received a good education, after which he was apprenticed to Rhodes, the bookseller, who had been wardrobe-keeper to the Blackfriars Theatre. The latter obtained a license for a company of players at the Cockpit in Drury Lane, and there introduced his apprentice Betterton, who soon gave proofs of genius and merit. The plays of Beaumont and Fletcher were at that time in the ascendant, and the young actor —he was then little more than twenty years of age—gained the highest applause in *The Loyal Subject, Spanish Curate, Wild-Goose Chase*, &c., of those authors. When the theatre was opened in Lincoln's Inn Fields, in 1662, by Sir William Davenant, Betterton removed thither, and considerably increased his reputation. He was here noticed by Charles II., by whom he was sent to Paris to gain information relative to the French stage, with a view to the improvement of our own. Betterton was subsequently engaged in management, which he finally quitted as the infirmities of age increased. He then appeared but seldom upon the stage, his last performance being given in April, 1710, on the occasion of his benefit. Just previously he was suddenly seized with gout, and, fearful of disappointing his friends, he applied stimulants to reduce the swelling, which drove the distemper into his head, and terminated his life three days subsequently to his last performance. Betterton's remains were interred in the cloisters, the ceremony being performed with great solemnity.

In our search for the graves of the players we must not overlook those ladies of the theatre whose talent secured them interment in the Abbey. Here slumbers one—

MRS. ANNA OLDFIELD,

who, like Betterton, was born in Westminster: her father held at the time a commission in the Guards. Farquhar, the dramatist, one day overhearing her read a play, was so pleased with the emphasis and agreeable turn she gave to each character, that he pronounced her at once "cut out for the stage." This opinion was communicated to Captain Vanbrugh (afterwards Sir John), by whom Miss Nancy was recommended to Christopher Rich, and introduced to the theatre. This was in 1699, and, having the advantage of a good figure and a fine voice, the town soon gave her the preference to all the young actresses of the day. The Duke of Bedford was likewise pleased to speak to the manager on her behalf, when her weekly salary—hear this, ye captivating " stars " of the present day!—was advanced from fifteen shillings to twenty! The first prominent display of talent made by Mrs. Oldfield was in 1704, in the part of Lady Betty Modish, in the *Careless Husband;* and a few years later, Addison awarded her the character of Marcia upon the production of his *Cato.* She continued for some years to occupy a distinguished station in public favour, but died in 1730, at the age of forty-seven. Her remains lay in state, and, attended by two noblemen, were removed to their final deposit, a monument being raised to her memory. We are told that she was buried in a "very fine Brussels lace head-dress, a holland shift, with a tucker and double ruffles of the same lace, a pair of new kid gloves," &c., a conceit which Pope has satirised in the following lines :—

> "Odious! in woollen! 'twould a saint provoke!"
> Were the last words that poor Narcissa spoke.
> " No, let a charming chintz and Brussels lace
> Wrap my cold limbs and shade my lifeless face;
> One would not, sure, be frightful when one's dead!
> And—Betty—give this cheek a little red."

Mrs. Oldfield's contemporary, and rival in one character at least, reposes near her. Such was

MRS. BRACEGIRDLE,

one of the most fascinating women of her age, when it became a kind of fashion for the gallants of the day to avow a tenderness for her. When scarcely six years old she played the page in *The Orphan;* and in maturer years she secured a name that has ever been mentioned with respect, both on account of her professional merit and her private virtues. Mrs. Bracegirdle was the representative of Mrs. Brittle, in Betterton's *Amorous Widow,* which part Mrs. Oldfield likewise played. On a contest taking place between them in this character, the town decided in favour of the latter lady, upon which Mrs. Bracegirdle quitted the stage. There is no rivalry, however, in the grave. Henderson and Garrick have yielded up their tragic crowns, and they lie side by side in " Poets' Corner;" whilst the rival Mrs. Brittles forget their jealousy, and are here beneath our feet. Byron, in the following lines, points to the graves of Pitt and Fox —slumbering beneath the beauteous roof to which we occasionally direct a glance—but the juxtaposition admits of a wider applicability :—

> " A few feet
> Of sullen earth divide each winding-sheet :
> How peaceful and how powerful is the grave,
> That hushes all!"

One of Mrs. Bracegirdle's favourite characters was Statira, in Nat Lee's *Alexander the Great*, the hero being enacted by Mountford, who resided in Norfolk Street, Strand. A Captain Hill—a drunkard and a reprobate—was one of the many fascinated by the charms of the favoured actress ; and as Mountford was frequently her theatrical lover, against him did Hill meditate a jealous revenge. For this diabolical purpose he secured the cooperation of the noted duellist, Lord Mohun, waylaid the unfortunate actor in the street, and ran him through the body. Hill fled from justice, and his end was unknown ; whilst Mohun, his companion, fell in his duel with the Duke of Hamilton—an encounter fatal to both.

Mrs. Bracegirdle died in 1748, having exceeded the fourscore years alluded to by the Psalmist.

The stage ladies over whose graves we have thus gossiped

were of the age of Congreve and Betterton. There rests near them one who was the dramatic associate of Garrick and Barry, namely,

MRS. CIBBER.

She was sister to Dr. Arne, the composer, whose "Rule Britannia" has lately been listened to and admired all over the world. Born in 1715, she first appeared upon the stage as a singer, and in 1734 became the wife of Theophilus Cibber (son of the renowned Colley), from whom she was compelled to separate, in consequence of his dissipated course of life. Attempting tragedy, she experienced so much success that she resigned all vocal honours, and in the race for tragic fame outstripped her competitors, with the exception of Mrs. Pritchard, to whom a tablet has been raised in "Poets' Corner," adjoining the monument to Shakspeare. Mrs. Cibber died in 1766. During the latter years of her life she was much afflicted with ill-health, which considerably impeded her efforts. She was a most exquisite actress, excelling in parts of tenderness and deep pathos. Garrick, on hearing of her death, emphatically remarked, " Barry and I still remain, but tragedy is dead on one side."

In the cloisters likewise rest the remains of a lady who in her day was a reigning favourite,—

MRS. APHRA BEHN.

The poetical name of this writer was Astrea, by which she was known and addressed by her contemporaries. Born of a good family during the reign of Charles I., she was taken in her youth to Surinam, where she became acquainted with the Prince Oroonoko, whose adventures she recorded in a novel, the subject of which was afterwards dramatised by Southern. On her returning to England she married Mr. Behn, a merchant of Dutch extraction. Her wit and abilities next brought her into notice at court; and during the Dutch war Charles II. selected her to transact some important affairs. She accordingly visited Antwerp, and by her intrigues and gallantry secured essential information. Once more in England, she divided her remaining days between gaiety and the Muses. Her works are exceedingly numerous, including seventeen dramatic pieces, principally comedies. In these pieces faults and perfections stand in strong opposition to each other. Her dialogue sparkles with dazzling wit, but indelicacy forms therein a prominent feature, showing the truth of Pope's line,—

"The stage how loosely does Astrea tread."

Mrs. Behn's life was intermingled with numerous disappointments, and finally closed in 1689. She lies interred against the first pillar in the ambulatory, and the following inscription marks the spot:—

"Mrs. Aphra Behn
Died April the 16th, 1689.
Here lies a proof that wit can never be
Defence enough against mortality."

Sir Walter Scott relates the following anecdote, in connection with Mrs. Behn, which exhibits a striking proof of the change of manners in this country since the days of the fair Astrea :—

"A grand-aunt of my own, Mrs. Keith, of Ravenstone, who was a person of some condition, being a daughter of Sir John Swinton, of Swinton, lived with unabated vigour of intellect to a very advanced age. She was very fond of reading, and enjoyed it to the very last of her long life. One day she asked me, when we happened to be alone together, whether I had ever seen Mrs. Behn's novels? I confessed the charge. Whether I could get her a sight of them? I said, with some hesitation, I believed I could, but that I did not think that she would like either the manners or the language, which approached too near that of Charles II.'s time to be quite proper reading. 'Nevertheless,' said the good old lady, 'I remember their being so much admired, and being so much interested in them myself, that I wish to look at them again.' To hear was to obey. So I sent Mrs. Aphra Behn, curiously sealed up, with 'private and confidential' on the packet, to my gay old grand-aunt. The next time I saw her afterwards she gave me back Aphra, properly wrapped up, with nearly these words :—'Take back your bonny Mrs. Behn ; and, if you will take my advice, put her in the fire, for I found it impossible to get through the very first novel. But is it not,' she said, 'a very odd thing that I, an old woman of eighty and upwards, sitting alone, feel myself ashamed to read a book which sixty years ago I have heard read aloud for the amusement of large circles, consisting of the first and most creditable society in London?'"

The Abbey cloisters received from the theatre another lady, a clever woman and an actress of note,—

MRS. BARRY,

who for many years reigned in Ireland as queen of the drama, often sharing in the triumphs acquired by her husband, the elegant Spranger, whose grave we shall next visit. After his demise—and though she herself reckoned years exceeding half a century—she entered into a second matrimonial engagement with an Irish barrister named Crawford, and who, by this union, became proprietor of the Crow-street Theatre, Dublin. After an absence of five years she returned to the stage (Covent Garden, 1783), appearing as Lady Randolph, Henderson playing Old Norval. Mrs. Crawford was secured as a counter-attraction to Drury Lane, where John Kemble had then just appeared, and, in conjunction with Mrs. Siddons, was drawing great houses. She performed for the last time in 1797, and died four years subsequently in distress. Dibdin says she had much of Garrick's merit in tragedy, excelling in the exposition of the terrible and turbulent passions. Common grief was too tame for her expression; she knew not how to insinuate herself into the heart; her mode was to seize it. Mrs. Crawford's remains are interred near those of her first husband,

SPRANGER BARRY,

whose silver voice has assisted to perpetuate his memory. He was born in Dublin, in which city he first tried his powers upon the stage in 1744, in the character of Othello. Two years later he removed to the British metropolis, and was soon recognised as an able rival of Garrick. In the character of Othello he was especially preferred to the Roscius, exhibiting therein such striking excellence that from the severest critic was drawn the most unqualified approbation. In this part Garrick failed to make an impression—the wits of the day remarking that he resembled a black page running about after Desdemona! Barry has been thus described:—"In person he was about five feet eleven inches high, finely formed, and possessing a countenance in which manliness and sweetness were so happily blended as formed one of the best imitations of Apollo Belvidere."

"In person taller than the common size,
Behold where Barry draws admiring eyes.
What man could give, if Barry was not here,
Such well-applauded tenderness to Lear?"—CHURCHILL.

He died in January, 1777, and lies within a few yards of the steps leading from the Abbey to the cloisters.

Towards the close of the same year (1777) a new grave was made in the cloisters, to which were consigned the remains of

SAMUEL FOOTE,

"the English Aristophanes," whom Cornwall claims to have given birth to. His education was received from Worcester College, from whence, being designed for the law, he was removed to the Temple. At this period of his life he is thus referred to by a contemporary writer:—
" He came into the room in a frock suit of green and silver,

bag wig, sword, bouquet, and point ruffles, and immediately joined the critical circle at the upper end. Nobody knew him, but he soon entered boldly into conversation, and by the brilliance of his wit, the justness of his remarks, and his unembarrassed freedom of manners, attracted the general notice. The buzz of the room went round, 'Who is he? whence came he?' which nobody could answer, until a handsome carriage, stopping at the door to take him to the assembly of fashion, they learned from the servants that his name was Foote, that he was a young man of family and fortune, and a student of the Inner Temple." To Foote, however, the law presented but few allurements, and the home of the Templars was forsaken for the " little theatre in the Haymarket." Here he first appeared in 1774, in the character of Othello. This path of the drama he subsequently forsook, selecting one in which—as author, mimic, and wit—he secured considerable reputation. In 1766, while on a visit to Lord Mexborough, Foote was thrown from his horse, by which accident his leg was broken, and amputation rendered necessary; but, with the aid of an artificial limb, he performed with no less spirit and agility than before.

In reference to Foote's lost member, George Colman has left us the following bit of pleasantry upon its substitute :—" This prop to his person I once saw standing by his bedside, richly dressed in a handsome silk stocking, with a polished shoe and gold buckle, awaiting the owner's getting up. It had a kind of tragic-comical appearance, and I leave to inveterate wags the ingenuity of punning upon a Foote in bed and a leg out of it. The proxy for a limb thus decorated, though ludicrous, is too strong a reminder of amputation to be very laughable. His undressed supporter was the common wooden stick, which was not a little injurious to a well-kept pleasure ground. I remember following him, after a shower of rain, upon a nicely-rolled terrace, in which he stumped a deep round hole at every step he took, till it appeared as if the gardener had been there with his dibble, preparing, against all horticultural practice, to plant a long row of cabbages in a gravel walk."

Immediately following Foote's accident an effort was made by his distinguished friends to obtain for him a patent for the Haymarket Theatre, which was secured on the 9th of July, 1766, when that house was duly established as a summer theatre. Here Foote continued to play until the season preceding his death, when he disposed of the theatre to the elder Colman. Being seized with paralysis whilst upon the stage, he was advised, upon a partial recovery, to remove to France. He had proceeded, however, only as far as Dover, when a second attack proved fatal. His remains were removed to London, and interred in the Abbey, with much solemnity, by torchlight. Foote was the author of about two dozen pieces. His death occurred on the 21st of October, 1777.

Twenty years later another of Garrick's supporters was honoured with interment in the cloisters. This was

MRS. POPE,

formerly Miss Younge, who was born in Southwark in 1740. Apprenticed to a milliner, she devoted her leisure moments to the study of dramatic poetry, and was ultimately engaged by Garrick for Drury Lane. At this house she appeared in October, 1768, in the character of Imogen, and soon attracted much notice as the representative of the poetic drama; whilst the production of Mrs. Cowley's *Belle's Stratagem*, in which she played Lætitia Hardy, advanced her reputation as the first comedy actress of the day. In August, 1785, Miss Younge was united to Alexander Pope—the actor, not the poet—famed for his love of the good things of the world. Expatiating at table once on the excellence of ham, he remarked, " Ham, sir, is the same improvement upon bacon that steel is upon iron. In fact, sir, ham is the poetry of bacon." Mrs. Pope continued to perform until the 26th of January, 1797, her last character being Ellen Vortex, in *The Cure for the Heartache*. She died on the ensuing 15th of March.

The last time Garrick acted Lear—the crown of all his achievements—Mrs. Pope, then Miss Younge, was his Cordelia, and her hand, as is usual, was fast locked in his at the dropping of the curtain. He led her thus into the green-room, and, remembering with a sigh that one more night would terminate his dramatic existence, he observed to her, " Ah, Bess! this is the last time of MY being your father. You must now look out, therefore, to be adopted by some one else." " Well, then, sir," responded Miss Younge, " give me a father's blessing," at the same time throwing herself gracefully upon her knees before him. Garrick, kindled with the enthusiasm of his favourite actress, replied, with great energy, " God bless you!" Then, raising his eyes to the rest of the performers, he solemnly added, " And may God bless you all!" His emotion now became too great to trust longer to language, and he instantly retired.

We have now visited the graves we were in quest of; and as we cast a lingering look upon the beauties of the Abbey, our thoughts wander again to the occupants of the south transept at which we entered. The sun is adding to the solemnity of the scene his soft, departing rays, and in its pure light we seem to trace the shades of the poets, as we dwell upon the rich legacies of thought which they have bequeathed us. Shakspeare we again behold with his unparalleled opulence; Milton with his sacred harmony; Spenser with his gentle fancy; Dryden with his nervous energy; Gray with his daring flights; Goldsmith with his tender flow of feeling; and Cowper with his moral gravity. To some of these the Abbey offers honorary memorials, whilst their graves are to be found elsewhere, soon to be visited by us. Shakspeare sleeps at his native Stratford, the gentle Avon flowing by the spot as peaceably as of old. Milton lies in the crowded city; and Byron—whose statue has been denied admittance here—sleeps at Hucknall, near to Newstead Abbey, Ada ("sole daughter of his house and heart") by his side. There is a monument here to Samuel Butler. When the poet died an effort was made by his executor to have his remains interred here; but, failing to raise a sufficient subscription, they found an asylum in the churchyard of St. Paul, Covent Garden. The monument to the author of "Hudibras" was erected in the Abbey, in 1721, by Alderman John Barber, a printer of London. The latter

part of its Latin inscription drew from Samuel Wesley the
following epigram:—

> "While Butler, needy wretch, was yet alive,
> No generous patron would a dinner give;
> See him, when starved to death, and turn'd to dust,
> Presented with a monumental bust.
> The poet's fate is here in emblem shown,—
> He ask'd for bread, and he received a stone."

It is pleasurable to be enabled to remark that the story of
Butler's poverty, so frequently referred to, appears to be
unfounded.

The monument to Shakspeare was placed here in 1740:
it was designed by Kent, and executed by Scheemakers,
the expense being defrayed by performances given for the
purpose at Drury Lane and Covent Garden Theatres.
There are memorials here to two disciples of Shakspeare—
John Kemble and Mrs. Siddons. The former is resting in
a consecrated piece of ground situate on the road to
Berne, in Switzerland: the grave of his gifted sister we
shall find elsewhere—in our own metropolis. There is a
monument here to Isaac Watts, whom a critic recently
styled "a good man, but a bad poet." The doctor's grave
will be included in our visits. We must not omit a passing thought to the great philosopher Newton, who lies
near the entrance to the choir; and the English musician,
Purcell, reposes not far from thence, where his sublime
anthems have so often sounded.

> "Sometimes a hero in an age appears,
> But scarce a Purcell in a thousand years."

This epitaph to the musician is said to have been supplied by Dryden:—"Here lies Henry Purcell, Esq., who left this life, and is gone to that blessed place where only his harmony can be exceeded." It is recorded that the bereaved widow of a pyrotechnist, anxious to give her departed lord a befitting testimony of her regard, alighted upon the above inscription, with which she was so pleased that a portion was transferred to her husband's tomb, which informed all survivors that he was gone to that blessed place where only his fireworks could be exceeded !

A memorial to a painter is here to be found — the "coxcomb Kneller," who, however, slumbers at Twickenham, refusing to be interred in the Abbey, because "they do bury fools there." Thomson has a memento here, but sleeps at Richmond, near to the spot where he " sang the ' Seasons' and their change." Goldsmith is likewise remembered, though his body rests with the knights of old in the Temple. Gray has here his bust, but the churchyard of Stoke, in Buckinghamshire, received his remains.

Mason, Wordsworth, and Southey, too, are perpetuated in the Abbey, though the first sleeps at Aston, in Yorkshire, and his two brethren near to their favourite lakes. Other master-spirits come crowding upon us : though favoured with no memorial here, they have their names engraven on Nature's temple with those over whose ashes we have thus long tarried. Pope enjoys his rest at Twickenham, in the vicinity of his once favourite grotto ; Swift, whose genius was as wild as dazzling, rests near his Stella at St. Patrick's Cathedral, Dublin ; Cowper, at East Dereham ; Parnell, at Chester ; Waller, at Beaconsfield ; Collins, at Chichester ; Young, at Welwyn ; Crabbe, at Trowbridge. Blair occupies a " Grave" in the churchyard of Athelstaneford, where he was long the parish minister. Keats—whose hope was smitten in its earliest dawn—lies in the Protestant burying-ground at Rome, where his monument, it has been remarked, throws a greater chill over the English heart than the ruins by which it is surrounded. Shelley went down beneath the waves, but his ashes found their way to the sweet spot he had so loved when living, and now mingle with those of Keats, who, like himself, warbled his songs in the spring, destined to know no summer. Of the Scottish minstrels Burns lies in St. Michael's churchyard, Dumfries; Allan Ramsay has his tomb in the cemetery of the Grey Friars, where the martyrs of the Covenant have their memorial; Hogg fills a grave in Ettrick churchyard, where the shepherd and his dog, in earlier days, may have sat and mused; and Scott sleeps amid the old abbey ruins of Dryburgh, which for years he had looked upon as his place of burial.

After this lengthened gossip, in which centuries have been handed about, and in which we have wandered from old Geoffrey Chaucer to Walter Scott, we quit the Abbey for the adjoining church,—

ST. MARGARET'S, WESTMINSTER.

Upon the rebuilding of the Abbey by the Confessor, with so much magnificence, inconvenience attended its use as a parish church, to obviate which the sacred building into which we have entered was founded. It was rebuilt in the reign of the fourth Edward, and from that erection the present structure may be dated, though extensive and incongruous have been the repairs both in the past and present centuries.

The first monument by which our notice is attracted, was not raised to the memory of Poet, Painter, or Player, but to one to whom the three combined are indebted,—

WILLIAM CAXTON,

by whom printing was introduced into England, by the exercise of which art the aspirations of the Poet are widely diffused. The canvas of the Painter is pictured to those who can never behold its colours, whilst the Player, whose fame is based upon a feeble pedestal, may have his name occasionally repeated, long after himself and his admirers have quitted the scene for ever. Caxton—a name to be revered by those who love to trace the progress of mankind—was originally engaged in the business of a mercer. After passing some time abroad he returned to England about 1473, bringing with him the few, simple, and rude implements which had cost him wealth and labour to obtain; and from the precincts of Westminster Abbey was first given to this country the art of printing. Such at least is the popular opinion, though De Machliniâ, it has been said, printed in England even before Caxton. The latter produced sixty-two books, and worked with his pen as well as with his types, translating some works from the French, &c. He preserved until the end of his life (which terminated about 1491) the character of an honest and modest man. It was Caxton who sought out the manuscript of Chaucer's " Canterbury Tales," and his printing of the poem gave to it a greater permanence. It was

Caxton, likewise, who placed the original inscription over the poet's grave. To the "father of English printing," then, are we largely indebted: his memorial tablet has the following inscription:—

> "To the Memory
> of
> **William Caxton,**
> Who first introduced into Great Britain
> The Art of Printing,
> And who, A.D. 1477, or earlier,
> Exercised that Art
> In the Abbey of Westminster,
> THIS TABLET,
> In remembrance of One
> To whom
> The Literature of this Country
> Is so largely indebted,
> Was raised
> Anno Domini MDCCCXX.
> By the Roxburghe Club.
> Earl Spencer, K.G., President."

Another tablet arrests our attention, and which summons up a host of memories—of intrigues, plots, and finally the axe. Near to it rests

SIR WALTER RALEIGH,

the poet, soldier, and statesman, of whose youth but little is known. Born in Devonshire in 1552, he was sent to Oxford, where he secured high praise for the precocity of his talents. In 1569 he began his military career in the civil wars of France, as a volunteer in the Protestant cause. Subsequently he sought discoveries in the New World, but the enterprise was unsuccessful. He next became an attendant upon Elizabeth, and the young courtier is related to have spread his rich cloak upon the miry road, when his royal mistress hesitated to proceed— his cloak procuring for him, it has been observed, many a good suit. Raleigh displayed his chivalrous spirit when the Spanish Armada passed up our Channel; but he was ultimately driven from court, according to some authorities, by the enmity of the Earl of Essex. Removing to Ireland, he renewed his intimacy with Spenser, who celebrated the reunion in a beautiful pastoral. A private marriage with Elizabeth Throckmorton, one of the queen's maids of honour, incurred him more severe court displeasure, and he was committed to the Tower. Again released, he employed his leisure in maturing an expedition to Guiana, and sailed from Plymouth in 1595, in search of the " El Dorado," where inexhaustible wealth was thought to exist. The promised land, however, was never reached; but general praise was subsequently awarded to Raleigh for his share in the expedition by which the Spanish fleet was destroyed in the harbour of Cadiz, and he continued to enjoy much favour until the death of Elizabeth.

When James succeeded to the throne, the rivals of Raleigh renewed their malice, and eventually succeeded in bringing him to trial, charged with conspiring to kill the king and to raise a rebellion. Few trials have excited a deeper interest. Raleigh, in his defence, was self-possessed, poetical, and even witty; but he was found guilty, and sentenced to death, with all the usual barbarities. A reprieve, however, came, but Raleigh was doomed to pass thirteen years of bondage in the Tower—a captivity shared in by his wife, the union with whom first made him familiar with its gloomy walls. It was during this confinement that he became an ardent student, and the elevation and beauty of his life during that period are strongly marked. At length he was released from his confinement, and again set sail for the "mine of gold." Disasters, however, followed this new venture, and Raleigh returned to England and to incarceration. The Spaniards had been offended by this last expedition. Raleigh's death was demanded, and, failing in all other attempts to complete his ruin, the sentence passed thirteen years previously was revived, and Raleigh passed from the Tower to the scaffold :

"On through that gate misnamed, through which before
Went Sydney, Russell, Raleigh, Cranmer, More."

He was executed on Thursday, October 29th, 1618, in Old Palace Yard, Westminster. Feeling carefully the edge of the axe, he, smiling, said, "This is a sharp medicine, but it will cure all diseases." Raleigh went to his rest in the sixty-seventh year of his age, and St. Margaret's received his body.

In St. Margaret's church, also, were interred the remains of Skelton, the satirical poet of the reign of Henry VIII.; and likewise those of Catharine, the wife of Milton, buried here in February, 1657, and referred to in one of the poet's sonnets as his "late espoused saint." Whilst looking round upon the monuments of the church—and a sumptuous one is to be found here to Lord Howard of Effingham, the gallant lord high admiral of Elizabeth— the eastern window frequently attracts our attention.

The Crucifixion is here gorgeously represented. The history of the window is curious. The magistrates of Dort, in Holland, had it made, as a fitting present to Henry VII. for his chapel in the Abbey. Before its completion, however, Henry died, when the Abbot of Waltham received the window, which was retained by his church until the Dissolution. It was then sent into Wiltshire, was purchased with its new home by Thomas Villiers, Duke of Buckingham, and again sold to General Monk. To save it from destruction it was next buried. At the Restoration it again saw the light, and revisited New Hall, in Wiltshire, when fresh dangers threatened it, upon the chapel there being destroyed by a new possessor. Preserved and cased up, it found its way to Epping, and finally reached its present home in the church of St. Margaret, Westminster.

Leaving both church and window—with Caxton and Raleigh to their slumber—we may refer to a poet whose remains are said to have been thrust ignobly from the Abbey into the adjoining graveyard. That poet was

THOMAS MAY,

the friend of Ben Jonson, and the historian of the Long Parliament, of which, on his rupture with Charles, who had been his patron, he became the able secretary. He was the eldest son of Sir Thomas May, and was born at the ancient palace of St. Dunstan's, at Mayfield, Sussex, in 1595. In early youth he made great progress in the acquisition of the learned languages, and, on his removal to Cambridge, made himself acquainted with the best poets and historians of antiquity. He took his degree at the early age of seventeen, and three years later was admitted a student at Gray's Inn. The cultivation of poetry, however, occupied the principal attention of May, who, on the death of Jonson, was a candidate for the vacant laureateship, but which was conferred upon Dryden. He wrote both tragedies and comedies, but his merits appear the greatest in his translations, more especially in Lucan's " Pharsalia." His father having squandered his estate, May was left with limited resources ; but he brought his mind to his fortune, and was continually occupied with his parliamentary services and his compositions. He died suddenly on the 13th of November, 1650, and was buried, according to Dr. Fuller, " near a good and true historian indeed, viz., the great Mr. William Camden, in the west side of the south isle of Westminster Abbey." The ceremony was attended, by order of the parliament, with much pomp and solemnity; whilst an inscription on a marble monument recorded the historian's virtues. On the return, however, of Charles II. from his exile, this monument was torn down; and the body of Thomas May—after resting quietly for more than ten years—is said to have been disinterred, and thrust into a pit dug for the purpose in the churchyard of St. Margaret's.

In that same churchyard, with its numerous and time-worn gravestones, lie the remains of two who in their day were connected with the theatre. The memory of one,

THOMAS HULL,

has been materially preserved by his having originated the institutions known as " Theatrical Funds," by which the actor is taught to provide, in his more prosperous season, for the hour of affliction, or when in the "sere and yellow leaf" he falls into need. Hull was for many years the " father of the stage," and was the predecessor of the gay and sprightly Lewis as acting manager of Covent Garden Theatre. Whilst connected with the latter establishment he conceived the idea of making some provision for the distressed actor in his old age, and the plan was effected one year previously to its introduction at Drury Lane. At this period (1765) Garrick was upon the continent; and though displeased, upon his return, at not having been consulted on the question, he warmly espoused the cause. Hull was intimate with Shenstone, the poet. He died in April, 1808, and the following lines were written upon the occasion by John Taylor:—

"EPITAPH

ON THE LATE THOMAS HULL, FOUNDER OF THE THEATRICAL FUND.

HULL, long respected in his scenic art,
On life's great stage sustain'd a virtuous part;
And some memorial of his zeal to show,
For his loved art, and shelter age from woe,
He form'd that noble Fund which guards his name,
Embalm'd by gratitude, enshrined by fame."

The second member of the theatre who exchanged the footlights for the occupancy of a grave at St. Margaret's was

MRS. BLAND,

who in her day was acknowledged "England's best ballad singer." Her parents were Italian Jews, named Romanzini, and she was born at Caen, in Normandy, in 1770. Being brought to England, and developing some vocal powers, she was introduced to the public, when a mere child, at Sadler's Wells Theatre. Subsequent years found her at Drury Lane and at the Haymarket, where very many original characters were intrusted to her. It was in 1790 that Miss Romanzini exchanged her name for that of Bland, her husband being a brother of Mrs. Jordan. She continued before the public until 1822, when a malady which had occasionally evinced itself assumed a serious form. This was an aberration of intellect, from which, however, she recovered. The proceeds of a benefit given her at Drury Lane in 1824, augmented by private contributions, were invested by the late Earl of Egremont, from whose estate Mrs. Bland received £70 per annum until her death, which occurred in January, 1838, in the sixty-eighth year of her age. Mrs. Bland was an excellent musician, and gave popularity to many pleasing ballads. She was long the evening star of Vauxhall Gardens.

Whilst in the Abbey we gossiped over the grave of Chaucer, and have just left that of his first printer, Caxton. Let us now, disregarding any precise order in our rambles, seek a church in which we shall find Chaucer's contemporary, Gower, and likewise Fletcher, so linked in friendship with Beaumont, the companion of Chaucer in the Abbey. Such is the church of

ST. MARY OVERIE, OR ST. SAVIOUR, SOUTHWARK.

There is much poetical romance connected with the story of this cathedral-like edifice, a romance which, for nearly ten centuries, has spoken gratefully of Mary Overie, plying her little skiff between the two shores of the adjoining river, at a time when London could not boast of a single bridge, and devoting all her earnings, as well as those amassed by her parents, to the erection of a religious house upon its bank. To this romance old Stow, in the following notice, appears to give some confirmation :— " This church, or some other in place thereof, was of old time, long before the Conquest, a house of sisters, founded by a maiden named Mary. Unto the which house and sisters she left (as was left her by her parents) the oversight and profits of a cross ferry over the Thames, there kept before that any bridge was builded. This house of sisters was afterwards, by Swithin, a noble lady, converted into a college of priests, who, in place of the ferry, builded a bridge of timber." In 1106 this church received its second foundation for canons regular.

The priory was seriously injured in the great fire in Southwark in 1212, after which the canons founded a hospital in the neighbourhood, in which they performed all the services of their church until the repairs of St. Mary Overie were completed. At the commencement of the fourteenth century we hear of the poverty of this priory. King Edward I. makes an application for one of his aged servants to be admitted therein, but the answer is that the body is so poor that the whole of their goods, rents, and possessions cannot afford sufficient for their own maintenance without the " pious bounty of the faithful." Towards the close of that century the church was repaired and restored; and who was the contributor of the principal funds? The king? No; it was a poet! —John Gower. At the commencement of the sixteenth century (1510) we find this church first spoken of as St. Saviour's. In 1539 the priory was dissolved, and a few years later the church became connected with a religious persecution, carried to an extreme which this country never witnessed before or since. Within its walls there sat a dread tribunal, from which holy martyrs passed to the fiery stake at Smithfield—two or three hundred Protestant victims perishing in the course of three years. About 1578 the church was repaired in many parts, " and within throughout richly and very worthily beautified; " and about 1713 we learn that " this is now a very magnificent church, since the late reparation. It hath an huge organ, which was procured by voluntary subscription. The repair (it is said) cost the parish £2600, and that well laid out. The old monuments are all refreshed and new painted." During the present century upwards of £50,000 have been expended upon St. Saviour's. The far-famed Lady Chapel—which narrowly escaped destruction in preparing the approaches to London Bridge—occupies the eastern extremity of the church. It is the side pointed out by Stow as the ancient house of sisters " beyond the choir." Mary Overie is said to have been buried here, though no monument records her memory.

There are numerous monuments here to detain us, more especially the fine effigy in the choir of a knight cross-legged, probably one of those distinguished patrons who, in 1106, refounded the establishment; and formerly, in the Lady Chapel, stood the tomb of a grocer, with one of the quaint inscriptions of the place:—

> " Weep not for him, since he is gone before
> To heaven, where grocers there are many more."

We pass by, however, the many inviting monuments, and seek that sumptuous pile in the south transept raised to the memory of

JOHN GOWER,

the poet of the fourteenth century, the period which saw the revival of modern learning. Dante, Petrarch, and Boccaccio in Italy, and Chaucer in England, gave the impulse to the movement, and Gower was their contemporary. It was in this church, in 1397, that he was married to Alice Groundolf, the ceremony being performed by William of Wykeham. Gower was not the only poet who in this church received at the altar his selected bride. The minstrel king, James of Scotland, was likewise married here. Taken prisoner when a boy, he was detained for years in captivity, and from his window in Windsor Castle he beheld the beauteous Jane Beaufort, niece of the cardinal of that name, by whom his heart was immediately made captive. Gower's bride was here interred, but her monument has long since disappeared. There is little fear of the exquisite tomb before which we stand being preserved as long as the sacred building itself. As already related, Gower contributed the principal portion of the funds when the building needed restoration; and the canons marked their gratitude to their benefactor by long continuing to perform a yearly *obiit* to his memory, and by hanging up a tablet near to the tomb, with the inscription: " Whosoever prayeth for the soul of John Gower he shall, so oft as he so doth, have a M. and a D. days of pardon." In the front of this tomb is inscribed, " Here lies John

Gower, Esq., a celebrated English poet, also a benefactor to the sacred edifice in the time of Edward III. and Richard II." Gower's fame as a poet rests upon his " Confessio Amantis," his only published work, and which was written by him in accordance with the wishes of Richard II., the circumstance being thus related by the poet himself:—

> " In Themse [Thames] when it was flowende,
> As I by boat came rowend,
> So as Fortune her time set
> My liege lord perchance I met;
> And so befel as I came nigh
> Out of my boat, when he me sigh [saw]
> He bad me to come into his barge,
> And when I was with him at large
> Amonges other things he said,
> He hath this charge upon me laid,
> And bade me do my business,
> That to his high worthiness
> Some newe thing I should book."

The monument was removed to the present site, and repaired and coloured in 1832, at the expense of Gower, first Duke of Sutherland. Gower's monument has always been taken care of.

The remains of another poet were subsequently received into this church, namely,—

JOHN FLETCHER.

This fact we learn from the register of St. Mary Overie, which, under the date of 1625, records the burial of " Mr.

John Fletcher, a man, in the church." This was the friend of Beaumont, with whom his name is so indissolubly united. He was the son of the Rev. Dr. Fletcher, whom Elizabeth made Bishop of Bristol, and in 1593 removed to the more lucrative see of London. To upwards of fifty dramas are appended the names of Beaumont and Fletcher, though it is probable the latter did not assist his friend in more than half that number. Fletcher survived his brother dramatist ten years. The circumstances attending his death are thus described by Aubrey:—" In the great plague of 1625 a knight of Norfolk or Suffolk invited him into the country: he stayed but to make himself a suit of clothes, and, while it was making, fell sick and died. This I heard from the tailor, who is now a very old man and clerk of St. Mary Overie."

Within this church was likewise interred one who gloried in a name which will be forgotten only with time, but of whom, individually, little is known. We allude to

EDMUND SHAKSPEARE,

youngest brother to our great dramatic poet. Edmund was " a player," probably through his gifted relative's connection with the theatre. The register connected with the church at Stratford-upon-Avon informs us that he was there baptized on the 3rd of May, 1580; the church books of St. Mary Overie tell us that he was there interred on the 31st of December, 1607. Such is the brief detail of all that is known of Edmund Shakspeare!

Leaving the interior of the church for its adjoining graveyard, we shall find a dreary spot, which the green garb of nature appears to have entirely forsaken. We value the spot, notwithstanding, for beneath its desolation lies

PHILIP MASSINGER.

This dramatist was born at Salisbury in 1584, and at the age of eighteen was entered a fellow-commoner of St. Alban's Hall, Oxford, which he quitted, however, without taking any degree. Repairing to London, he applied himself to writing for the stage, which his pen furnished with nearly forty plays. He soon rose into high reputation, but combined with lofty endowments an unassuming modesty, which endeared him to all his contemporaries, many of whom joined with him in the composition of their works—of which number may be mentioned Dekker, Field, Rowley, and Middleton. Massinger was the more immediate successor of Shakspeare, to whom he is allowed to have approached as closely as any of his competitors. Notwithstanding the celebrity enjoyed by Massinger's productions in their earlier day, but few of them are known to the present race of playgoers. *A New Way to Pay Old Debts* is occasionally performed; whilst *The Fatal Dowry* and *Riches* (altered from *The City Madam*) have been found amongst the modern revivals. Massinger's days are thought to have been passed in comfort, though conflicting statements have been given as to many circumstances connected with his career. For a length of time the period of his demise was a problem; but this was at length solved by the records of this church, which contain the melancholy line, "March 20,

1639, buried Philip Massinger, a stranger," that is, a non-parishioner.

In graves unmarked were buried Sir Edward Dyer, the poet, in the chancel, May 11th, 1607: he lived and died in Winchester House adjoining. Lawrence Fletcher, one of the leading shareholders of the Globe and Blackfriars Theatres, and Shakspeare's "fellow," was buried in the church, September 12th, 1608; and Philip Henslowe, the well-known theatrical manager, was buried in the chancel, January, 1615-16.

Leaving Massinger's unmarked grave, we ascend the steps which conduct us to the busy thoroughfare of the Borough. Taking a parting glance at the exterior of St. Mary Overie, we cross the Thames, and find ourselves in the heart of the busy city. In a brief walk the spire and tower of many a church are to be distinguished, though the number is far less than it once was. The Reformation thinned the ranks of these sacred edifices; whilst the Great Fire, a century later, destroyed many that have not been rebuilt. Several that are still spared us are rich in historic associations. At the church of Allhallows, Barking, for instance, the headless body of the poet Surrey was temporarily deposited after his execution on Tower Hill. St. Andrew Undershaft has the honoured ashes of the fine old chronicler, Stow; whilst the church of St. Catharine Cree, Leadenhall Street, according to Strype, is the resting-place of Hans Holbein. This "great and inimitable" painter was born at Grünstadt, and on visiting England rose high in the favour of Henry VIII. Holbein died in London, of the plague, in 1554.

From the living stream constantly flowing through

the city we first turn, for quietude, into the picturesque old church of

ST. GILES, CRIPPLEGATE.

" Softly tread, 'tis hallow'd ground."

The name of this locality is derived from a gate which formerly stood in the vicinity of the church, near to which a number of cripples were accustomed to assemble for the solicitation of alms. Cripplegate appears to be of great age; and Maitland, in his " Survey," gives it as his opinion that in 1010 the gate then standing here was the only one in the north wall of the city. A record of its antiquity is preserved in an account of the translation of the relics of King Edmund the Martyr from their original place of repose to London. This occurred about sixty years before the Norman Conquest. It is stated that in their transit the bearers conveyed their precious burden into the city through this gate, which was supposed to have derived from the circumstance a miraculous virtue; and the lame and impotent resorted thither, trusting to be cured of their maladies by the contact of its consecrated pavement. The church was founded about 1090 by Alfunc, the first master of St. Bartholomew's Hospital. It is dedicated to St. Giles, the patron of the mendicant fraternity, which tutelage he divides with St. Martin. The building, with the exception of the tower, was destroyed by fire in 1545, and numerous alterations have been since effected. This is one of the few city churches which escaped the Great Fire of 1666; but, with the exception of the tower, little of the old church remains.

Among other associations of the place we must not forget that it was to this church the sturdy Cromwell brought Elizabeth Bourchier, who at this altar promised unto him to "love, cherish, and to obey." John Speed, the chronicler, rests here from his learned labours, and so does John Fox, from whom we received the " Book of Martyrs." But our present thoughts are with one on whom Cromwell, when Protector, bestowed his favour. Near the middle of the centre aisle, and on the north side, there is a pew which invites our attention, for beneath it are the remains of our great poet,—

JOHN MILTON.

The register of baptisms of Allhallows Church, Bread Street, contains the earliest notice of this distinguished man:—" The 20th day of December, 1608, was baptized John, the sonne of John Mylton, scrivener." It was on the preceding 9th of December that Milton was born, in Bread Street. After receiving instruction from a private tutor he was sent to St. Paul's School, and from thence to Christ's College, Cambridge. At this time of his life he was so eminently handsome, with his light brown hair hanging in curls upon his shoulders, that he was called " the lady of the college." Being a good Latin scholar, at the age of fifteen he versified two psalms, which were published, but gave evidence of no remarkable talent. After his return from Cambridge—where a mulberry tree, planted by his own hands, is still growing in the college gardens— he wrote his beautiful masque of *Comus*, which was first acted at Ludlow by the sons and daughters of the Earl of

Bridgewater. In 1638 he visited the Continent, but returned home on hearing of the dissension between Charles I. and his parliament. From lodgings in St. Bride's churchyard he removed to a pretty garden-house in Aldersgate-street, than which, at this period, there were few streets in London more free from noise. After a short time spent in giving scholastic instruction, he began to take part in the controversies of the times, enlisting himself on the side of the Puritans. In 1645 Milton's "Allegro" and "Penseroso" made their appearance, amongst a collection of his Latin and English poems. Under Cromwell's control of the nation our poet became secretary of foreign tongues to the council of state, and took up his residence at Whitehall. During the Protectorate the whole of the communications between England and foreign states were made in Latin, and those written by Milton were expressed in language remarkable for its nervous strength and classic elegance. When about forty-four he lost his sight. This was a terrible calamity; yet in one of his sonnets, addressed to Cyriack Skinner, he thus records his spirit of resignation :—

"I argue not
Against Heaven's hand or will, nor bate a jot
   Of heart or hope, but still bear up and steer
Right onward. What supports me, dost thou ask?
   The conscience, friend, to have lost them, overplied,
In Liberty's defence, my noble task,
   Of which all Europe rings from side to side:
This thought might lead me through the vain world's mask,
   Content, though blind, had I no better guide."

In 1652 Milton left Whitehall, and went to reside in

Petty France, now known as Queen Square Place, Westminster. It was during his residence here that Milton lost his wife, to whom we alluded when visiting the church of St. Margaret's. At the Restoration the blind bard was proscribed, but he contrived to escape the impending danger. When quiet was at length restored to the troubled nation, Milton was then more than fifty years of age, but he sat down in his blindness to a task, the vision of which had been with him through his life. This was the completion of his " Paradise Lost." On the 27th of April, 1667, an agreement was entered into by its author and Samuel Symons, a printer, which witnessed that—

" The said John Milton, in consideration of five pounds now paid by the said Samuel Symons, his executors, and assignees, all that booke-copy or manuscript of a poem intituled 'Paradize Lost,' or by whatsoever title or name the same may be called or distinguished, now lately liscensed to be printed, together with the full benefitt, profit, and advantage thereof, or wch shall or may arrise thereby; and the said John Milton, for him, his exrs., and asss., that he and they shall at all times hereafter have, hold, and enjoy the same and all impressions thereof accordingly, without the lett or hindrance of him, the said John Milton, his exrs., or asss., or any person or persons by his or their consent or privity."

In addition to this reward for a great poem its author was to receive an additional £5 when thirteen hundred copies had been " sold and retailed off to particular reading customers." The original document of this agreement is in the British Museum, to which it was presented

The Painters' Graves in the Crypt of St. Paul's Cathedral.

by the poet Rogers, who had purchased the same for one hundred guineas.

Milton subsequently wrote "Paradise Regained," a production which he himself valued more than its predecessor. His remaining days were passed in peaceful retirement, and in 1674 death came gently upon him, and found him — ready!

> "How beautiful is genius when combined
> With holiness! Oh, how divinely sweet
> The tones of earthly harp, whose chords are touched
> By the soft hand of piety, and hung
> Upon Religion's shrine, there vibrating
> With solemn music in the ear of God!"

The parish register of St. Giles has a line—"12th November, 1674, John Milton, gentleman, consumpc'on, chancel."

The poet's remains lay without a memorial until, in 1793, at the expense of the patriotic Samuel Whitbread, a bust of Milton by Bacon, with a tablet, was set up on the north side of the nave. From the grave of Milton—surrounded as it appears to be with a halo of intellectual grandeur—we reluctantly turn away; and, leaving Cripplegate, a vast and lofty dome becomes our guide to

ST. PAUL'S CATHEDRAL.

It would appear that from the most ancient times the vicinity of this magnificent church has been used as a burying-ground; consequently, whilst within its precinct, we tread upon the dust of Briton, Roman, and Saxon, and, above them all, the graves of later generations. Tradition speaks of the situation having been occupied by a temple dedicated to Diana or Jupiter; but Wren, in digging the foundation for the present structure, found no corroboration of such surmise. This metropolitan church is supposed by some writers to have been founded by the apostle Paul himself, though many questions have arisen upon the subject. Christianity would seem to have been introduced into Britain at a period contemporary with the apostles. Joseph of Arimathea was claimed by the monks of Glastonbury as having conveyed the Gospel into this country; but their authority rests only on a monkish legend. The question of the apostleship of Britain appears to lie between St. Peter and St. Paul, the Romish authors claiming on behalf of the former, and those of our church the latter.

The see of London was in existence at the latter part of the second century, but it was not until the beginning of the sixth century that we hear of a cathedral having been erected. To the adornment of this church many succeeding kings contributed, including Athelstan, Edgar, Canute, and the pious Confessor. At the Conquest it received the support of William; but during the Conqueror's reign (1086) the church was burned. Its rebuilding was commenced towards the close of the eleventh century. Like its predecessor, this structure continued to receive numerous additions and improvements. Thus, in 1221, a new steeple was completed, and nineteen years later a new choir was added. In 1444 the spire of St. Paul's was struck by lightning, and during the reign of Elizabeth (1561) the tall steeple, with the roof of the church and aisle, was destroyed. The accounts published at the time attributed this calamity to lightning, though later historians placed it to the neglect of a plumber in leaving a pan of lighted coals unprotected. Some repairs were subsequently effected, but from neglect the edifice was allowed to fall almost into ruins; and towards the close of the sixteenth century a dungheap was to be seen within its doors, whilst the steps of the choir were frequently occupied at night by beggars and drunkards! The middle aisle was at this time known as Paul's Walk, being the daily promenade of a motley group of persons of all ranks. In 1633 the work of improvement was commenced, Inigo Jones being engaged in its direction. In ten years these restorations were effected, with the exception of the steeple; but the Civil War speedily followed, and horse-soldiers became quartered in the nave of the sacred edifice! The second Charles commenced repairing the injuries perpetrated by civil discord; but the Great Fire of 1666 cared nothing for old St. Paul's, which added a triumph to its blazing progress.

One of the appendages of this old church was Paul's Cross, from which, about the year 1300, sermons were first preached. The mystic types used in printing were not then invented; and the newspaper, with its "fluctuations and its vast concerns," was not then found on the breakfast-table of the citizens. Proclamations were consequently read at the Cross, where information of a varied nature was imparted to the people. According to old Stow, it was "a pulpit cross of timber, mounted upon steps of stone, and covered with lead." It was here that the great preachers of the Reformation came — it was here that

Latimer and Ridley frequently proclaimed their faith. During Mary's reign St. Paul's Cross echoed with the doctrines of Rome; but in 1643 it was finally levelled with the ground by order of the Long Parliament, and thus the celebrated Cross became a thing of the past.

In the list of the buried dead of old St. Paul's are great names, including that of John of Gaunt, "time-honour'd Lancaster;" but, carrying out our original design, we seek in such list for the poets, and rejoice that our eye alights upon a distinguished name,—

SIR PHILIP SYDNEY.

This ornament of the court of Elizabeth is said to have been born on the 29th of November, 1554, at Penshurst, in Kent, and at an early age was sent to the grammar-school at Shrewsbury. He was subsequently entered as a student at Christ Church, Oxford, from whence, after completing his education, he proceeded to the Continent, and was concealed at Paris during the terrible massacre of St. Bartholomew. In Hungary, Germany, and Italy he studied graceful and warlike exercises, and returned to England an accomplished courtier, becoming soon a favourite of Elizabeth. A striking proof of that favour is to be found in the peremptory command of the queen that Sydney should not embark with Sir Francis Drake in his second expedition against the Spaniards in the West Indies, "lest she should lose the jewel of her dominions." It was during a temporary secession from court that Sydney wrote his "Arcadia," a pastoral romance, chiefly composed for the amusement of his sister, the Countess of Pembroke, the subject of Ben Jonson's celebrated epitaph. In his dedication to this beloved sister he says: "You desired me to do it, and your desire, to my heart, is an absolute commandment. Now, it is done only for you; if you keep it to yourself, or commend it to such friends who will weigh errors in the balance of good-will, I hope, for the father's sake, it will be pardoned, perchance made much of, though in itself it have deformities." Ultimately overcoming the disinclination of the queen, Sydney was employed on military service; and, after many successes, received a wound under the walls of Zutphen, which proved fatal on the 7th of October, 1586, he being then in the thirty-third year of his age. England mourned for the loss of her poet-hero, whose body was interred in old St. Paul's with great magnificence: a general mourning was observed throughout the country, it being the first occasion on which such a ceremony had been known in England. Sir Philip Sydney was one of the noblest men of whom England has to be proud. As a writer his principal work is the "Defence of Poesie." Raleigh designated him the "English Petrarch," whilst Cowper happily styles him the "warbler of poetic prose;" and a third writer remarks that "he trod from his cradle to his grave amid incense and flowers, and died in a dream of glory."

We look again into the list from which we selected this "hero of the lyre and sword," and find the name of another lyrist, one who was likewise distinguished as a Christian minister,—

DOCTOR JOHN DONNE,

Dean of St. Paul's, and the celebrated poet and preacher

of the reign of James I., some of whose pieces, both for thought and even melody, are absolute gems. Donne was born in London in 1573, and at the early age of eleven, being a good Latin scholar, was sent to the University of Oxford, and thence removed to Cambridge. He studied for the law in Lincoln's Inn, but subsequently, at the request of James I., he took holy orders. Walton describes Donne as "always preaching as an angel *from* a cloud, but not *in* a cloud." Of his poetical pieces, many written in lyric measures are perfect music. Ben Jonson predicted that Donne would perish as a poet for want of being understood. His "Poems, Letters, and Elegies" are now little read; but his "Satires" are models of strength and energy, and their merits were discovered by Pope, who "translated them into English!"

Donne died in 1631. In his last illness he designed his own monument, and, having caused a wooden urn to be carved, he stood upon the urn with his winding-sheet "put on him, and so tied with knots at his head and feet, and his hands so placed, as dead bodies are usually fitted, to be shrouded and put into their coffin or grave. Upon this urn he thus stood, with his eyes shut, and with so much of the sheet turned aside as might show his lean, pale, and deathlike face, which was purposely turned towards the east, from whence he expected the second coming of his and our Saviour Jesus." When the picture was finished he caused it to be set by his bedside, where it continued, and became his hourly object till his death, and was then given to his dearest friend and executor, Dr. Henry King, who caused Donne to be thus carved in one entire piece of marble, for which he dictated an epitaph in elegant

Latin. He was accordingly buried in the old cathedral, followed by great numbers of "persons of nobility and of eminency for learning, who did love and honour him in his life, and did show it at his death by a voluntary and sad attendance of his body to the grave, where nothing was so remarkable as a public sorrow." The reader will find a touching account of these last honours to Donne in Isaac Walton's life of the great preacher and poet. His effigy lies here upon a stone bench, and as the turmoil of the street finds its way through the iron *grille* of the arched window, breaking the solemn silence of the crypt, one cannot help regretting that more care has not been taken to preserve the memorial of the poet in the position in which he took such pains to be portrayed in marble two centuries and a quarter since.

He was subsequently appointed chaplain to the king, and likewise became dean of St. Paul's. One of his earliest supporters was Sir Robert Drewry, who was "a cherisher of his studies, and such a friend as sympathised with him and his in all their joys and sorrows." Donne accompanied this patron to Paris, and some of his finest verses commemorate the separation of himself from his wife. Referring in these verses to his own and his wife's soul, he says:—

> " If they be two, they are too so
>   As stiff twin compasses are two.
> Thy soul, the fix'd foot, makes no show
>   To move, but doth if the other do.
> And though it in the centre sit,
>   Yet, when the other far doth roam,
> It leans, and hearkens after it,
>   And grows erect when that comes home."

Another name—it is that of a great painter—and we lower the curtain upon old St. Paul's. The name is an illustrious one,—

SIR ANTHONY VANDYCK.

Born at Antwerp in March, 1598, this artist was first placed with Henry Van Balen, but afterwards with Rubens. Under this last master he made such progress as to be able to assist in the works from which he studied. Rubens advised him to devote himself to portraits, in which he foresaw he would excel. After making the tour of Italy, Vandyck returned to Antwerp, and then visited England. Failing, at first, in securing the notice of Charles I., he quitted this country in chagrin, but was subsequently invited by that monarch to return. On this second visit he was lodged at Blackfriars among the king's artists, where he was frequently visited by Charles, who was so well pleased with his works that he conferred the honour of knighthood upon him at St. James's in July, 1632. Vandyck had his studio at Whitehall, and painted numerous pictures for his royal and unfortunate master. He died in 1641, leaving an infant daughter and heiress. As a painter, in portraits, he is allowed to have but one superior—Titian. He was indefatigable in his application: he painted a portrait in a day. Notwithstanding his expensive habits, he died worth about £20,000. He was an accomplished man, amiable and generous, but, at the same time, was petulant and vain. He was interred in old St. Paul's, near to the remains of John of Gaunt. The Civil War, however, which speedily followed his demise, prevented the erection of any tomb to his memory.

It was on the 21st of June, 1675, that the first stone of the present St. Paul's was laid by Sir Christopher Wren. Despite innumerable difficulties, that architect was enabled to complete his designs, though it occupied nearly forty years of his life. In this respect our cathedral was more fortunate than its rival, St. Peter's, at Rome, which was the work of more than twenty architects, supported by the treasure of the Christian world, under the pontificates of nineteen successive popes. The expense incurred in the erection of St. Paul's was about £750,000, equal to nearly £1,250,000 present money. In 1710 Wren had reached his seventy-eighth year, and with a gratified heart he then attended his son, and witnessed the placing by him of the highest stone of the lantern on the cupola. England had seen many changes during the forty-four years which had then elapsed since the Great Fire, thirty-five of which had passed since the first stone of the building had been laid; and three sovereigns had terminated their reign. Divine service was performed in the new church, for the first time, on the 5th of December, 1697.

St. Paul's has no "Poets' Corner"* like the Western Minster. There are monuments, it is true, numbering about fifty, but of that number seven or eight only are to be found which record eminence reached by the arts of peace; the remainder, to use the phrase of Flaxman, are "paragraphs of military gazettes" cut in stone. Yes; in this temple, dedicated to Religion and to all that is asso-

* The late Douglas Jerrold says, in his play of *The Heart of Gold*, with strange humour and pathos: "The Corner where they put the poets. Poor things! What have they done that they should always be put in a corner?"

ciated with Peace, we encounter at every step memorials of war and slaughter. Nelson and Wellington are sleeping here, and around them are sculptured the deeds of Collingwood, Cornwallis, Abercromby, Rodney, Howe, Ponsonby, Picton, St. Vincent, Jervis, Duncan, Moore, Dundas, &c. These monuments were erected at the public expense, the cost exceeding £100,000. Lives passed in the service of their country merited this acknowledgment; but our present thoughts are with

" A different race of men,
Who loathed the sword and loved the pen."

We therefore seek the small minority of monuments. Here is a colossal statue of the illustrious philanthropist, Howard, erected in 1791, being the first monument admitted into the cathedral. Here is another to Sir William Jones, the accomplished scholar, and in part a poet. The statue raised to the memory of Johnson is by Bacon,* and has been the subject of much praise; but we have already stood over the grave of the great lexicographer in Westminster Abbey. Mr. Leslie, R.A., says : " If Westminster Abbey has its *Poets' Corner*, so has St. Paul's its *Painters' Corner*. Sir Joshua Reynolds lies buried here, and Barry, and Opie, and Lawrence are around him; and, above all, the ashes of the great Vandyck are in the earth under the cathedral."

* John Bacon was a popular sculptor in his day. He died on the 7th of August, 1799, at the age of fifty-nine. In Whitefield's Chapel, Tottenham Court Road, will be found a plain tablet, with his own characteristic inscription :—" What I was as an artist seemed to me of some importance while I lived; but what I was as a believer in Jesus Christ is the only thing of importance to me now."

The painters' graves are in the crypt of the cathedral, which is now only used as a place of interment; and in the south aisle, not far from the eastern end, at certain periods of the day, the sunlight sheds its glory upon these resting-places of the sons of genius who, by their beautiful art, have sought to refine, ennoble, and exalt mankind.* First is the grave of

SIR JOSHUA REYNOLDS.

This great artist was born at Plympton, in Devonshire, on the 10th of July, 1723, his father being the rector and master of the grammar-school of the parish. He was at first intended for the medical profession; but, as he very early evinced a taste for art, his resolution of becoming a painter was adopted. In 1741 he was accordingly placed with Hudson, then a portrait-painter of some eminence in London. Thomas Hudson was born in 1701, and outstepped his rivals in the race for distinction. Visiting Rome with Roubiliac, he entered Italy as Reynolds was leaving it; and it was at Mount Cenis, in their passage over the Alps, that the rising and setting stars of portraiture in England encountered each other. With Hudson (who died in 1779) Reynolds remained two years, and then commenced painting "on his own account" at Devonport, at that time known as Plymouth Dock. In 1746 he began to practise his art in London, having taken apartments in St. Martin's Lane. He ultimately became the most distinguished portrait-painter in England, and

* This hallowed spot is engraved from a sketch made for the present volume.

in 1786 was unanimously chosen president of the then newly-established Royal Academy, receiving the honour of knighthood upon the occasion. Sir Joshua died at his house, No. 47, in Leicester Square, on the 23rd of February, 1792, and was buried with great pomp in St. Paul's.

Burke passed a high eulogium upon the merits of Reynolds as a painter, remarking that "in taste, in grace, and facility, in happy invention, and in the richness and harmony of colouring, he was equal to the greatest masters of the renowned ages." Cunningham, in his memoir of Sir Joshua, relates the following instance of the force of habit. Reynolds had been taught by his old master, Hudson, to paint portraits in a certain position; the gentleman, for instance, holding his hat under his arm. Before he had thrown off the trammels of habit, and began to exhibit that free and bold manner that afterwards distinguished him, a customer desired to be painted with his hat on. His wish was gratified, but when the portrait was sent home the gentleman's wife was not a little astonished to perceive that her husband had two hats, one on his head and another under his arm!

In the nave of the cathedral above is placed the portrait statue of Reynolds, one of the finest works of Flaxman, our greatest English sculptor.

Leftward in the crypt is the grave of the most distinguished historical painter of the English school,—

BENJAMIN WEST,

who was born at Springfield, in Pennsylvania, on the 10th of October, 1738. At the age of eighteen he commenced as a portrait-painter in Philadelphia, whence he removed to New York. He next visited the classic shrines of Italy, where he remained three years; and in 1763 he placed his foot upon the soil of England. One of his first patrons in this country was Dr. Drummond, Archbishop of York, who introduced the young artist to George III., by whom he was almost exclusively employed for more than thirty years, from 1767 until 1802. In the last-named year he lost the patronage of the court through the illness of the king. West was then sixty-four years of age,* but commenced a series of religious pictures on a large scale, the first of this series being " Christ Healing the Sick," which is now in the National Gallery. West painted this picture for the Quakers (to which denomination he belonged) of Philadelphia, to aid them in the erection of a hospital. It was first exhibited in London, where its excellence was considered so great that three thousand guineas were offered for it by the British Insti-

* " It is never too late to mend," says the homely adage. Milton, in his blindness, when past the age of fifty, sat down to complete his world-known epic; and Scott, at fifty-five, took up his pen to redeem an enormous liability. " I am still learning," said Michael Angelo, when threescore years and ten were past, and he had long attained the highest triumph of the pencil. John Kemble is said to have written out the part of Hamlet thirty times, and each time discovered something which had previously escaped him; and during his last season he remarked, " Now that I am retiring I am only beginning thoroughly to understand my art." His gifted sister, Mrs. Siddons, after she had left the stage, was waited upon by a friend, who found her in her garden musing over a book. " I am reading over Lady Macbeth," said the incomparable actress, " and I am amazed to discover some new point in the character which I never found out while acting it."

G

tution. West accepted the offer, on condition that he might be allowed to execute a copy for Philadelphia. He painted altogether, including his coloured sketches, about four hundred pictures. One of his most celebrated works is the "Death of General Wolfe," in which the characters are dressed in their proper costume. This was considered, when being adopted, an innovation; it having been the practice of painters to dress their figures, in historical compositions, in the Greek or Roman costume. West was one of the original members of the Royal Academy, and in 1792 succeeded Sir Joshua Reynolds as its president. He died in Newman-street on the 11th of March, 1820, being then in his eighty-second year. The honour of knighthood had been offered to West, but declined. "No man," he remarked, "entertains a higher respect than myself for political honours and distinctions, but I really think I have earned more eminence by my pen already than knighthood could confer on me."

Immediately on the left of Reynolds lies

JAMES BARRY,

who was born in the city of Cork in 1741, his father at that time being engaged in the coasting trade between England and Ireland. A love of drawing rescued the son from the same employment. A picture, some years later, was accepted for an exhibition of art in Dublin, the subject being an incident in the history of St. Patrick. The exhibition opened, and inquiry was made by every one, "Who is the painter?" The question could not be answered until a poorly-clad young man, with trembling lips, confessed it to be his own work, and then hurried away. That young man was Barry. There was one present, however, who hurried after the modest artist, and became his patron. This was Edmund Burke. By the aid of the great orator the young painter was sent to Rome, and, after studying for three years the great masters in Italy, he returned to England, and became a member of the Royal Academy.

Barry's works include the pictures which adorn the "great room" of the Society of Arts in the Adelphi. When he commenced these paintings he was worth just sixteen shillings; the undertaking occupied him six years, during which time he never borrowed a sixpence, but subsisted upon the employment he was enabled to obtain and to accomplish by night. From these facts it is to be feared that the eccentric artist was troubled at times to appease what old Homer calls "the sacred rage of hunger." When completed, the exhibition of Barry's labours produced him nearly £1000. Jonas Hanway, the benevolent merchant and traveller, was an early visitor to these wonderful paintings. Having taken a slight survey, he hurried back to the door, and insisted upon paying a guinea for admission, instead of the shilling he had already deposited. Barry died on the 21st of February, 1806.

On the right of Reynolds rest the remains of

JOHN OPIE,

who was born in Cornwall in 1761, and was intended for the humble calling of his father, that of a carpenter. When very young, however, he evinced a taste for drawing, and began to take likenesses of his relations and neighbours, which attracted the notice of Dr. Wolcot (Peter Pindar), who possessed considerable knowledge of painting, and with whom Opie arrived in London in 1781. He was introduced to Sir Joshua Reynolds; and through Wolcot's aid, Opie soon rose into fame as the "Cornish wonder," and was elected an academician. He was twice married, his second wife being Amelia Alderson, the possessor of one of the kindliest hearts in the world, and who became so favourably known in the field of literature. John Opie holds a respectable station among English painters: his historical pictures are remarkable for their vivid reality and truthful colouring. He died on the 9th of April, 1807: his amiable widow survived him until 1853.

In the summer of 1806 Mr. and Mrs. Opie, with David Wilkie, were among the guests assembled at Southhill, the seat of Samuel Whitbread. The wife of our painter there formed an intimacy with the fascinating Lady Roslyn, whose premature death prevented a more ripened friendship. Ten years later, Mrs. Opie visited the grave of that lady in the beautiful but ruined chapel of Roslyn Castle, and stood upon the stone that covered her remains. An "auld wifie" accompanied her as guide to the spot, of whom she inquired whether she had known Lady Roslyn. "Knew her!" replied the woman, almost pettishly; "ah! to be sure I did, and many others knew her too; and there were as many tears shed at her death as would ha' washed out a shirt or a sack." The eulogy, homely as it was, was earnest and touching; and, said Mrs. Opie, "With a tearful eye and a quivering lip I turned away, for it had gone to my heart."

HENRY FUSELI,

whose remains lie next to Reynolds, was born at Zurich, in Switzerland, and was intended for the church. The palette, however, was preferred by him to the pulpit, and in 1765 he settled in London. Some of his sketches were here shown to Reynolds, from whom they elicited the warmest praise. This was decisive of his after-course in life. He studied in Rome, one of his fellow-students in the "Eternal City" being James Northcote. These artists subsequently became Royal Academicians, and both were engaged upon Boydell's Shakspeare Gallery. For this work Fuseli painted eight of his best pictures. A series of forty-seven of his paintings was at one time exhibited as the Milton Gallery. Fuseli died on the 16th of April, 1825.

Five years later, and another president of the Academy rejoined his predecessors, Reynolds and West. This was

SIR THOMAS LAWRENCE,

who was born at Bristol on the 4th of May, 1769, and early exhibited great ability in drawing. His father was landlord of the Black Bear at Devizes, where young Lawrence attracted notice by sketching in chalk some of the customers at the inn. When little more than ten years old he set up as a portrait-painter in crayons at Oxford, whence he removed to Bath, where he experienced considerable success. At the age of seventeen he commenced oil-painting, and one year later (1787) he settled in London, and became a student in the Royal Academy. Of this institution he was elected an associate in 1791, an academician in 1795; on the death of West he was unanimously chosen its president, and he was knighted by the Prince Regent in 1815. Lawrence died at his house in Russell Square on the 7th of January, 1830. During his career he was unrivalled as a portrait-painter, and the Waterloo Gallery at Windsor Castle is a noble monument of his skill.

The painter last added to this artistic companionship was

J. M. W. TURNER.

This celebrated artist was born in 1773, at the corner of Hand Court, in Maiden Lane, Covent Garden, where his father was a hair-dresser. He first studied architectural design, and in 1790 exhibited at the Academy a water-coloured drawing of the entrance to Lambeth. This was followed, three years later, by his first oil-painting. He became an associate of the Academy in 1799, and in 1802 was elected academician. Great works now proceeded rapidly from his pencil, and drawings were furnished by him for the illustration of the works of Milton, Scott, Rogers, and others of our poets. To some of these drawings a high value is attached: a small sketch in water colours has been sold for one hundred and twenty guineas; whilst a sketch-book of one of Turner's river tours on the Continent has realised six hundred guineas. He ultimately secured the reputation of being one of the greatest landscape painters that England has produced. His pictures are remarkable for truth, and effects which were produced by means that few could discover.

Campbell relates of our painter the following:—" Turner is a ready wit. Once at a dinner where several artists, amateurs, and literary men were convened, a poet, by way of being facetious, proposed, as a toast, the health of the *painters* and *glaziers* of Great Britain. The toast was drunk ; and Turner, after returning thanks for it, proposed the health of the British *paper-stainers.*"

If Turner was one of the greatest artists of his day, he was at the same time one of the most eccentric of men. He loved retirement, and one of his peculiarities was his dislike of having his place of abode known. He possessed a mansion in Queen Anne-street, but at the time of his death (December 19th, 1851) he occupied apartments at Chelsea. It is related that he saw these rooms, and, approving both of their appearance and of their cheapness (the latter a great recommendation), he immediately secured them. The landlady, as was natural, required a reference. This was met by the somewhat angry response, " I will buy your house outright, my good woman." An agreement was now requisite. Out came a handful of bank-notes and sovereigns, with an offer to pay the rent in advance. Another difficulty still. The landlady wished to know her lodger's name, " in case any gentleman should call." This was a serious dilemma. " Name—name !" Turner muttered to himself ; " what is *your* name ? " " My name is Mrs. Brook." " Oh !" was his reply ; " then I am Mr. Brook." And as a " Mr. Brook " our artist occupied and died in those apartments. Turner's parsimonious habits enabled him to amass property to the amount of £100,000, which, at his death, he left to found almshouses for the benefit of unfortunate and meritorious artists. His pictures he likewise bequeathed to the nation, on the express condition that, within a given period, a suitable place should be provided for their deposit and exhibition. Turner's remains were interred in the crypt of the cathedral, close to the grave of Sir Christopher Wren.

Here is a mural tablet, with a medallic portrait, to Barry; and upon the opposite pier is a memorial to the daughter of Sir Christopher Wren, who is said to have made many of the drawings, and assisted in the designs, of her father's greatest works.

' Passing onward to the left, you reach the chamber of the crypt, wherein rests the great Duke of Wellington in a porphyry sarcophagus; and in the dim distance is seen the sarcophagus wherein are deposited the remains of Nelson. This juxtaposition of England's two greatest heroes is very impressive.

We were about to quit our metropolitan church, first obeying the instruction on the tomb of its architect,—

"Si monumentum requiris, circumspice;"

but, remembering that a "poor player" slumbers in the adjacent burial-ground, we linger a few moments over the grave of

RICHARD SUETT.

This child of mirth was born at Chelsea in 1755, and became, ten years later, one of the choir at St. Paul's. He would in after-life speak of his chorister days, when he was "cherub Dicky." In 1769 he was engaged as a vocalist at the then celebrated Ranelagh Gardens, and in the following year his services were secured by Foote for the Haymarket Theatre. He next joined the York circuit, and was ultimately transferred therefrom to the boards of Drury Lane. Suett excelled in old men, and in the clowns and jesters of Shakspeare; but his irregularities retarded the maturity of his abilities and hastened his demise, which occurred on the 5th of July, 1805. "Dicky Suett"—for so in his lifetime he was best pleased to be called—was the "Robin Goodfellow" of the stage, and a personal favourite with the town. "He lieth buried," says Charles Lamb, "on the north side of the cemetery of Holy Paul."

We now pass down the busy stream of Ludgate Hill to

ST. BRIDE'S, FLEET STREET.

To Sir Christopher Wren we are likewise indebted for this church, with its fine spire, erected in the year 1680. The structure which originally occupied the site was destroyed in the Great Fire of 1666. In St. Bride's churchyard Milton once had lodgings, "at the house of one Russel, a Taylor, where he first undertook the education and instruction of his sister's two sons." In the old church were buried the remains of Wynkyn de Worde, the famous printer, who was the associate and successor of Caxton; Thomas Sackville, Earl of Dorset, the poet; Sir Richard Baker, author of the "Chronicles of the Kings of England;" and, with others, two writers over whose memory we may linger. The first was the most accomplished and popular gallant of his day,—

RICHARD LOVELACE,

who was the eldest son of Sir William Lovelace, of Woolwich, and was himself born in Kent. After receiving his "grammar learning" at the Charterhouse, he became a gentleman commoner of Gloucester Hall, Oxford. At this period (1634), according to Anthony à Wood, he was "accounted the most amiable and beautiful person that eye ever beheld; a person also of innate modesty, virtue, and courtly deportment, which made him then, but especially after when he retired to the great city, much admired and adored by the female sex." Richard Lovelace, whose early life abounded with such promise, entered the military service of Charles I., being at first an ensign, and afterwards a captain. Ardent in the royal cause, and living beyond his means, he subsequently became an object of charity. When he "was in glory he wore cloth of gold and silver," but now he "went in ragged clothes;" and finally died, in 1658, at an obscure lodging in Gunpowder Alley, leading from Shoe Lane. He was the author of a tragedy and a comedy, and several songs: of the latter, the song "To Althea, from Prison," will live, says Southey, "as long as the English language."

In the present church lies Ogilby, the translator of Homer; and near the communion table Hatman, the poet and painter.

About the middle of the centre aisle lies the once popular novelist,—

SAMUEL RICHARDSON,

who was born in Devonshire in 1689, and at the usual age was apprenticed to a London printer. It was in the neighbourhood of his final resting-place, in the centre of Salisbury Square, that in after-years his own printing-office was to be found, in which he "composed at case," without copy, some portions of his "Pamela" and "Clarissa Harlowe." Richardson died on the 4th of July, 1761, at the age of seventy-two. He was a man of much benevolence and moral worth, and was constantly visited by Johnson, Hogarth, Dr. Young, and other eminent men of the day; and by Mrs. Barbauld, when a playful child.

Though little read at the present time, the works of Richardson were once exceedingly popular, in proof of which Sir John Herschel adduces the following record:—
" I recollect an anecdote told me by a late highly respectable inhabitant of Windsor, as a fact which he could personally testify to, having occurred in a village where he resided several years, and where he actually was at the time it took place. The blacksmith of the village had got hold of Richardson's novel of ' Pamela, or Virtue Rewarded,' and used to read it aloud in the long summer evenings, seated on his anvil, and never failed to have a large and attentive audience. It is a pretty long-winded book, but their patience was fully a match for the author's prolixity, and they fairly listened to all. At length, when the happy turn of fortune arrived which brings the hero and heroine together, and sets them living long and happily, according to the most approved rules, the congregation was so delighted as to raise a great shout, and, procuring the church keys, actually set the parish bells a ringing!"

Crossing Fleet-street, and wending our way through Shoe Lane, we reach

ST. ANDREW'S, HOLBORN.

In the survey made in the reign of the Conqueror

Holborn is specified as a village situate in the hundred of Osulvestane (Ossulston), and is denominated Holebrune. Reference is made to the church about the year 1297, but how long it had existed previously is not known. The rectory of St. Andrew's was at one time in the gift of the abbots of Bermondsey, but was taken from them at the dissolution of the religious houses by Henry VIII. It was then bestowed upon the Lord Chancellor, Thomas Wriothesley, Earl of Southampton, from whose family it descended by marriage to the Duke of Montague. Bishops Hacket* and Stillingfleet, and Dr. Sacheverel are to be found in the list of its rectors. The present edifice was rebuilt in 1686, under the superintendence of Sir Christopher Wren.

St. Andrew's has been called "the Poets' Church," from the sons of Song connected with it. John Webster, the dramatic poet, a late contemporary of Shakspeare, is said to have been parish-clerk here, but this is not attested by the register. Richard Savage was christened here, January 18th, 1696-7. In the churchyard lies Henry Neele, the poet, the gravestone bearing a touching epitaph written by him on his father. And the church register records, "August 28th, 1770, *William* (Thomas) Chatterton," with "the poet," added by a later hand, interred in the burial-ground of the workhouse in Shoe Lane, now the site of Farringdon Market.

---

* One Sunday, while Hacket was reading the common prayer in St. Andrew's, a soldier of the Earl of Essex came and clapped a pistol to his breast, and commanded him to read no further. Not at all terrified, Hacket said he would do what became a divine, and he might do what became a soldier! He was permitted to proceed.

THOMAS CHATTERTON.

The "marvellous boy" was born at Bristol in November, 1752, his father being the sexton at the church of St. Mary Redcliff in that city. Eight years after his birth he was admitted into Colston's Blue-coat School, and soon after began to present to the world that which puzzled the learned and most acute. Day after day did he produce poems of considerable length and great beauty, the obsolete spelling and the diffuse, quaint style bearing the stamp of a bygone age. He occasionally contributed to newspapers and magazines under assumed names. The obscure Bristol boy saw no attraction in his own name, and therefore were his early productions given to the world as the emanations of a monk named Rowley, these poems exhibiting a grandeur of conception with a boldness and sweetness combined. Chatterton was at length taken into the office of a scrivener, which he was compelled to leave in consequence of the discovery of the extraordinary document known as his " Will," and which is still preserved. He was now in his seventeenth year, and quitted Bristol for London, full of high expectation. Here he managed to procure, for a short time, a precarious existence by his pen, writing political and satirical articles, burlettas for Vauxhall, and sermons for clergymen! But his hopes soon passed away; he was abused, and savagely attacked for his " Rowley Poems ;" he had passed five months in the metropolis, and the reward of severe toil and patient endurance was to be found in the frequent lack of bread! His humble lodgings were in Brook-street, Holborn, and his sustenance for three days was a crust of dry bread and a little water. But August, 1770, brought this "drama of a life" to its close. Heart-sick of the world and of its gilded promises, he expended the last penny he possessed in the purchase of arsenic, and was found on his wretched pallet a corpse, lacking at the time three months of his eighteenth year. We have no "storied urn" to direct us to the spot of his sepulture, for above the pauper, unblessed grave of Chatterton no stone was placed. To his name, however, honour has been given by the most gifted of men: Byron lauded him; Shelley wrote of his "solemn agency;" Coleridge indited to him a noble monody; Keats dedicated "Endymion" to his memory; and Bristol, in posthumous atonement for the neglect of her Blue-coat boy, presented him with a monument seventy-five years after his death. We conclude our brief notice of this wondrous youth by reciting a little poem, which was "A Thought" upon the death of Keats, and the subsequent recognition of his talents:—

"' We heed thee not!—give o'er, give o'er!'
Said the World, as the Poet pour'd
The wealth of his soul and its glory forth
In burning thought and word—
' Give o'er, give o'er!'

" Then a darkness fell on the Poet's face,
An omen of death and doom.
Ah me! ah me! what tears rain'd down
When soon, in the shadowy tomb,
His rest was won.

"' We will weave a crown for this Poet's brow,'
Said the World, 'we will build a throne
For his kingly fame; and from shore to shore
For aye shall his name be known—
For aye, for aye!'

"Amen to that loving deed, O World!
Amen! brave world art thou!
With thy bitter scorn for the beating heart,
And thy crown for the corpse's brow—
Amen! O World!"

But we have to search for a player, and in the churchyard we find the honoured grave of

JOHN EMERY.

This favourite actor was born at Sunderland in December, 1777, his parents being members of the histrionic profession. Though intended for a musician, he himself preferred the pursuit adopted by his parents, and became an actor. At Sheffield, in 1790, he ventured upon a song on the occasion of his father's benefit; and three years later he obtained an engagement at the Brighton Theatre, where he appended to his duties as a comedian those of a scene-painter. Emery was next engaged by the warm-hearted, but eccentric Tate Wilkinson for the York circuit, in which he continued until 1798: in this year he made his *début* in the metropolis, at Covent Garden, as Frank Oatlands, in Morton's *Cure for the Heartache.* He had at this period scarcely reached his majority, yet was his success most decisive. His subsequent career was marked with public approval, which he continued to enjoy until his death, which occurred somewhat suddenly on the 25th of July, 1822, having then reached only his forty-fifth year. As an actor Emery had scarcely a competitor in his day, and left no successor possessing, as he did, a natural and rich humour, untainted by vapid trickery or grimace. He was strikingly effective in serious characters, and his Robert Tyke, in the *School of Reform*, was a masterpiece of acting. Many an old actor has been encountered in the course of these "visits," upon whom could be traced the marks of sixty or seventy summers; but poor John Emery was suddenly snatched from the footlights in the prime of his life. There is a tablet to his memory in the south aisle of St Andrew's church.

We have now to visit another church which the fertile genius of Wren assisted in giving to the metropolis—that of St. Clement Danes. To reach this from St. Andrew's we will ascend Holborn Hill, and pass through Lincoln's Inn Fields, the name of which is derived from the founder of the adjacent inn, Henry Lacy, Earl of Lincoln, who died here in 1312. It was in these "Fields" that William Lord Russell lost his head upon the block in 1683. Tradition has a story that Ben Jonson worked here as a bricklayer on the garden-wall next to Chancery Lane. Aubrey is an authority for this story, and Fuller also says, "He helped in the building of the new structure of Lincoln's Inn, where, having a trowel in his hand, he had a book in his pocket." Gifford, however, in his edition of Jonson's works, denies that the poet ever worked as a bricklayer, and treats the entire story as a "figment." In that little thoroughfare opening on the western side (Duke-street) Benjamin Franklin occupied apartments when employed in the neighbourhood as a journeyman printer.

We will for a few moments turn into Portugal-street, on the south side of the square, and so named in compliment to the queen of Charles II. Here stood the Duke's Theatre; and here, consequently, Congreve, Betterton, and Mrs. Bracegirdle—over whose ashes we have paused in Westminster Abbey—frequently acted before Charles and his gay court. That inclosure on the side opposite to where the theatre stood, the site of which now forms part of the hall of the College of Surgeons, was long the upper burying-ground of the parish of St. Clement Danes; and here were interred the remains of the world-renowned

JOSEPH MILLER.

The first notice of the stage career of this parent of all orphan jests appears in a bill announcing the performance of *The Constant Couple*, in which he played Young Clincher. This was in 1715. His last appearance upon the stage was on the 30th of May, 1738, when he played the parts of Clodpole (*Amorous Widow*), and the Miller (*King and the Miller of Mansfield*). He was such a favourite at court that Caroline, queen of George II., commanded a play for his benefit, and disposed of a great many tickets at one of her drawing-rooms. He died on the 15th of August, 1738, having then reached his fifty-fourth year. The stone which once marked his grave has been preserved: its inscription is as follows:—

" Here lye the remains of
Honest Joe Miller,
WHO WAS
A tender Husband,
A sincere Friend,

A facetious Companion,
And an excellent Comedian.
He departed this life the 15th day of August, 1738, aged 54 years.
If humour, wit, and honesty could save
The humorous, witty, honest, from the grave,
The grave had not so soon this tenant found,
Whom honesty, and wit, and humour crown'd.
Could but esteem and love preserve our breath,
And guard us longer from the stroke of Death,
The stroke of Death on him had later fell,
Whom all mankind esteem'd and loved so well."

These lines are attributed to Stephen Duck, the "thrasher poet."

Miller was not the wit for which he has received the credit of posterity. He was accustomed to visit "the Black Jack," in Portsmouth-street, where numerous tradesmen were wont to assemble and exercise their mirthful fancies. Their pleasantry, however, fell harmless upon the ears of Joseph Miller, whose taciturn countenance relaxed not from its accustomed gravity From this peculiarity his name (*lucus à non lucendo*) became linked with some of the jests of the day, a collection of which was made at his death by John Mottley, the author of several dramatic pieces. To this collection the name of "Joe Miller" was appended, and the work was published for the benefit of his family. The first edition appeared in December, 1738 (the year of Miller's death), although no date was affixed to it. A copy of this edition, at the Bindley sale, was sold for eleven pounds five shillings.

Previously to visiting the church of St. Clement Danes let us enter Chancery Lane, the great legal thoroughfare of London. A few doors from Fleet-street, on the left-hand side, is the site of the shop of Izaak Walton,—

"Happy old man, whose worth all mankind knows
Except himself."

The shop of the respected hosier has long been swept away. In a house which abutted upon Sergeants' Inn, but which has likewise disappeared, the poet Cowley was born; and Cowper was at one time here located in the capacity of an attorney's clerk.

We have now reached the bottom of Chancery Lane, and, crossing Fleet-street to the Inner Temple gate, at the bottom of the Lane is the

TEMPLE CHURCH.

This round, half-fortress-looking structure was founded by the Templars, the famous warriors, whose professed object was to "conquer the Holy Land, and to befriend all oppressed Christians." These knights of old blended piety with military skill and courage, and formed a mighty fellowship known through every country of Christian Europe. It was in the year 1128 that this band of men established themselves in London, their first house being in Holborn—the spot now occupied by Southampton Buildings—whence they removed to the present site, where they erected this beautiful church and other buildings on a scale of great splendour. The church was consecrated in 1185 by Heraclius, patriarch of Jerusalem, whose presence in this country was owing to a battle fought on the banks of the Jordan in 1179, when the Knight Templars were almost all annihilated by Saladin, and the grand master taken prisoner. To seek fresh aid throughout Europe was the object of the visit of Heraclius to England. The order of the Templars was finally abolished in 1312: the site and buildings of the Temple shortly after became the property of the students of the law, who have enjoyed the same for a period exceeding five centuries.

> "Where now the studious lawyers have their bowers,
> There whilom wont the Templar knights to bide,
> Till they decay'd through pride."—SPENSER.

The Temple suffered greatly in the rebellion of Wat Tyler, and narrowly escaped destruction, in the following century, during the outbreak under Jack Cade. Mutilations were subsequently effected, occasionally under the name of "improvements." In 1840, however, the work of restoration was commenced in the right spirit, and three years later the present interesting and beautiful church was completed. There, on the floor, lie the recumbent figures of Crusaders "in cross-legged effigy devoutly stretched;" whilst from the entrance door, looking towards the altar, there is presented, on a small scale, a specimen of the great ecclesiastical structures of the thirteenth century.

Connected with the Temple were the old poets, Chaucer, Gower, and Spenser. The learned and patriotic Selden came from Oxford to the Inner Temple, and in its precincts ultimately found a grave. Of others who have inhabited the Temple we might mention Sackville, Earl of Dorset, one of the authors of *Gorboduc*, the earliest English tragedy; Beaumont, Congreve, Wycherley, Edmund Burke, and Cowper. Samuel Johnson at one time resided on the first floor of the house No. 1, Inner Temple Lane, taken down in 1857. The poet Blair was here introduced to him, and subsequently described how he had "found the giant in his den."

The banking-house of Messrs. Child, adjoining Temple Bar, is supposed to occupy the site of the famous Devil Tavern, the resort of the wits from the days of Ben Jonson to those of Addison. Swift, in one of his letters to Stella, says: "I dined to-day with Dr. Garth and Mr. Addison at the Devil Tavern, near Temple Bar, and Garth treated."

Though teeming with so much beauty and so many historic associations, we quit the Temple Church for the paved court which until recently was its burying-ground. Here, beneath the pavement east of the choir, lies

OLIVER GOLDSMITH.

This universal favourite of those who read and feel was born in Ireland, at Pallas, county of Longford. The 10th of November, 1728, is stated to have been the day of his birth, though some uncertainty exists upon this as to the day. His father was the Rev. Charles Goldsmith, who, from an early and improvident marriage, was for many years dependent upon the kindness of a relative. It was at Lissoy, near to Athlone—to which place his parents removed—that Oliver received the first rudiments of education, and acquired the character of being "impenetrably stupid." He was next removed to a school of a higher class at Athlone, from thence to one at Edgeworth's Town, and finally (June 11th, 1745) was admitted into Trinity College, Dublin. Here he remained four years, with mutual dissatisfaction to himself and his tutors. It would seem that, at this period of his career, Goldsmith had a natural aptness for singing a song well, and likewise exceedingly enjoyed a good dinner. He consequently trifled away much of his time, and the books that should have been studied were pawned for "dinners and dances." A kind uncle, prior to his leaving college, tried his influence in inducing him to qualify for holy orders. "But," said Goldsmith subsequently, "to be obliged to wear a long wig when I liked a short one, or a black coat when I generally dressed in brown, I thought such a restraint upon my liberty that I absolutely rejected the proposal." He did, notwithstanding, consent to qualify, but was rejected on his application to the Bishop of Elphin for ordination. It is pretty certain that but little thought had been devoted to his qualification, and on his application to the bishop he appeared before that dignitary in "scarlet breeches!" Goldsmith next had several rambling expeditions, and from his first, at the end of three or four weeks, he returned to his astonished friends with a poor unfortunate pony, whom he had christened "Fiddleback."

The law was now thought of, then medicine, and, to complete his studies for the latter science, he started for Leyden. This city, in its turn, was quitted by our restless hero for a tour of the continent, his worldly possessions comprising "one shirt, one guinea, and one flute." Blessed with these auxiliaries, he continued his travels for some time, and finally entered London, where he commenced his course of literary drudgery. That career was at first marked by destitution and severe struggles with poverty. At length reputation came, though in its train was seen no substantial emolument. With a generous heart, Goldsmith thought but little of the morrow, and sorrow and disappointment were his frequent companions. He had a genial love for every kind of sport and enjoyment. At one time he resided at Islington, and was in the habit of making what he called a "shoemaker's holiday" with a few friends. He would, on those occasions, dine at Highbury Barn, adjourn to White Conduit House to tea, and conclude the evening at the Globe in Fleet-street. Garrick once remarked, " He wrote like an angel, and talked like poor Poll."

Goldsmith had a thousand faults, with many virtues to place in the opposite scale. Forgetting his own wants, he could appreciate the wants of others, whilst his love of truth and virtue was unchanging. He died at No. 2, Brick-court, April 4th, 1774, not far from the spot we feel reluctant to leave. Goldsmith left no species of writing untouched or unadorned by his pen; and if he could not boast of the correct and extended knowledge of some writers, he possessed a kindliness of feeling and truthfulness of description that yield a calm pleasure in the perusal of his works, which are full of artless benevolence and amiable views of human life.

In his days of poverty he was to be found in a chemist's shop at the corner of Monument-yard; he subsequently practised medicine for himself in a small way in the neighbourhood of Bankside, Southwark. His green coat was now exchanged for a black one, but which unfortunately exhibited a patch on the left breast. When conversing with a patient, the poet ingeniously concealed this defect in his garment by holding over the spot affected his cocked hat. A friend once kindly sought to remedy the inconvenience, but the hat was pressed more devoutly than ever to his heart!

Quitting the Temple, and returning into Fleet-street,

we pass through Temple Bar into the Strand; and before us, in the centre of this great thoroughfare, stands the capacious church of

ST. CLEMENT DANES.

In discussing the origin of this name much ink and paper have been used, and, what is far worse, much angry feeling has been exhibited. By the old historian, William of Malmesbury, we are told that the Danes burned down the church that in their day stood on this spot; but that, "desirous at length to return to Denmark, they were about to embark, when they were, by the judgment of God, all slain at London, in a place which has since been called the church of the Danes." From other sources we are led to infer that, when the Danes were driven out of England, a few who were married to Englishwomen were allowed to remain, provided that they resided between Ludgate and our present Westminster. They are said to have availed themselves of this leniency, and to have erected a church, which was called *Ecclesia Clementis Danorum*. Whatever be the origin of the name, it would appear certain that for more than eight hundred years a church has occupied the site of the present one, which was rebuilt in 1682, under the direction of Sir Christopher Wren. The chimes of this sacred building, which are still continued, are referred to by Falstaff and Justice Shallow.

Of the persons in connection with our present subject who have found sepulture in St. Clement Danes, we need only select two or three who have figured more prominently than the rest upon the great stage of the world. And first we can notice old

JOHN LOWEN,

the frequent companion of Shakspeare, and one of the original actors in the plays of the bard. His picture in the Ashmolean Museum at Oxford gives 1576 as the date of his birth. Wright mentions, in his "Historia Histrionica," that "before the wars he used to act the part of Falstaff with mighty applause." It is doubtful, however, whether the fat knight was first played by Lowen, the probability being that Heminge or some other actor originally acted the character, and that a few years later the part was given to Lowen, who, in a copy of verses written in 1632, is referred to as one of the most popular actors of the day. After the suppression of stage representations he appears to have fallen into poverty, but is said to have taken a small inn, by the aid of a few friends —the Three Pigeons—at Brentford. He is supposed to have died at the latter place, but it is certain that he was buried at Clement Danes on the 24th of August, 1653. The register designates him "player."

A poet, more unfortunate still than poor old Lowen, was likewise interred here,—

THOMAS OTWAY,

who was born on the 3rd of March, 1651, at Trotton, in Sussex, of which parish his father was at that time curate, though subsequently promoted to the rectorship of the adjoining parish of Wolbeding. Much attention was paid to Otway's early education. At Winchester he received his first lessons in classical learning, and was then entered a commoner of Christ Church, Oxford, where his wit and attainments made him much courted as an associate. Otway was intended for the church, but, as his father died without bequeathing him a patrimony, he repaired to London in 1651, having at that time no resources or any direct object. Necessity, as well as inclination, led him to the theatre, where he at first appeared as an actor, but the result was a failure. He then became the companion of men of rank and fashion, among whom was the young Earl of Plymouth, natural son of Charles II. These noble associates, however, did not relieve his necessities. He mixed in their revelries, but his pecuniary difficulties continued to increase. He attempted dramatic composition, and in 1675 produced *Alcibiades*. His second tragedy, *Don Carlos*, effected some improvement in his fortune, and brought him into competition with writers of the first rank.

Subsequently he obtained a cornet's commission in a new regiment of horse, which formed part of the army commanded by the Duke of Monmouth, and with which Otway went to Flanders. He soon after returned to England in extreme indigence, and found himself deserted by his former patrons: by Rochester he was even lampooned. Otway continued, notwithstanding, to write for the theatre, and in 1680-1 produced the work which keeps possession of the stage—*Venice Preserved*—for the copyright of which he received from the booksellers the sum of fifteen pounds. His latest production was given to the public in 1684. This was *The Atheist*, a continuation of a preceding play—*The Soldier's Fortune*. In April, 1685, Otway closed his chequered career. Experiencing many reverses of fortune, disheartened and cast down, he is said to have retired to the Bull public-house on Tower-hill to avoid his creditors, and there died in a state of great destitution. Such, at least, is the statement which has gained credence. Whatever be its truth, there is no doubt but that despondency and want embittered his later days.

Otway ranks high as a dramatic writer. By some critics he has been placed among the poets of the first order, and credit awarded him for being a master of the tragic passion. Sir Walter Scott says: "The talents of Otway, in his scenes of passionate affection, rival at least, and sometimes excel, those of Shakspeare."

St. Clement's Church received also the remains of at least "one more unfortunate," whose career, limited to thirty-five years, was marked by insanity. This was

NATHANIEL LEE.

A minister at Hatfield, Dr. Lee, was the father of this writer, who received a liberal education. After gaining the rudiments of his instruction at Westminster School* he was admitted a scholar on the foundation of Trinity College,

* From this school (Westminster) we received Ben Jonson, Cowley, Dryden, Rowe, Prior, Churchill, Colman, and others, whose memory we are seeking to renew; whilst from St. Paul's School came Camden and Milton. The Charterhouse gave us Addison and Steele; Christ's Hospital, Coleridge and Lamb; and Harrow furnished Sheridan, Byron, and Sir Robert Peel. At the High School of Edinburgh, Luke Fraser, from three successive classes of four years each, had the good fortune to turn out Walter Scott, Jeffrey, and Brougham. In Hans Place, Chelsea, was a seminary at which Mary Russell Mitford was a scholar: one of the pupils (Miss Rowden) subsequently became a governess, and at

Cambridge. Not succeeding to a fellowship, he tried his talents upon the stage, and in 1672 made his first appearance as an actor at the Duke's Theatre, as Duncan, in Davenant's alteration of *Macbeth*. He soon, however, quitted the stage, in despair of, ever " making a profitable figure there," and subsequently tried dramatic composition, his first play being produced in 1675. Ten others followed, in addition to two in which he was assisted by Dryden. In 1684 Lee exhibited symptoms of insanity, and was received into Bethlem Hospital, whence he was discharged upon the recovery of his reason. He did not, however, long enjoy his enlargement. Being unfortunately addicted to intemperance, he on one occasion partook of too much wine, and, returning to his lodgings in Duke-street, he stumbled and fell in the snow, and was carried to the Bear and Harrow, in Butcher-row, Strand, where he died. Lee appears to have had some talent for dramatic writing, though his unbridled impetuosity too often carried him beyond all bounds of nature and probability. One of his plays, *Alexander the Great*, is occasionally represented.

Of the several Thespians who played out their part and finally tarried at St. Clement Danes, we may mention William Mountford, murdered in the adjoining street, as referred to at the grave of Mrs. Bracegirdle; and in a vault

---

the old school gave her first instruction to Letitia Landon, and her latest to Fanny Kemble. And L. E. L. is sleeping at Cape Coast Castle,

"Where they made her a grave, too cold and damp
For a heart so warm and true."

beneath the church lies one not altogether forgotten by the old playgoer of the present day,—

WILLIAM OXBERRY.

This actor was born in London in December, 1784, and in his young days followed the art and mystery of printing. Types, however, were forsaken for the theatre, and in 1804 the young printer was to be found in the company of Manager Jerrold (father of the wit and dramatist, Douglas Jerrold, who, in his time, likewise handled the types), disputing with Edmund Kean—then unknown to the metropolis—the tragic heroes of the drama. He at length threw down the truncheon, and assumed the comic mask, and in November, 1807, appeared at Covent Garden in the character of Robin Roughhead. For many years he was connected with the theatres of the metropolis, and was likewise engaged in other pursuits. For instance, he was the host of the Craven Head in Drury Lane, the author of some dramas, and the editor of an edition of plays. It was at one time remarked that he might be termed the " Five P's—Printer, Poet, Publisher, Publican, and Player." William Oxberry possessed talents as an actor, but appears to have cared little for their culture or advancement. His last appearance was in May, 1824 (Munden's farewell night), and in the following month the vault to which we have referred received his remains.

We must not quit this church without a thought of one who here occupies a vault—the eccentric and kind-hearted

DR. KITCHINER.

Having received his education at Eton, he adopted

the medical profession, and took his degree of M.D.; but he appears to have subsequently used the pen instead of practising the healing art. He had three grand hobbies—cookery, optics, and music. A love of the latter accompanied him through life, and he played and sang with considerable taste. He was an epicure, fond of experiments in cooking, and his "public dinners," as they were termed, were marked by pomp and circumstance. From his house in Warren-street, Fitzroy-square, were issued "notes of preparation" summoning "a committee of taste," signed by himself as secretary—"the specimens to be placed upon the table at five o'clock precisely, when the business of the day will immediately commence." The doctor's *conversazioni* were delightful meetings, composed of men of letters, and of professors and amateurs of the liberal arts. As the first visitors arrived the humorous host received them seated at the grand piano-forte, and struck up "See the conquering hero comes," accompanying the air, by placing his feet on the pedals, with a peal on the kettle-drums beneath the instrument. For the regulation of these meetings Dr. Kitchiner used to fix a placard over his chimney-piece inscribed—

"At seven come—
At eleven go."

It is said that upon one of these occasions George Colman, on observing the admonitory injunction, availed himself of an opportunity to add the pronoun IT, making the last line "At eleven go it." Quiet in manner and apparently timid, Dr. Kitchiner possessed the estimable virtue of never speaking ill of any one, and was a great lover of conciliation.

Leaving the church of St. Clement Danes, we pursue our way westward, and a few steps bring us to its neighbour, St. Mary-le-Strand. The first stone of this church was laid by its architect, Gibbs, on the 25th of February, 1714. It was completed in less than four years, though the building was not consecrated until January 1st, 1723. Here is a tablet to James Bindley, the great book collector. We do not tarry to search the register of St. Mary, for our present journey is to

ST. PAUL'S, COVENT GARDEN.

This church was first erected in 1633, from designs by Inigo Jones, the father of modern English architecture, who was born in London in 1572, and died at old Somerset House in 1652. His tomb in St. Bennet's, Paul's Wharf, was swept away by the Great Fire, fourteen years later. In 1727 alterations and repairs were effected in St. Paul's; but on the 17th of September, 1795, the building was almost destroyed by fire. It was then rebuilt, from the same primitive designs and dimensions, by Hardwick, and opened for its sacred purpose on the 1st of August, 1798. Though twice almost rebuilt, it retains the east front as in the original work by Inigo Jones. Here are monumental mementos of " poets, painters, and players " in great variety, the neighbourhood having long been the resort of literary and other celebrities, a few reminiscences of whom, prior to entering the church, may be acceptable.

In Covent Garden, at the Bedford Arms, Fielding, Hogarth, Churchill, and Goldsmith have congregated at a gossiping shilling-rubber club. At Will's, in Bow-street, the wits of the day were wont to assemble—Rochester,

Cowley, Waller, and Davenant being of the number—with Dryden in his select and favourite chair. It was in Covent Garden (Great Russell-street) that Boswell first made the acquaintance of Johnson. Addison was the patron of Button's coffee-house (situate in the same street), and attracted thither the great literary Whigs of his period. Colley Cibber was a frequenter of the latter establishment, as were Pope, Swift, Steele, and Savage. Garrick, Macklin, Kneller, Mrs. Oldfield, Wycherley, and Mrs. Clive were residents in Covent Garden. Dr. Arne, the composer, and his sister, Mrs. Cibber, were both born in King-street; whilst Voltaire, after his release from the Bastile, and upon his visit to England, selected Maiden Lane for his residence.

Entering at length the sacred precincts of the church, we find sleeping in the graveyard (his friends not being able to afford to bury him in Westminster Abbey), the author of "Hudibras,"—

SAMUEL BUTLER.

In the parish church of Strensham, in Worcestershire, was baptized this celebrated writer, on the 8th of February, 1612. His father was a large farmer, an active and intelligent man, and sent his son to the college school at Worcester. It is not known how long Butler remained here, nor where his education was completed; though, from the great learning he possessed, he must have been a diligent scholar somewhere. He appears to have acquired a good acquaintance with the law, and one of his first positions in life was that of clerk to a magistrate in his native county. There are numerous blanks in the biography of Butler which careful research has been unable to supply. It is not known, for instance, where many of his years were passed, nor the exact period of his death. It was shortly after the Restoration that his chief work, " Hudibras," appeared. The fecundity of wit and the infinite variety of knowledge displayed in this poem have been universally admitted. Butler was now introduced at court, and enjoyed the intimacy of many of the most eminent wits and courtiers of the day. He died some time in 1680, having resided during his later years in Rose-street, Long Acre, " retired and studious." His remains were interred in the churchyard of St. Paul's, but no memorial marked the spot.* In 1786, however, when the church was being repaired, a marble monument was raised to his memory by some of the parishioners.

The house in which our poet was born, known as " Butler's cot," and situate near to the banks of the Avon, is still preserved. It has not, however, that we have yet heard, experienced the strange fate which has befallen other cottages connected with the poets, and been converted into a beershop. The native cottage of Burns, a few years back, was a little public-house ; at the same time Shelley's house at Great Marlowe was a beershop ; Moore's native abode was a whiskey-shop ; the cottage inhabited by Coleridge was a beershop ; whilst a public-house was erected on the spot where Scott was born. It was in Coleridge's cottage, thus unpoetically transformed,

* Aubrey states, "in the north part of the churchyard, next the church, at the east end. His feet touch the wall. His grave, 2 yards distant from the pilaster of the dore (by his desire), 6 foot deepe."

I

that its occupant penned his "Ode to the Nightingale," in which occurs the line,—

"Jug, jug, jug, and that low note more sweet than all;"

but which, to the consternation of the poet, was thus rendered by the printer:—

"Jug, jug, jug, and that low note more sweet than *ale*."

We look around the church of St. Paul's, and in a vault discover the resting-place of one of Butler's contemporaries,—

WILLIAM WYCHERLEY,

the dramatist, who was born about 1640, and was intended for the law. From legal pursuits, however, he was allured by the gay amusements of the town, and commenced writing for the stage. Obtaining a prominent position by his wit and felicitous writing, he gained the favour of Charles II., who once paid him a visit in Bow-street. During the later portion of Wycherley's life he was involved in difficulties, and passed some years in the old Fleet prison, from which confinement he was released by James II. He died on the 1st of January, 1715. He was at one time considered the greatest of comic writers; but his productions, suiting a dissolute age, are tinged with much licentiousness. Wycherley's plays are four in number—*The Plain Dealer*, *Love in a Wood*, *The Gentleman Dancing-Master*, and *The Country Wife*.

Another dramatist is sleeping here, Thomas Southern, who gave to the stage eleven plays, including the tragedies of *Oroonoko* and *Isabella*. He was born in Dublin in

1660, and died in May, 1746. Being a resident in the neighbourhood, he attended the religious services of this church, where he was distinguished by his "silver hair and his silver buckles." Here, too, is one of Wycherley's contemporaries, the painter,—

SIR PETER LELY.

Born at Soest, in Westphalia, in 1617, this artist studied painting at Haerlem, and first visited England in 1641. He was patronised both by Charles I. and Cromwell, whose portraits he finished. At the restoration of Charles II. he rose to fame and prosperity, and was knighted by the new monarch. Sir Peter now revelled amongst the beauties of the court, and the grace and delicacy of his pencil are exhibited in his portraits of the divinities of that period, all of whom seem to possess

"The sleepy eye that speaks the melting soul."

Sir Peter Lely finally laid down his palette in 1680. His monument, with the bust by Gibbons, and his epitaph by Flatman, shared the fate of the church when destroyed by fire in 1795.

Here lies one to whom the fourscore years of the Psalmist were awarded, and yet for another quarter of a century did the wheels of life carry him on, namely,—

CHARLES MACKLIN.

The real name of this veteran of the stage was M'Laughlin, which was Englished by himself on his coming to this country. He was born in Ireland in 1690, and first visited London in 1720, appearing three years subsequently at the Lincoln's Inn Fields Theatre. From that time until May, 1789, an interval of sixty-six years, he continued occasionally to perform, and likewise gave to the stage eight pieces, the principal of which is the *Man of the World*. His defects of temper and his great vanity led him into perpetual disputes with managers and brother actors. Macklin died on the 11th of July, 1797, at the right-hand corner of Tavistock-street, having reached the great age of one hundred and seven years. In 1741 he restored to the stage Shakspeare's *Merchant of Venice*, which had long been superseded by Lansdowne's *Jew of Venice;* and in his later days, when mourning the decay of his powers, he consoled himself with the reflection that it was he of whom Pope uttered his celebrated couplet,—

"This is the Jew
That Shakspeare drew."

His remains are in the vault under the communion table, and there is a tablet to his memory in the church.

In the western graveyard, near to the iron railings which inclose it from the busy pavement, reposes the once lively but thoughtless

JOHN EDWIN.

This favourite of the comic muse was born in London in August, 1749. After leaving school he obtained an appointment in the Pension-office of the Exchequer. Being here occupied but for a brief portion of the day, he devoted its remaining hours to thoughts of the stage, spouting clubs, &c. He soon embarked upon the stage; and, after the usual provincial practice, was engaged for the Haymarket, where he first appeared in June, 1776. Next season he removed to the boards of Covent Garden. His last performance was at the Haymarket, August 2nd, 1790 : he died on the ensuing 31st of October. John Edwin was a clever actor, but most intemperate in his habits, and the grave received him before he had reached his forty-second year. When you visit the adjacent market, gentle reader, look for one moment upon his grave, seen through the railings to which we have referred, and read this epitaph:—

"Each social meed which honours humankind,
 The dust beneath this frail memorial bore;
If pride of excellence uplift thy mind,
 Subdue the weakness, and be vain no more.

"A nation's mirth was subject to his art,
 Ere icy Death had smote this child of glee;
And Care resumed his empire o'er the heart,
 When Heaven issued—' Edwin shall not be.'"

Here lies another humorist, whose wit, however, was given to the laughter-loving world through the medium of his pen. We had better introduce him by his *nom de plume*, Peter Pindar. The writer so known was

JOHN WOLCOT,

who was born at Dodbrock, Devon, in 1738, and was articled to an apothecary. At an early age he evinced attachment to poetry. He visited London to attend the hospitals, and in 1767 obtained the degree of doctor of medicine. He next repaired to Jamaica, where, failing to secure a practice, he entered into holy orders, and preached to a congregation composed of "blacks." Returning to England, he practised as a physician at Truro, and has the merit of having discovered the talent of Opie, the painter, whom we lately left in St. Paul's Cathedral. With this artist he revisited London, and soon rendered himself conspicuous by those satirical compositions which he published under the name of "Peter Pindar," and which, from their drollery, became highly popular. Dr. Wolcot died in 1819, in his eighty-first year. Throughout his career he was noted for his frugality of living. It is known that he laughed at George III., but he laughed equally loud at the faculty. He would analyse the drugs which he prescribed for his patients before he would permit them to swallow them; he sanctioned the plentiful use of water; and maintained that, in most cases, there was nothing required on the doctor's part but "to watch nature, and when she was going right to give her a shove behind." Molière was not more enamoured of the sons of Esculapius than was Peter Pindar. Though an habitual valetudinarian, the French dramatist relied wholly on the temperament of his diet for the re-establishment of his health. "What use do you make of your physician?" said the king to him one day. "We chat together, sire," replied the poet. "He gives me his prescriptions; I never follow them, and so I get well." To return to Dr. Wolcot. As a poet he exhibited much freshness of humour, though his works have lost much of their interest from the temporary and personal nature of their subjects.

We scarcely move a step in our survey of this depository of the dead without alighting upon the memorial of some distinguished actor. To point out the little narrow homes of all is impossible; but, before we close the gate, let us call to remembrance some half-dozen who signalised themselves among their compeers. Here, then, in the churchyard, lies the facetious "Joe Haines." This comedian, when a youth, was sent to Oxford by some gentlemen who had noticed his "quickness of parts." At the university he blended learning with a great fund of humour; but ultimately he threw aside his cap and band, and became an actor. His inimitable performances on the stage, and his vivacity and pleasantry in private society, secured him the friendship of persons of high rank. Haines died in April, 1701.

In 1731, came to his last home, in the north aisle, Robert Wilkes, who was associated with Cibber, Booth, Dogget, and Steele in the management of Drury Lane Theatre: he was the original Sir Harry Wildair, and was celebrated by Steele for acting with the easy frankness of a gentleman. His kindness procured a befitting grave for the dramatist Farquhar, to whose orphan daughters he became a second father, whilst his generous nature was ever engaged in alleviating distress.—In 1776 was interred here, near to the grave of Edwin, the remains of Edward Shuter, who, like his companion in the tomb, was a good actor, but thoughtless and dissipated. Of humble origin, he was in early life a potboy in the neighbourhood of Covent Garden. Introduced to the stage, his merits were first developed at Smithfield. In 1750 he was a member of the Drury Lane company, and enjoyed the favour of the public until the close of his career. "Ned" Shuter had an irresistible drollery, while his conception

of character and perpetual diversity were peculiarly
captivating:

"Shuter, who never cared a single pin,
Whether he left out nonsense, or put in."—CHURCHILL.

—In 1794 this consecrated ground received another comedian, Robert Baddely, famous in his day in Jews, Frenchmen, &c. He was taken ill whilst dressing for the part of Moses in the *School for Scandal*, and died on the following day, at the age of sixty-one. Baddely left the sum of three pounds to be annually appropriated to the purchase of cake and wine for the performers of Drury Lane Theatre, which he desired should be partaken of in the green-room every Twelfth-night, in remembrance of the donor.—The following year (1795) saw buried here William Farren, the father of the present comedian, who possessed considerable abilities as a tragedian, and held a high station both at Drury Lane and Covent Garden.—In 1805 the companionship of these Thespians was joined by the veteran Thomas King, unrivalled in several characters— Shakspeare's *Touchstone*, for instance, being said to be entombed with his remains. His first appearance in the metropolis was at Drury Lane in October, 1748, as Alworth (*A New Way to Pay Old Debts*). His advancement in the profession was rapid, and in 1782 he became acting-manager of Drury Lane. He enjoyed more of Garrick's friendship than any of his contemporaries, and was presented with the dress foil worn by the Roscius upon the night of his retirement from the stage. Having been before the public for fifty-four years, King uttered his farewell words on the 24th of May, 1802; and in three years closed his account with life, at the age of seventy-six.

> "If he be not fellow with the best King,
> Thou shalt find him the best King of good fellows."

—In September, 1820, a new grave was made here to receive the remains of Alexander Rae, favourably known to the metropolitan public, to whom he was first introduced at the Haymarket, in the character of Octavian. He subsequently opened in *Hamlet* at Drury Lane, where he officiated as stage-manager. About the time of Rae's demise, Edmund Kean quitted England for America, the following lines appearing upon the occasion:—

> "Mourn, Drury, mourn, thy half-deserted scene,
> Thy triumph once, thy sorrow now is Kean;
> And in fresh gloom to wrap thy setting day,
> Lost is thy other son, extinct thy Rae:
> Hope's anchor raised, her swelling sails unfurl'd,
> *This* seeks 'another'—*that* 'a better world.'"

Kelly, the musical composer, likewise sleeps here. Michael came out as a singer in 1779. After visiting the principal cities of France and Italy, he appeared at Drury Lane in April, 1787. In addition to his merits as a vocalist, he supplied the music to no less than sixty-two dramas. Kelly appeared for the last time upon the Drury Lane boards in 1808, and made his final bow at Dublin, three years later. He died at Margate in 1826.

On the eastern side of the church we alight upon a stone which covers the remains of Mrs. Davenport, who, for thirty-six years was attached to Covent Garden Theatre, and was one of the most diligent and diverting performers that ever devoted their time to the amusement of the public. She first appeared at the neighbouring theatre in 1794, in the character of Mrs. Hardcastle (*She Stoops to Conquer*); and her farewell words were uttered at the same house in May, 1830, when she played the Nurse in *Romeo and Juliet*. Mrs. Davenport died in 1843, having been engaged upon the great stage of the world for eighty-four years.

As lovers of Art, which will ever have its ennobling influence, whatever be the form it assumes, we must give a thought to Grinling Gibbons, the celebrated sculptor and carver in wood. In the chapel at Windsor, in the choir of St. Paul's, at Chatsworth, and elsewhere, much of his ornamental carving is to be found. Grinling Gibbons died on the 3rd of August, 1721.

Here, also, was interred Edward Kynaston, the celebrated actor of female parts at the Restoration. Downes states that it is disputable "whether any woman that succeeded him so sensibly touched the audience as he."

We now close the gate of the church of St. Paul's, and take the direction of King-street. The house No. 35, on our right hand, is occupied by the Garrick Club, the walls of which establishment are hung with portraits of most of those actors whose graves we have just visited. The gallery was formed by the late Charles Mathews, and bequeathed to the club by one of its members. We are now in St. Martin's Lane, where, at "Old Slaughter's Coffee-house," Hogarth, West, and other artists were wont to assemble; and see, in the distance is the beautiful portico of

ST. MARTIN'S-IN-THE-FIELDS.

A small church was erected near this spot in the reign of Henry VIII., the parish at that time being very poor and but thinly inhabited. In 1607 the parishioners had materially increased, and additions were consequently made to the building. In 1721, from a still greater increase, further accommodation was required, and it was deemed advisable to take down the old building and erect a new one. The present handsome structure was consequently commenced, and was completed in 1726, at an expense of £37,000. Gibbs was the architect employed, and on this building his fame chiefly rests. The principal feature of the exterior is the classical portico, the design of which is copied from an ancient temple.

On visiting this church,—

"Where God delights to dwell, and man to praise,"—

we shall find the player divested of his motley garb; Hamlet no longer jesting with the grave-digger; the dramatist indifferent to the reception of his productions; and the sculptor who had placed over many a grave the triumphs of his art. But hark! the bells of the church are ringing, reminding us of one who bequeathed to the "ringers" a small sum for their weekly entertainment, and finally rested within the precincts of the earlier church. This was the frail but charitable

NELL GWYNNE.

The name of this theatrical heroine of a former day is supposed to have been an assumption, her real patronymic being Margaret Symcott. But little is known of her early career, save what is gathered from the lampoons of the times. She was first noticed when selling oranges in the playhouse, and whilst in that employment she formed an acquaintance with Hart, the actor, by whom she was introduced to the stage about 1663. She subsequently captivated the "merry monarch," and by him was soon raised to distinction. Her residence was in Pall Mall, upon the site of the present house No. 79. Nell Gwynne lived at a time when vice was considered an accomplishment, but yet maintained a good name. She continued faithful to her licentious sovereign, and continually shared the contents of her purse with the unfortunate.

There is occasionally developed a good trait in the character of Charles II., of which the following is an instance. Thomas Ken refused to allow Nell Gwynne to occupy apartments assigned to her in his prebendal house at Winchester, upon the occasion of Charles's visit to that city. This refusal, of course, must have reached the royal ears. Well, anon the bishopric of Bath and Wells becomes vacant; a host of cringing loyalists is in the field with cap in hand, but Charles straightway calls for "the good little man who would not give poor Nelly a lodging," and Thomas Ken becomes Bishop of Bath and Wells.

In 1651 the warm-hearted Nelly was, doubtless, to be found in the lowest grade of poverty; in 1851, two centuries later, her initials to an Exchequer warrant ("E. G.") were sold for £3 11s.

Near to the old church of St. Martin were likewise interred the remains of the dramatist,—

GEORGE FARQUHAR.

This excellent dramatic writer was born in Ireland, and was educated at Trinity College, Dublin. He embraced the stage, but failed; and about 1696 quitted his native island for London, where he began to write for the theatre. Farquhar produced eight pieces, which include the *Constant Couple* and the *Beaux' Stratagem*. He completed the latter comedy in six weeks, suffering at the time under a serious illness. The play was presented to the public, but before its first "run" was over, its author was entombed in the silence of St. Martin. Farquhar, who has been termed the Fielding of the drama, died at the early age of twenty-nine.

Another dramatist is sleeping here,—

MRS. CENTLIVRE,

who was also born in Ireland in 1667. Being of a romantic turn of mind, she quitted home on the death of her mother, and came to England, where her career, for some time, was marked by much singularity. She was married at sixteen to a nephew of Sir Stephen Fox, who died in the following year. Her wit and beauty soon procured her a second husband, an officer named Carrol, who, within eighteen months, was killed in a duel. As the means of subsistence she then attempted dramatic composition, and likewise tried the stage. In 1706 she married a third time, selecting Mr. Centlivre, who was "yeoman of the mouth" to Queen Anne. She then wrote several comedies, some of which have enjoyed great popularity. Three are still to be found in the playbills of the present day—*The Wonder*, *The Busy Body*, and *A Bold Stroke for a Wife*.

Mrs. Centlivre was the associate of the literary celebrities of her time. Pope, however, she offended, and was, in consequence, visited with a notice in his "Dunciad." Mrs. Centlivre died at her house in Spring Gardens, on the 1st of December, 1723.

Under the south-west corner of the portico of St. Martin's, within a few yards of each other, lie

CHARLES BANNISTER—JOHN BANNISTER.

The elder of these comedians was born in Gloucestershire in June, 1740, but early in life was removed to Deptford, his father having been placed in the Victualling office there. Gifted with an ardent mind and a great flow of spirits, Charles attached himself to a company of players who visited his new place of residence. He became an actor, played Romeo, &c.; but tragedy was soon thrown aside, and he was engaged by Foote for the Haymarket, where he first appeared in 1762. Charles Bannister soon established himself a reputation in comedy, and was acknowledged an admirable mimic, added to which he possessed considerable powers as a singer, although one of an untaught class. In 1767 he was secured by Garrick for Drury Lane. He was now in high repute, and was an especial favourite at Ranelagh and Marylebone Gardens: he was likewise the centre of the gay and spirited clubs of the day, and often " the sun of the table" of the Prince of Wales at Carlton House. He retired from the stage at the commencement of the present century. Throughout his professional career he had been deficient in one virtue—prudence, his gains being generally anticipated. Charles Bannister died on the 26th of October, 1803, his later days having been made comfortable by the kindness of his son, who rests here by his side.

Jack Bannister—he would not have known his name, says Mary Russell Mitford, had he been called John—was born at Deptford on the 12th of May, 1760. Intended for an artist, he studied for some time under De Loutherbourg, and became a student at the Royal Academy. His handsome face, however, might often be seen in the greenroom of Drury Lane Theatre, and before he had reached his eighteenth year he stood before Garrick, expressing a desire to relinquish painting and to embrace the stage. Garrick felt an interest in the young applicant, and instructed him in three or four tragic characters ; and at the Haymarket, on the occasion of his father's benefit (August 27th, 1778), Charles Bannister made his *début* as Dick, in the farce of *The Apprentice*. He played at Drury Lane in the ensuing November, and for some time personated high tragedy. The appearance of John Kemble, however, in 1783, took from him some portion of his tragic dignity ; and when Mrs. Jordan came, two years later, Bannister proved himself a powerful auxiliary in comedy. He then entirely forsook Melpomene, and continued, until the close of his professional career, to pay court to her sprightly sister, being recognised as one of her especial favourites.

Bannister quitted the stage on the 1st of June, 1815, having been a member of the metropolitan boards for a period of thirty-six years. Twenty-one years were subsequently passed by him in the enjoyment of competence and a happy family. He resided in Gower-street, Bedford-street, where he was once accosted by Sir George Rose, known for his wit and vivacity as well as for his legal attainments. Being on the opposite side of the way, Bannister cried out, "Stop a moment, Sir George, and I will come over to you." " No," said the good-humoured punster, " I never made you *cross* yet, and I will not begin now." He accordingly joined the valetudinarian, and, after a short conversation, returned home and penned the following lines, which he left at Bannister's door:—

> " With seventy years upon his back,
> Still is my honest friend 'Young Jack,'
> Nor spirits check'd, nor fancy slack,
>   But fresh as any daisy;
> Though Time has knock'd his stumps about,
> He cannot bowl his temper out,
> And all the Bannister is stout,
>   Although the steps be crazy."

" Honest Jack Bannister" died on the 7th of November, 1836, and was buried by the side of his father.

Reposing near to the Bannisters are the remains of

ROBERT PALMER,

who appeared at Drury Lane, when but six years old, as Mustard Seed, in *Midsummer Night's Dream*. This was in 1763; twelve years later he came out at the Haymarket as James, in the farce of *The Bankrupt*. The characters in which he excelled were the fops of the stage. Charles Lamb, in one of his admirable essays, remarks: " Bob Palmer was a gentleman, with a slight infusion of the footman. When you saw Bobby in the Duke's Servant (*High Life Below Stairs*) you said, what a pity such a pretty fellow was only a servant."

We must not quit this church without noticing that it furnished a grave to

LOUIS FRANCIS ROUBILIAC,

the celebrated sculptor. He was a native of Lyons, but settled in England during the reign of George I., and was principally employed on sepulchral monuments. His last work was the Nightingale tomb, one of the most remarkable monuments in Westminster Abbey, and in which is pictured an agonised husband, clasping his dying wife with one arm, and with the other seeking to ward off the fatal shaft. This fine work was raised in 1762, and Roubiliac died the following year. Whilst engaged upon this last work the sculptor was one day observed by Gayfere, the Abbey mason, standing with his arms folded, gazing intently upon the tomb of Sir Francis Vere, where four kneeling knights support a table and a group of armour over the recumbent figure of the warrior. Roubiliac was looking at one of these knights, and, observing the approach of Gayfere, the enthusiastic Frenchman laid his hand on his arm, pointed to the figure, and said in a whisper, " Hush ! hush ! he will speak presently."

Our next visit is to the church of

ST. JAMES'S, PICCADILLY.

This edifice, erected in 1680, is about the largest of Wren's structures, and has nearly the meanest of his exteriors. The architect, however, in the arrangement of the interior, has displayed the union of beauty and fitness in a most consummate manner. All Wren's churches, fifty in number, replaced old ones, except St. James's, which was a new parish taken out of St. Martin's, and which had itself, in the time of Henry VIII., been taken out of St. Margaret's, Westminster. Of Wren's churches —the erection of which extended from 1668 to 1705— six have disappeared.

In St. James's Church is interred the classic poet,—

MARK AKENSIDE,

who was born in November, 1721, at Newcastle-upon-Tyne, receiving his education at the local grammar-school, and proceeding to Edinburgh to qualify for the ministry. Subsequently he relinquished the idea of a sacred profession, and turned his attention to medicine. With this view he proceeded to Leyden, where, in 1744, he took the degree of M.D. In the same year Akenside produced his "Pleasures of Imagination." He received the degree of M.D., by royal mandate, from the University of Cambridge. He first began to practise as a physician at Northampton, but removed from thence to Hampstead, and finally to London. Fortune, however, smiled but rarely upon his efforts, and when, at length, a better prospect opened to his view, poor Akenside was hurried off by a fever. He was a man of great learning, and the style of his poetry is lofty, chaste, and classical.

But who rests here, so different in his life from the preceding? It is

TOM D'URFEY,

as he has ever been familiarly called. Time was when his humorous writings were exceedingly popular. D'Urfey was born at Exeter, where his parents, who were French refugees, had settled. He at first thought of the law, but threw aside the chance of legal preferment, turned dramatist, and ultimately gave to the stage more than thirty comedies. These productions, however, sought to gratify the licentiousness of the age, and are now scarcely heard of. D'Urfey's satires and irregular odes—in addition to his plays—gained him considerable reputation, whilst his good humour and natural vivacity secured him the favour of all ranks. From the *Guardian* we learn that Charles II. was once seen leaning upon his arm, humming over a song with him. His witty catches and songs of humour greatly diverted Queen Anne. D'Urfey is said to have been a good-natured, honest, cheerful man, and was certainly the delight of the most polite companies from the commencement of the reign of Charles II. to the latter part of the reign of George I. In his later days he was beset by difficulties, for creditors, he discovered, would not be paid with a song. Addison was instrumental in securing him a benefit at the theatre, and this is thought to have cheered his remaining hours, for he continued to write with liveliness and humour to the last. His poem of " Pills to Purge Melancholy " is extremely rare. A small stone let into the outer south wall of St. James's Church tower informs us

" Tom d'Urfey
dyed Feb. ye 26th, 1723."

This church likewise received the remains of David Ross, an actor of the past century. He was born in 1728, and was disinherited by his father, a lawyer in Scotland, for going upon the stage. He was bred at Westminster School, and appeared at Covent Garden in 1753. Ross possessed merit, but indolence and a love of pleasure proved detrimental to his abilities. He died on the 14th of September, 1790.

ST. PETER'S, PIMLICO.

To this church we are directed from its having received the remains of Richard Jones, an admirable comedian and an accomplished gentleman. Born in Worcestershire in March, 1778, he was articled to an architect, but whilst at school he had received considerable applause for his elocutionary efforts, the remembrance of which induced him, at the age of eighteen, to throw architecture aside, for the purpose of "drawing houses" in another way. He embraced the stage, conceiving that tragedy was his forte. Accident at length introduced him to comedy, and then his earlier mistake was discovered. Richard Jones first came to London in October, 1807 : he appeared at Covent Garden as Goldfinch, in *The Road to Ruin*, and eventually became one of the greatest favourites the metropolis has ever had. His latest performances were given in 1833. No formal leave was taken, and he was subsequently known as a teacher of elocution. He was the author of three dramatic pieces—*The Green Man, Too Late for Dinner*, and *The School for Gallantry*. "Gentleman Jones," as he was sometimes styled, was treated kindly by time ; for, at the age of seventy, he was favoured with the full possession of his polished address, and exhibited the same careful attention to personal appearance which marked him half a century before. He died on the 30th of August, 1851.

From the church of St. James we proceed to visit that of

ST. GILES-IN-THE-FIELDS.

In a Report furnished to the House of Commons by the Church Commissioners the design of this church is attributed to Hawksmoor; whilst Horace Walpole and other authorities award the merit of the work to Flitcroft, whose reputation is materially derived from the same. We enter at one corner of the churchyard, through the "Resurrection Gate," so called from the representation of that event being sculptured on its upper portion. This was executed about 1687, and, consequently, was an adjunct to the church which then occupied the site, the predecessor of the present edifice. Still earlier the same ground was occupied by a hospital, founded by Matilda, wife of Henry I., for lepers. Of the monuments appertaining to the old church (which was consecrated by Archbishop Laud in 1630), one still remains in perpetuation of the memory of Sir Roger L'Estrange, the loyalist and political writer; and of others whose ashes are here preserved we may instance the old dramatist,—

GEORGE CHAPMAN,

who was born in the year 1577, and received an academical education at Oxford, where he acquired considerable proficiency in the Greek and Latin languages. When still young he was found in the metropolis, entering into the arena of authorship with Shakspeare, Jonson, and their celebrated compeers. Seventeen plays are attributed to Chapman's pen—the first (*The Blind Beggar of Alexandria*) bearing date 1598, and the last (*The Revenge for Honour*), 1654. In his play of *Eastward Ho!* he was assisted by Ben Jonson and Marston. For writing this piece these authors, without trial, were thrown into prison, certain passages being considered to reflect upon the Scotch, thereby offending the nationality of King James. To this sovereign more flattering reference is made in "The Booke of Bulls, 1636," it being there related that "when King James was lying sicke, one prayed in publicke that hee might raigne as long as the sun and moone should endure, and the prince, his sonne, after him." Chapman was a man of great learning, and translated the "Iliad" and other works of Homer, with portions of Hesiod, Musæus, &c. He died in May, 1654, at the age of seventy-seven, esteemed throughout his career for moral rectitude and amiability of character. His remains found a resting-place on the south side of the church, where Inigo Jones, at his own expense, erected an altar-tomb to Chapman's memory.

Two years after the demise of this old dramatist he was joined in death by one of his contemporaries,—

JAMES SHIRLEY.

This dramatist was born in London about 1594, and was educated at the Merchant Tailors' School, whence he was removed to Oxford. He next proceeded to Cambridge, entered into holy orders, and was presented with a living near St. Alban's. Changing his religion for that of the

Church of Rome, he next taught in a grammar-school, but soon after repaired to London, and became a writer of plays. Upon the closing of the theatres by the severe ordinances of the Long Parliament, Shirley resumed his grammar-school, but at the Restoration he returned to his more favourite pursuit. At the Great Fire of 1666 he was burnt out of his house near Fleet-street, and removed into the parish of St. Giles-in-the-Fields; but the losses and sorrow occasioned by the conflagration, added to the increasing infirmities of himself and wife, greatly impaired their spirits, and they laid themselves down and died on the same day, one grave receiving their remains. Shirley was the author of forty-two plays, and was considered one of the most famous dramatic writers of his day. In the register of burials in St. Giles's Church the following entry is to be found:—

"October, 1666.

29 { Mr. JAMES SHERLEY
Mrs. FFRAUNCES SHERLEY, his wife."

Still more honoured dust is preserved in the present church, for here is interred the poet and patriot,—

ANDREW MARVELL.

It was at Hull, on the 15th of November, 1620, that this true advocate of honesty and patriotism was born, his father being at the time master of the grammar-school there. At the age of fifteen he was admitted of Trinity College, Cambridge, where he made great progress in learning. In 1641 he was, with four others, conditionally expelled the university, and shortly after visited Rome, where he formed with Milton an enduring friendship.

Marvell returned to England, and found the Civil War raging in all its fury. In 1657 he was appointed Assistant Latin Secretary to Milton, and in 1660 was returned to the House of Commons by his native town of Hull. His parliamentary duties, however, did not prevent his occasional use of his poetic pen, and the devotion of his energies to friendship. Evil days had fallen upon Milton. Not only was the light shut out from him for ever, but persecution followed his steps, menacing imprisonment and even death. Andrew Marvell shielded the sightless poet, and with generous and tender care alleviated his sufferings. Venerated be his ashes for such noble sympathy. Marvell died on the 16th of August, 1678, in the fifty-eighth year of his age. Gossiping old Aubrey, who knew him well, says, "He was of middling stature, pretty strong set, roundish faced, cherry-cheeked, hazel-eyed, brown-haired. In his conversation he was modest, and of very few words." Marvell lived in an age of apostacy from truth and principle, but his patriotism and eminent moral worth retained their purity to the last. It was in this contest for Right that Russell and Algernon Sydney went to the scaffold, the trial of the former presenting the affecting scene of the noble wife stepping forward to act as secretary to her husband. The latter patriot is referred to in Wordsworth's lines:—

"Great men have been among us—hands that penn'd
And tongues that utter'd wisdom; better none:
The later Sydney, Marvell, Harrington,
Young Vane, and others who call'd Milton friend."

We must not quit this church without referring to the tomb of our most eminent British sculptor,—

JOHN FLAXMAN, R.A.,

born in the city of York on the 6th of July, 1755, where his father was a plaster figure-maker. He was brought to London when an infant, and very early exhibited that observation and love for works of art which distinguished him in after-life. Before reaching his twelfth year he obtained a prize from the Society of Arts (their silver palette) for a model. He subsequently visited Rome, returned to England, built a studio, and commenced his monument to Lord Mansfield, which is in Westminster Abbey. For this work he received £2500. Flaxman continued to labour in his avocation, and produced many works of high merit. His remains were followed by the President and Council of the Royal Academy to St. Giles's burial-ground, adjoining Old St. Pancras Church, where an altar or table-tomb bears the following remarkable inscription :—"John Flaxman, R.A., P.S., whose mortal life was a constant preparation for a blessed immortality: his angelic spirit returned to the Divine Giver on the 7th of December, 1826, in the seventy-second year of his age."

In addition to the churches we have visited there are yet to be found, scattered throughout this metropolis, numerous other sacred edifices which have received in trust the ashes of many who should be held in remembrance. This is more especially due to the

"Poor player,
That struts and frets his hour upon the stage,
And then is heard no more."

For, whilst the poet and the painter live in their works, the Thespian has no such record to bequeath, and is consequently too soon forgotten. Garrick alluded to this fleeting popularity of the actor, shortly after the death of Hogarth, in the following lines:—

> "The painter dead, yet still he charms the eye;
> While England lives his fame can never die;
> But he who struts his hour upon the stage
> Can scarce extend his fame to half an age:
> No pen nor pencil can the actor save,
> The arts and artist share one common grave."

Let us, therefore, seek out a few of those who have passed away. It may tend, in some slight degree, to perpetuate their memory, however humble be the scroll on which we inscribe their names. With this object in view, we will first visit

ST. LEONARD'S, SHOREDITCH.

This church is known to have been founded as early as the reign of Henry II., when a dispute having arisen between that monarch and the prior and canons of the Holy Trinity in London concerning the advowson, the question was decided in favour of the king. Here are interred the remains of

RICHARD BURBAGE,

the companion of Shakspeare in his management of the Blackfriars Theatre, and the original representative of many of the bard's principal characters. Sir Richard Baker pronounces him "such an actor as no age must ever look to see the like." He resided in Holywell-street, St. Leonard's, and was buried in the church in March, 1619. The British Museum possesses, in manuscript, the following

"𝕰𝖕𝖎𝖙𝖆𝖕𝖍

On Mr. RICHARD BURBAGE, *the Player.*

This life's a play, scean'd out by nature's arte,
Where every man hath his allotted parte.
This man hath now (as many more can tell)
Ended his part, and he hath acted well.
The play now ended, think his grave to be
The detiring howse of his sad tragedie:
Where to give his fame this, be not afraid,
Here lies the best tragedian ever plaid."

RICHARD TARLTON,

the popular clown of the days of Elizabeth, is also interred here. He acted at the temporary theatre at the Bull Inn, Bishopsgate-street, and likewise at the galleried inn, the Belle Sauvage. This was in the days of the itinerant drama, and prior to the advent of Shakspeare. Tarlton was so popular in his time that his portrait was selected as a sign for numerous alehouses. Bishop Hall, in his "Satires," has this line,—

"To sit with Tarlton on an alehouse signe!"

ST. LUKE'S, CHELSEA.

This church is the burial-place of many eminent persons, but of none more distinguished than

SIR THOMAS MORE.

Whether his ashes lie here is uncertain, though often so recorded. He was beheaded on the 6th of July, 1535, and, according to a revolting custom, his head was exhibited for some months on London Bridge, and was ultimately purchased by his pious daughter, Margaret Roper. Now, as this filial act subjected her to much trouble, as well as to imprisonment, it is exceedingly doubtful whether, in those troublous times, her affection enabled her to obtain the body of her revered parent from the Tower. The sacred relic which she did obtain was ultimately buried with her in the church of St. Dunstan's, Canterbury—a city which contains the last trace of the shrine of the martyr à Becket, the pavement worn down by the worshippers who there for centuries offered their oblations. It is known that More intended to lie at Chelsea, and that he erected for himself a tomb, which is preserved in the church. To the inscription thereon, written by himself in Latin prose and verse, the following is the conclusion:—" Good reader, I beseech thee that thy pious prayers may attend me while living, and follow me when dead, that I may not have done this in vain; nor trembling may dread the approach of death, but willingly, for Christ's sake, undergo it; and that death to me may not be altogether death, but a door to everlasting life." More is entitled to record here for his poetic genius. When at Oxford he composed several English poems, which, though deficient in harmony and ease of versification, are spoken of by Ben Jonson as some of the best in the English language.

In St. Luke's Church is interred, without a monument,

THOMAS SHADWELL,

the dramatic author and hero of Dryden's "Mac Flecknoe." Shadwell was born in Norfolk in 1610, and was bred to the law, which he left to write for the stage, and became so notable as to be set up by the Whigs as a rival of Dryden, upon whose secession from the laureateship Rochester recommended Shadwell to the place. He wrote

so rapidly as often to produce a play a month. He took
Ben Jonson for his model, but he owes his notoriety to
the ridicule of Dryden. He died in 1692, it is said, from
taking an over-dose of opium. His funeral sermon was
preached in St. Luke's Church by Nicholas Brady, Nahum
Tate's associate in the Psalms.

In this church also rests

HENRY MOSSOP,

one of the heroes of "The Rosciad." He received his
education at Trinity College, Dublin, and first appeared
in London, at Drury Lane, in October, 1751, in the
character of Richard III. He was highly successful;
but after a time he conceived himself injured by
Garrick, quitted London, turned manager, and found
himself ruined. Returning to the metropolis, broken
in spirits and constitution, he was advised to apply to
Garrick. Pride, however, would not allow of this, and
Mossop conceived the dreadful idea of starving himself to
death. This he accomplished in December, 1774, being
then forty-seven years of age.

In the churchyard of New St. Luke's, Chelsea, lie, side
by side, Blanchard and Egerton, the actors of our time.

HOLY TRINITY, BROMPTON.

In the churchyard of this district we find the grave of

JOHN REEVE,

the " Magnet of the Adelphi — the Momus of the Metropolis." He was educated at Charterhouse School, where he displayed more comicality than aptitude for learning. The hosiery business having been selected for him by his relatives, he was placed at a warehouse in Maiden-lane, Wood-street, Cheapside, where he appears to have paid more attention to Shakspeare than to his trade. He was accustomed, for instance, with a youth whose love of acting was kindred with his own, to repair at night to the leaded roof of the premises, and there rehearse scenes which had previously captivated them. On some occasions, however, they indulged so much in "rant," that complaints were made by the neighbours of these nocturnal outpourings, and John Reeve made his exit from the hosiery establishment. He was next placed with Messrs. Gosling and Co., the bankers, of Fleet-street; but the bent of his genius led him frequently to a private theatre, his success upon the boards of which was so great (more especially in the part of Sylvester Daggerwood), that he was requested by the elder Mr. Rodwell, the father of the musical composer, and the then box book-keeper of Drury Lane Theatre, to play the character for his benefit at that house, July 8th, 1819.

The amateur soon became a professional, and fulfilled engagements at the English Opera House (the Lyceum) and the Adelphi. It was at the latter house, in subsequent years, that this laughter-loving and laughter-moving actor principally distinguished himself, and became the favourite of the town. He was a clever droll, but had little claim to the title of an artist. Of the text of his author he sometimes evinced disregard, and even pretended to play parts he had never read through; but he would occasionally redeem his incorrectness by a marvellous note, and convulse the house by a twinkle of the eye. He had a personal acquaintance with his auditors, with whom he appeared constantly to converse. One night, during the run of *The Wreck Ashore* at the Adelphi, the house was so inconveniently crowded that the occupants of the gallery were very uproarious. Our comedian was on the stage when the noise was at its height, and whispered to one of the actors, " What is it the gentlemen upstairs want?" "Room, room, room!" cried several voices. "You shall have *mine*," replied John, bounding off the stage as promptly as he had been answered. As an actor Reeve was but a *farceur:* failing in the higher order of the drama, he sought principally to excite the mirth of his audience. In private life he was pleasant and unaffected, possessing many excellent qualities. His love of gay company led him, unhappily, into habits of convivial indulgence, to which he fell a sacrifice at an early age, finally quitting the scene in January, 1838, in his thirty-ninth year.

KENSINGTON CHURCH.

In a vault beneath this sacred edifice lie

THE COLMANS,

—the elder and the younger. The former was born at Florence early in 1732, his father having been his Majesty's resident minister for some time at Vienna. On the demise of this parent, young Colman was generously sent to Westminster School at the expense of the Earl of Bath. The dramatist Cumberland was at the same time a student there, as well as Warren Hastings, who survived to be saluted by the parliament before which he had been for years impeached. Colman, whilst at Westminster, commenced writing verses. In 1751 he was one of the scholars sent to Oxford, where he obtained his degree of B.A. He was next called to the bar; but his subsequent life was chiefly devoted to literature, the theatre occupying much of his attention. He produced some thirty dramas, including alterations, the most prominent being the *Jealous Wife* and the *Clandestine Marriage*. In 1789 he exhibited unquestionable proofs of mental derangement, to which reference is thus made in his friend Churchill's Epistle to Hogarth :—

> " Sure 'tis a curse which angry fates impose
> To mortify man's arrogance, that those
> Who're fashion'd of some better sort of clay,
> Much sooner than the common herd decay.
> With curious art the brain too finely wrought
> Preys on herself, and is destroy'd by thought.
> Constant attention wears the active mind,
> Blots out her powers, and leaves a blank behind."

Colman died on the 14th of August, 1794, at the age of sixty-two, and was succeeded, both in the profession of the pen and in the conduct of the theatre, by George the second, surnamed the " Younger." The latter gave to the stage about twenty pieces, many of which retain their position on the acting list, including the *Iron Chest*, *John Bull*, &c. He died on the 17th of October, 1836. In private life Colman was social and intelligent, but as a writer he was tainted by much jealousy. Not being able to endure obscurity, he would rather be abused, however scurrilously, than unnoticed. He was a great punster, and won from Sheridan the remark, " I hate a pun, but Colman almost reconciles me sometimes to the infliction." At the table of George IV., when Prince Regent, the royal host once said, "Why, Colman, you are older than I am." "O no, sir," replied our wit; "I could not take the liberty of coming into the world before your royal highness."

In Kensington churchyard is a monument to Mrs. Inchbald, "a beauty, a virtue, a player, and authoress of 'A Simple Story.'" She commenced her career as an actress in 1777, in Tate Wilkinson's York circuit, but quitted the stage in 1789, continuing, however, to entertain the public in the character of a dramatist. Mrs. Inchbald died on the 1st of March, 1821.

ST. MARY'S, PADDINGTON.

This church, the third erected for the district, was built upon the Green in 1788-91, "finely embosomed in venerable elms." In the churchyard lie many noteworthy persons, but none more celebrated than

MRS. SIDDONS.

This incomparable actress was born in July, 1755, at Brecon, in South Wales. Daughter of old Roger Kemble, the provincial manager, she was introduced to the stage at an early age as a member of her father's company. She was at length advanced to the Liverpool theatre, and in November, 1775, ventured her powers before a London audience at Drury Lane, in the character of Portia. Failing to attract, she returned, at the end of the season, to the provinces, where she continued seven years. Genius then prompted her a second time to try the metropolis, and on the 10th of October, 1782, she re-appeared at Drury Lane as Isabella (*Fatal Marriage*). From that night is dated the commencement of her splendid career; for, although the old playgoers of the period battled hard for the fame of the Cibbers, Yateses, and Crawfords, the verdict was in favour of the Siddons, in whom every excellence appeared to be centred. She possessed a voice at once sweet and powerful, a conception instinctively true, combined with a tragic faculty which exercised a singular force over every feeling :

> " Mistress of each soft art, with matchless skill
> To turn and wind the passions at her will;
> To melt the heart with sympathetic woe,
> Awake the sigh, and teach the tear to flow;
> To put on frenzy's wild, distracted glare,
> And freeze the soul with horror and despair;
> With just desert, enroll'd in endless fame,
> Conscious of worth superior, Siddons came."

Mrs. Siddons continued without a rival near her tragic throne until June, 1812, when she uttered to her patrons her farewell words. She was induced, however, on a few subsequent occasions, to re-appear upon the boards, but in 1819 finally passed into retirement. The faculties of this gifted woman were retained to the latest hour, and long after her retirement she would delight society by reading entire plays of Shakspeare. The following simple inscription indicates the resting-place of this celebrated actress :—

> " Sacred to the Memory of
> 𝕾𝖆𝖗𝖆𝖍 𝕾𝖎𝖉𝖉𝖔𝖓𝖘,
> Who departed this life June 8, 1831, in her 76th year.
>
> Blessed are the dead who die in the Lord."

In the church is also a tablet to her memory.

Near the grave of Mrs. Siddons lies the ill-fated painter,

BENJAMIN ROBERT HAYDON,

who "devoted forty-two years to the improvement of the taste of the English people in high art." He was born at Plymouth in 1786; became a student at the Royal Academy in 1804; in 1807 he exhibited his first picture, "A Riposo of the Holy Family;" and in 1809 his "Dentatus," which was followed by the "Judgment of Solomon," sold for seven hundred guineas. He had previously quarrelled with the Royal Academy, or he might now have become a member. His ambition was to be the founder of an elevated school of art. He had the mind, the knowledge, and the energy suited for the purpose; but he had to contend with settled prejudices, and the opposing influences of persons of station and position, who took advantage of Haydon's overweening conceit to depreciate his attempts to improve the art. His struggles for this great object involved him in pecuniary embarrassments; and in 1827, when a subscription was opened to aid the distressed painter, he gave this melancholy account of the fate of his great pictures:—" My 'Judgment of Solomon' is rolled up in a warehouse in the Borough; my 'Entry into Jerusalem,' once graced by the enthusiasm of the rank and beauty of the three kingdoms, is doubled up in a back room in Holborn; my 'Lazarus' is in an upholsterer's shop in Mount-street; and my 'Crucifixion' in a hayloft in Lisson Grove." He next became an inmate of the King's Bench prison, where he painted a "Mock Election" that was held there. This picture was purchased by George IV. for £500. Haydon painted a companion, "The Chairing of the Member;" but the king declined to purchase it, and it was subsequently sold for three hundred guineas. Among his works, which are more remarkable for historical interest than artistic character, are his large pictures of the "Reform Banquet" and the "Anti-Slavery Society." The chalk studies for the former, of the heads of men of high intellect, are admirable. His "Napoleon Musing at St. Helena" was another success, of which he made four copies. He exhibited a cartoon as a candidate to paint a fresco for the New Houses of Parliament, but in this he was unsuccessful. This proved almost the death-blow to his hopes. He made another effort, in his "Banishment of Aristides;" but its exhibition was coldly neglected by the public, and the painter's spirit was broken; and, on June 22nd, 1846, with his own hand he put an end to "life's fitful fever" at Burwood Place, where he had resided many years. He scarcely left his equal as an English historical painter, and to him must be conceded the genius of instantly appreciating the beauty of the Elgin Marbles.

In a grave marked by a marble cross lies

WILLIAM COLLINS, R.A.,

one of the most thoroughly national of English painters, and distinguished for his seashore scenes. He was born in Great Titchfield-street, Marylebone, in 1787, and soon showed his skill in drawing, and delighted to watch Morland paint. He entered, in 1807, as a student of the Royal Academy: in the same year he exhibited two small "Views on Millbank," and, with the exception of two years, did not miss an exhibition for the remaining nine-and-thirty years of his life. For some time after his father's death, in 1812, Collins painted portraits, but his landscapes and rustic groups soon made their way; and in 1814, when elected an Associate of the Royal Academy, he began to paint coast scenery, which led him to fame and fortune. He had, from the first, an excellent eye for form, chiar'-oscuro, and colour. He was elected R.A. in 1820. He passed from 1837 to 1839 in Italy, and on his return attempted historical painting, but with partial success. He, however, re-appeared with freshness and vigour in his original line, and continued to enjoy great popularity as a painter until his death, from disease of the heart, in 1847.

ST. GEORGE'S, BLOOMSBURY.

This church was erected by Hawksmoor, shortly after the construction of St. Martin's-in-the-Fields, the portico of which may have furnished an idea for some portion of the plans of the present structure, which is surmounted by a statue, in Roman costume, of George I. We find here interred Richard Wroughton, the meritorious actor, who was for many years stage-manager of Drury Lane Theatre. At the end of the season of 1815, through age and in firmity, he quitted the profession and retired into private life. He died in February, 1824.

Here rests from her extended career

MRS. GLOVER,

the "mother of the stage" in our own times. This excellent actress was born at Newry, in Ireland, and commenced her professional career almost before she could walk. She first appeared in London in October, 1797, and continued to display her varied excellence until July,

1850—a period of fifty-three years—when she died within a week from her farewell benefit at Drury Lane.

ST. JOHN'S, WATERLOO ROAD.

In this district church of the extensive borough of Lambeth are interred the remains of

ROBERT WILLIAM ELLISTON,

the popular comedian. He was born in Bloomsbury in 1774, and was educated at St. Paul's School, being intended for the church. In his boyhood, however, he encountered the late Charles Mathews, and both yearned for dramatic distinction. On the first floor of a pastrycook's house, near Bedford-street, Strand, did young Elliston "hold forth" with his friend Mathews, the lady of the little band being Miss Flaxman, daughter of the celebrated sculptor, whose tomb we recently visited at the burial-ground of St. Giles-in-the-Fields. Elliston next played at Bath and in the York circuit, and in June, 1796, secured the favour of the metropolitan public, first appearing at the Haymarket in the character of Octavian (*The Mountaineers*). That favour was enjoyed by him until the close of his career in July, 1831. Elliston, "joyousest of once embodied spirits," was an extraordinary actor—excellent in tragedy, unrivalled in comedy, and admirable in farce. He had a merry, twinkling eye, still remembered by many; and in his managerial capacity he would often favour the audience with a rich specimen of the style grandiloquent—a style immortalised by Charles Lamb in one of his many delightful essays.

CAMDEN TOWN.

A burying-ground to be found in this district, and connected with the church of St. Martin, already visited, preserves the ashes of Charles Dibdin, the actor and dramatist, but who is more especially known by his naval songs, about twelve hundred of which are placed to his credit. He was born at Southampton in 1745, appeared in London as an actor in 1764, and closed his varied career, in indigent circumstances, in 1814. We copy from his gravestone the following inscription:—

" Sacred to the Memory of
Charles Dibdin,
The celebrated Author and Composer,
Who departed this life July 25th, 1814,
Aged Sixty-nine.
This stone is placed by his disconsolate wife and daughter,
as a dutiful token to the most affectionate and best of husbands.
His form was of the manliest beauty,
His heart was kind and soft;
Faithful below he did his duty,
And now he's gone aloft."

ST. JAMES'S, PENTONVILLE HILL.

In the burying-ground of this chapel repose the remains of

JOSEPH GRIMALDI.

This celebrated pantomimist was born on the 18th of December, 1779, and appeared on the stage before he had completed his third year. He continued to amuse the public until 1823, when his energies were subdued by an illness which had long previously threatened him. At a farewell benefit given him at Drury Lane on the 27th of

June, 1828, he feelingly remarked that, if he had then any aptitude for tumbling, it was through bodily infirmity. "To-night has seen me assume the motley," he then observed, "for a short time. It clung to my skin as I took it off, and the old cap and bells rang mournfully as I quitted them for ever." Grimaldi died on the 31st of May, 1837, being then in his fifty-eighth year. He was a man of the kindest heart, and of childlike simplicity. Of his performances, which were extraordinary, no adequate idea can be given to those who never witnessed them, and his excellences were all his own. Shakspeare seems to have considered some portion of wisdom essential even in the requisites of a clown:—

> "This fellow's wise enough to play the fool,
> And to do that well craves a kind of wit:
> He must observe their mood on whom he jests,
> The quality of persons, and the time;
> And, like the haggard, checks at every feather
> That comes before his eye. This is a practice
> As full of labour as a wise man's art."

OLD ST. PANCRAS.

This church was rebuilt a few years since. Among the materials of the preceding edifice, which presented features of great antiquity, was a quantity of Roman tiles, indicating the existence of a church here, or some edifice near at hand, in Roman times. The building then removed exhibited traces of having been repaired in different centuries, the fourteenth, probably, being the period of its erection. The church of St. Pancras, consequently, must have been founded at a very early date. The register records, among the burials of several distinguished persons, that of Lady Slingsby, an actress of Dryden and Lee's plays from 1681 to 1689; and Parker, who died in 1806, and is said to have performed 4852 times. The church contains one of the most interesting artist memorials in the metropolis, in a tablet to

SAMUEL COOPER,

the eminent miniature painter, known as "the miniature Vandyke." He was born in London in 1609, and was instructed in his art by his uncle Hoskins, whom he soon surpassed. He was the first artist in this country who gave to miniature strength and freedom approaching the vigour of oil-painting. The purity of his tints, the beauty of his carnations, and his loose and flowing manner of painting the hair, render the heads of his portraits worthy of imitation; but his execution of the figure was less successful. According to Lord Orford, Cooper visited the court of France, where he painted several portraits. Among his sitters in England were Cromwell, Charles II. and his queen, James Duke of York, and others of the court, for painting which Cooper's widow was promised a pension, which was not paid. She was aunt to the celebrated poet Pope. Louis XIV. is said to have offered Cooper 3750 francs for his famous miniature of Cromwell, which, however, he could not be induced to part with. He also painted Milton: the portrait has lately been discovered, and is in the possession of the Duke of Buccleuch. Cooper died in London in 1672. His memorial at St. Pancras is a mural tablet, surmounted with a pair of cherubim heads, and the painter's emblazoned arms, surmounted by his palette and brushes.

MARYLEBONE CEMETERY, FINCHLEY.

This is one of the latest of " God's fields " planted in the suburbs of London, having been consecrated so recently as 1855.

One of the earliest occupants of the new ground was

SIR HENRY ROWLEY BISHOP, Mus. Doc.

Music is the twin-sister of the drama, and is ofttimes wedded to immortal verse; in our "visits," therefore, we must not pass without a comment the grave of one to whom the musical art is so much indebted. This popular composer was a native of London, and received his principal musical tuition from Francesco Bianchi. In 1806 he was employed at the Opera House in the composition of ballet music, and two years later began to write for the English theatres by producing the music for a pantomimic ballet at Drury Lane. In 1809 his first regular piece, the *Circassian Bride*, was produced at Covent Garden Theatre. It was played but once, for on the day succeeding its production the theatre was destroyed by fire, the score of the music forming a portion of its ruins. More than seventy successful musical pieces followed this inauspicious commencement, as well as glees and ballads in ample number. For nearly half a century Sir Henry Bishop laboured in his beautiful art, enriching our stores of English concerted music with many admirable contributions. A great portion of his compositions have lived through all the changing fashion in music, and must ever captivate the lovers of pure harmony and graceful melody. Of the many effusions calculated to maintain an enduring interest we may note, " Blow, gentle gales; " " Lo ! here the gentle lark;" "Foresters sound the bugle horn;" "The winds whistle cold;" "Tell me, my heart;" "Under the greenwood tree;" and "When the wind blows."

BUNHILL FIELDS, CITY ROAD.

This graveyard of old London, surrounded on all sides by dwelling-houses, was at one time in the suburbs. It was opened by the City of London in the seventeenth century, being first used in 1665, at the time of the Plague, and became a favourite burying-ground of the Dissenters.

ISAAC WATTS.

Born at Southampton on the 17th of July, 1674, he early inclined to the Dissenters, and in 1698 was chosen assistant minister of an Independent congregation, to the full charge of which he succeeded. Ill health checked his services as a minister, and in 1712 he was received into the house of Sir Thomas Abney, of Abney Park, in which hospitable home he passed thirty-six years, until the period of his demise, November 25th, 1748. In this retirement he composed some theological works, together with many devotional hymns, which each returning Sabbath hears warbled by countless voices. In addition to the monument in Westminster Abbey, Abney Park Cemetery possesses a statue of Isaac Watts, in memory of his residence on the estate now included in the cemetery, and after which it is named.

An early occupant of Bunhill Fields was

JOHN BUNYAN,

who in 1688 surmounted his "Hill of Difficulty," and rested here after his labours. His allegory of "Pilgrim's Progress" stole silently into the world, and it is doubtful whether a single copy of the first edition of the work is in existence. It has, however, perpetuated the name of its author, which perhaps may be remembered as long as that of the sovereign by whom he was designated a "poor ignorant tinker." Bunyan was unquestionably a great genius, and by the forced spring of intellectual power rose far above the sphere in which he was originally placed.

Near to Bunyan lies one of his contemporaries,—

DANIEL DEFOE.

Born in 1661, in London, he early stood forth a champion of popular rights. Sincere in his opinions, and honest in his purpose, he passed a life of trial and persecution, endured, however, with patience. He was confined in Newgate for nearly two years, and, in addition to other indignities, was placed in the pillory. From such trials he was finally released on the 24th of April, 1731. Of Defoe's two hundred publications one alone has been sufficient to render his name familiar. Like Bunyan, he has but little chance of being forgotten, for the day is exceedingly remote that will not bring forth its reader of "Robinson Crusoe."

Here rest two artists of eminence, Stothard the painter, and Blake the engraver.

THOMAS STOTHARD, R.A.,

was born in Long Acre in 1755. When a child he evinced a taste for drawing, and having been educated at Stretton, near Tadcaster, he was apprenticed in London to a pattern drawer for brocaded silks. His first efforts in a higher branch of art were designs for Harrison's *Town and Country Magazine;* and such was his success in this class of book-illustration, that during his long life he is supposed to have made upwards of five thousand designs, of which three thousand have been engraved!

Stothard studied diligently at the Royal Academy, was elected an Associate in 1785, and Academician in 1794. Among his most important works are his designs for Boydell's Shakspeare, his " Canterbury Pilgrims," his " Flitch of Bacon," and the " Wellington Shield." His first style of painting was closely copied from Mortimer's vigorous manner; but he subsequently followed the bent of his own genius, which was essentially gentle: his humour was chaste, and his drawing of female beauty extremely pure. Among his latest works were his designs for a beautiful frieze in Buckingham Palace, representing "The Wars of the Roses." Stothard died in his seventy-ninth year at his house in Newman-street, where he had resided more than forty years.

WILLIAM BLAKE

was born in London in 1757, and at the age of fourteen was apprenticed to Basire, the engraver. The day he devoted to the graver, the night to writing poetry— " to make glorious shapes, expressing godlike sentiments;" and a collection of his poems was printed for his benefit, partly at the expense of Flaxman, the sculptor. Blake subsequently published his own poems, remarkable for their true pathos and mystical character, and illustrated by his own etchings, which are full of strange genius. His mind is thought to have been confirmed in chronic insanity: he persuaded himself that he conversed with the spirits of the departed great, many of whom sat to him for their portraits. He made a journey to Jerusalem, and on his return published one hundred designs of figures of men, spirits, gods, and angels. He painted in water-colour or distemper; and his "Canterbury Pilgrimage" possesses wonderful power and spirit. Among his best engravings are his "Illustrations of the Book of Job" and of Blair's "Grave." Blake died in poverty in Fountain-court, Strand, in 1828. As an artist his happiest efforts are in his conceptions. He left many volumes of poems in manuscript, full of extravagancies, and showing a want of discipline, which was the extent of Blake's madness.

KENSALL GREEN CEMETERY.

In closing the dark and crowded graveyards of cities, and opening cemeteries in their suburbs, Change has taken a healthy and wise direction. These "gardens of death" are productive of calm thought, for the memory of the dead is there embalmed with a pure sentiment; and the white tomb, with its clustering flowers, is sanctified by repose and quiet. Kensall Green Cemetery comprises about fifty acres of ground, and within the first ten years of its opening there took place in it six thousand interments.

Among those connected with literature and the arts we find Thomas Barnes, many years editor of the *Times* newspaper: the inscription upon his altar-tomb records that

"As a politician he conducted public opinion with great moral courage, inflexible integrity, and genuine patriotism. While he was distinguished by fine talents and a graceful elocution, learning in him was united with facility, criticism with taste, and elegance with ease."

Here, too, lies

THE REV. SYDNEY SMITH,

the witty canon of St. Paul's, designated "the most patriotic of Sydneys—the neatest-handed of Smiths." This possessor of honour, wit, and goodness was born in 1771, in Essex, and was educated at Winchester College, from whence, as Captain, he was sent to New College, Oxford, where he obtained a fellowship. The church became his profession, and his first curacy was that of a small village in the midst of Salisbury Plain. To this secluded spot a butcher's cart from Salisbury found its way but once a week, and then only was meat to be obtained: the worthy curate had, consequently, often to dine upon potatoes sprinkled with a little catsup. Sydney Smith next settled at Edinburgh as a private tutor, and was welcomed into the intellectual circle filled by Brougham, Jeffrey, Horner, Playfair, Scott, and others. Here he married, and one day after commencing housekeeping he went dancing joyously to his young bride, with six little silver teaspoons, which, from much wear, had become mere shadows of their former selves. "There, Kate," said he, throwing the spoons into her lap, "you lucky girl, I give you all my fortune." Sydney Smith came to London, and for some years struggled with genteel poverty. At length he gained promotion, and the kind-hearted curate of Salisbury Plain occupied a cathedral pulpit. He was one who claimed brotherhood with Christians of every denomination. Born for a teacher of the people, he rose to be the assertor of truth and justice, and the world loved him for his wit and kindness.

At Kensall Green also rests

ALLAN CUNNINGHAM,

a happy imitation of the old Scottish ballads, and a man of various talents. He was born in Dumfriesshire in 1784, and was apprenticed to his uncle, a country builder or mason. In 1810 he removed to London, and connected himself with the newspaper press. In 1814 he was engaged as superintendent of the establishment of Chantrey, the sculptor, where he remained till his death in 1842. Allan Cunningham was an indefatigable writer: he composed innumerable songs, warlike, amatory, and devotional, and abounding in traits of Scottish rural life and primitive manners, natural grace and tenderness. He wrote a rustic epic, and dramatic poems, romantic novels, and biographies of artists, with equal facility, and in intervals of his avocations in Chantrey's studio. His leading traits were strong nationality and inextinguishable ardour. "Altogether," says a contemporary, "Mr. Cunningham's life was a fine example of successful original talent and perseverance, undebased by any of the alloys by which the former is too often accompanied."

Has no spirit from Dryburgh Abbey ever " hovered around these graves ? "—In Kensall Green rests from his learned labours Dr. Valpy, beneath an inscription written by his former pupil, Judge Talfourd.—Here also we find Rosamond Mountain, the once popular songstress, with a voice hushed into silence, and all unconscious of the melody of the birds that surrounds her.—In a gaudy tomb-house lies another from the theatre, Andrew Ducrow, famous in his day as an equestrian, and long the proprietor of the establishment known as Astley's Amphitheatre.—Two Academicians are interred here—Sir A. Calcott and W. R. Daniell; and Winthrop Praed, the poet. The latter, when at Cambridge, was the pride of Trinity, from whence he brought numerous prizes for Greek ode and Latin epigram. His poems are finished and graceful; but he passed into these catacombs before his powers had fully developed themselves. Praed died young; but here lies one to whom eighty-six summers were intrusted—George Dyer, the friend of Charles Lamb —the G. D. with whom he held such long literary and social conference.

> " Above the scholar's fame, the poet's bays,
> Thus, Dyer, on thy tomb we write thy praise—
> A life of truth, a heart from guile as free,
> In manhood and in age, as infancy;
> And brotherly affection, unconfined
> By partial creeds, and open to mankind;
> Even here did Heaven, to recompense thee, send
> Long life uncensured, and a tranquil end. "

Here is another memorial around which we linger— that of

THOMAS HOOD,

the humorist and the poet. With generous heart and benevolent spirit animating his verse, Hood could not escape the infirmities which beset genius, and his latter years were clouded with sorrows, in addition to the affliction of ill health. He died in May, 1845; and for nine years his grave remained unmarked by any fit memorial of his genius, until, in July, 1854, was raised, by public subscription, a monument, surmounted by the poet's bust, in bronze, by Matthew Noble; and upon the sides of the massive pedestal are two medallions, one illustrating Hood's poem of "The Bridge of Sighs," and the other "The Dream of Eugene Aram," also sculptured by Noble. Immediately beneath the bust is inscribed, " He sang the Song of the Shirt; " and at the base of the pedestal are a bronze lyre and comic mask. Hood was born on the 23rd of May, 1798, and was the son of the well-known bookseller and publisher in the Poultry. Hood is most extensively known by his comic humour; but his earlier lyrics show him to have excelled in the imaginative, the serious, and the romantic. Douglas Jerrold, in dedicating his "Cakes and Ale" to Thomas Hood, thus eloquently expressed the public sentiment—regretting " that it was necessary for Thomas Hood still to do one thing ere the wide circle and the profound depth of his genius were to be fully acknowledged : that one thing was—to die."

We have just passed the grave of Mrs. Mountain, the singer. Here also lie Thomas Cooke, the clever composer and pleasant wit; and Mrs. Fitzwilliam, who passed from her cradle to the stage, from which she was suddenly removed after more than half a century of popular favour. Here, too, sleeps an adopted son of Momus,—

JOHN LISTON,

who, from 1805 till 1837, gladdened the London public with his *vis comica*. For many years he considered tragedy to be his forte, and with deep regret gave up Hamlet to play the Gravedigger. Even when recognised by the metropolis as its favourite comedian, he would still occasionally indulge his penchant for the serious. Thus in 1809 he played Octavian; the audience, from being accustomed to roar at his comedy, being puzzled what to make of it. Three years later the passion returned, and he appeared as Romeo! Liston died at Knightsbridge, March, 1846. Here, too, rests

CHARLES KEMBLE,

a brother of John Kemble. Charles first appeared as Malcolm, in *Macbeth*, in 1794, at Covent Garden Theatre, and took his leave of the public upon the same stage as Benedick, in *Much Ado about Nothing*, in 1836. By unremitting and patient labour and study he became a great actor, and for some years he supported the high reputation inseparable from his name in the annals of the drama. In his histrionic portraitures he exhibited a lofty conception and an exquisite refinement, with a taste at once pure and classic. After a professional career of more than forty years he passed into retirement, having been presented by his friends and admirers with a magnificent silver vase, modelled by Chantrey: its cost was £450. Charles

Kemble died at the close of 1854, thus adding an instance to the proverbial longevity of actors.

Early in the autumn of 1858 was brought to this peaceful bourne another popular player of our time,—

JOHN PRITT HARLEY,

who trod the stage for more than half a century. He was born in London in 1785, where he first appeared at the Lyceum in 1815, and in the same year at Drury Lane. He remained there until he joined Mr. Charles Kean at the Princess's Theatre, and proved himself a most efficient representative of Shakspeare's clowns, "the grotesque drollery of his manner seeming exactly made to suit the grotesque humour of the poet's dialogue." The very last words which Mr. Harley uttered seemed to mark his identity with the old Shakspearian drolls. On Friday, August 20th, he was struck with paralysis during his performance of Launcelot Gobbo in the *Merchant of Venice*: as he was conducted from the theatre he said, "I have an exposition of sleep come over me"—the words used by Bottom in *Midsummer Night's Dream;* and from that moment he remained speechless to the hour of his death. He had acted the character of Launcelot Gobbo with more than wonted vivacity on Friday night, August 20th; but the roar occasioned by his exit had scarcely subsided when he lay paralysed behind the scenes, deprived of the power of distinct articulation, and terrifying those who took his hand by the iciness of his grasp. He was conveyed home, and expired on August 22nd. His character for respectability and integrity always stood exceedingly high, and his tenure of office of Treasurer to the Drury Lane Theatrical

Fund rendered him almost as celebrated in theatrical circles as his drolleries made him familiar to the large public.

NORWOOD CEMETERY.

This is another of those beautiful depositories of the dead which are worthy of the German designation, " God's field." It is situated upon the Surrey hills, almost the loftiest suburb of London. The formation of these cemeteries is not a modern idea. The ancients did not, as we too long did, crowd their dead in the midst of their towns and cities, within the narrow precincts of a place deemed to be sacred. The Greeks and Romans had their burying-places at a distance from their towns, whilst the Jews had their sepulchres in gardens and in fields, and even among rocks and mountains.

Norwood Cemetery has received in trust the remains of several histrionic favourites. The rival managers, Davidge and Osbaldiston, are sleeping near to each other. Here, too, is reposing Harriet Waylett, whose ballads so often charmed us, and whose " Kate Kearney " is sounding in our ears as we drop a flower upon her grave. Here is the unadorned tomb of one who was allied to her in life, and in death is not far divided—Alexander Lee.

"Alas, poor Yorick!
I knew him well, Horatio."

Early in life he was introduced into fashionable society in Dublin, where his sweet voice and refined musical taste won him many friends. He adopted music as a profession, and sacrificed in the management of Drury Lane the labours of a life. His numerous musical compositions exhibit freshness and much originality of style. Harriet Waylett was brought to this sacred place of rest, after years of great suffering, in May, 1851, and in the following October was rejoined by Alexander Lee.

We pause over one more grave. It is that of

SIR THOMAS NOON TALFOURD,

an ornament to literature and to the seat of justice. His boyhood was spent at Reading, where he was born in 1795. At a befitting age he was placed at the excellent school there, under the direction of Dr. Valpy. He subsequently studied for the law, and in 1821 was called to the bar. Twelve years later he gained his silk gown, and in 1849 was elevated to the bench. It was whilst exercising his cultivated and manly powers as a judge at Stafford, on the 18th of March, 1854, pleading on behalf of the poor and degraded, that he was suddenly seized with apoplexy, and died with the accents of mercy on his lips.

"'Earth to earth,' and 'dust to dust,'
    The solemn priest hath said;
So we lay the turf above thee now,
    And we seal thy narrow bed.

" But thy spirit, brother, soars away
    Among the faithful bless'd,
Where the wicked cease from troubling,
    And the weary are at rest."

Judge Talfourd was a dramatic poet of great merit. His two classic plays—*Ion* and *The Athenian Captive*—are remarkable for gentle beauty, refinement, and pathos. *Ion* especially is an embodiment of the simplicity and grandeur of the Greek drama.

Here, too, is laid all that is mortal of one of a rare intellect—the wit and dramatist,—

DOUGLAS JERROLD,

who in early life essayed upon the stage, but rendered it more staple service by bequeathing to it some of the best-written dramas of the period. He was born in Greek-street, Soho, in 1803, and, in his own words, began the world at an age when, as a general rule, boys have not laid down their primers. The cockpit of a man-of-war was at thirteen exchanged for the struggle of London, and Jerrold appeared in print ere, perhaps, the meaning of words was duly mastered. Among his most popular dramas are *The Rent Day*, *The Housekeeper*, and *The Prisoner of War*. He greatly contributed to the stable literary success of *Punch*, and became otherwise popular as a journalist. He died June 8th, 1857, and was followed to the grave in the Norwood Cemetery by troops of friends, to whom he was endeared as well by his large charity as by the brilliancy of his wit and genius.

Mr. Jerrold edited a magazine which bears his name, his contributions to which, with papers from other journals, and tales, essays, and sketches, full of choice humour and pathos, and, "like a hedgehog, all points," have been collected and reprinted. Many of the good things which Jerrold said in support of struggling merit, and virtue battling with ill-gotten wealth and undeserved success, as well as his repartees and pleasantries, have been garnered into a volume, preceded by a memoir of the wit, gracefully written by his eldest son, William Blanchard Jerrold.

DISTANT GRAVES.

HAVING thus far visited the sacred depositories of the metropolis, we now take a wider range in search of the " Relics of Genius." Time and distance have been materially abridged by modern improvements, and we can readily exchange the busy hum of the city for more retired scenes, where the poet, the painter, or the player may have found a grave. It is in those quiet recesses that the worshipper of Nature should have his shrine, in the midst of objects which invoked his minstrelsy, and which remember his loss :

> " Call it not vain: they do not err
> Who say that, when the poet dies,
> Mute Nature mourns her worshipper,
> And celebrates his obsequies;
> Who say tall cliff and cavern lone
> For the departed bard make moan;
> That mountains weep in crystal rill;
> That flowers in tears of balm distil;
> Through his loved groves that breezes sigh,
> And oaks in deeper groan reply;
> And rivers teach their rushing wave
> To murmur dirges round his grave."

We cannot hope to visit the tombs of all the children of song, scattered as they are " behind the mountain and beyond the tide;" but we will endeavour to seek out the more prominent of those whose names are household words. Without observing any defined course, either in respect to district or chronology, we recommence our pilgrimage in the suburbs of the metropolis.

The tomb of Orpheus was shown in Greece, and by the ancients was honoured by the beautiful fiction that the nightingales in the branches around it excelled all others in the sweetness of song. The tomb faded into dust, but the melody was still heard. Napoleon, in his admiration of the gallant deeds of Desaix, sought from Nature a monument for his favourite general. "To so much heroism and virtue," said the great Corsican, in the flush of his power, "I will grant honours such as no mortal ever received. I will give to Desaix the Alps for a pedestal, and the monks of the Grand St. Bernard for keepers."

DULWICH.

In this quiet hamlet was the "College of God's Gift," founded by

EDWARD ALLEYN,

an actor in the days of Shakspeare, but whose histrionic excellence must yield the palm to his liberality as a man. Born in the parish of St. Botolph, Bishopsgate, Alleyn devoted himself very early to the drama, and soon acquired not only the approbation of the public, but the peculiar regard and esteem of his contemporaries. Thus, in the prologue to Marlowe's *Jew of Malta*, we find him styled the "best of actors," and likewise complimented with

"Being a man
Whom we may rank with, doing no man wrong,—
Proteus for shape, and Roscius for a tongue."

Alleyn became one of the proprietors of the Fortune Theatre, situate between Whitecross-street and Golden-lane, not far from the resting-place of Milton. In this neighbourhood are to be found almshouses erected by Alleyn, whose greater work, the College at Dulwich, was accomplished in 1616. On the 21st of June in that year the license was granted by James I. for its establishment and reception of one master, one warden, four fellows, six poor brethren, six poor sisters, and twelve scholars. At first there was a surplus of two hundred pounds per year, which has increased to some thousands. The administration of the funds of this excellent institution has latterly been greatly amended, by the extension of its educational benefits.

Alleyn—the excellent actor and more excellent man—quitted the stage of life in 1626, and laid down between the boy who was preparing for the journey of life, and the old man who had travelled far upon the way, and had come here to rest. Over his grave we read: "Here lyeth the body of Edward Alleyn, Esq., the Founder of this Church and College, who died the twenty-fifth of November, A.D. 1626, ætat. 61."

"When by a good man's grave I muse alone,
Methinks an angel sits upon the stone,
Like those of old, on that thrice-hallow'd night,
Who sat and watch'd in raiment heavenly bright;
And, with a voice inspiring joy, not fear,
Says, pointing upward, ' Know, he is not here!' "

CHISWICK

has a picturesque little church, situate near to the villa of the Duke of Devonshire, wherein breathed their last Fox and Canning. The church and churchyard present us with many a record of the distinguished dead. First is the depository of the remains of our " painting moralist,"

WILLIAM HOGARTH.

This celebrated artist was born in London at the close of the year 1697, and at the usual age was apprenticed to a silversmith in Cranbourn-street, Leicester-square. The occupation, however, of engraving crests on silver and baser metals did not suit his taste, and at the expiration of his apprenticeship Hogarth directed his attention to engraving on copper for booksellers. He first attracted attention by twelve small illustrations to Butler's "Hudibras," published in 1726. He subsequently commenced as a portrait-painter, and it was during his early career in this department of art that he painted the series of pictures known as the "Harlot's Progress." Other works followed, and Hogarth became recognised as an artist of high repute, both as a painter and as a satirist. Horace Walpole says: " He had no model to follow and improve upon. He created his art, and used colours instead of language. His place is between the Italians, whom we may consider as epic poets and tragedians, and the Flemish painters, who are as writers of farce and editors of burlesque nature." Hogarth died on the 26th of October, 1764, at his house in Leicester-fields.

On the south side of Chiswick churchyard is the characteristic monument to Hogarth. On its north face, in bass-relief, are grouped the laurel wreath, rest-stick, palette with " the line of beauty," and pencils ; a book inscribed " Analysis of Beauty ; " a mask, and a portfolio decorated with oak leaves and acorns. Beneath are the following lines :—

> " Farewell, great painter of mankind,
>   Who reach'd the noblest point of art ;
> Whose pictured morals charm the mind,
>   And through the eye correct the heart.
>
> " If genius fire thee, reader, stay ;
>   If nature move thee, drop a tear ;
> If neither touch thee, turn away,
>   For Hogarth's honour'd dust lies here."

This epitaph was furnished by Garrick, but Johnson's share in the same will be seen by the following letter, addressed by him to the Roscius, and dated Streatham, December 12th, 1771 :—

" I have thought upon your epitaph, but without much effect : an epitaph is no easy thing. Of your three stanzas the third is utterly unworthy of you. The first and third together give no discriminative character. If the first alone were to stand, Hogarth would not be distinguished from any other man of intellectual eminence. Suppose you worked upon something like this :—

> " The hand of Art here torpid lies
>   That traced the essential form of grace ;
> Here death has closed the curious eyes
>   That saw the manners in the face.

"If genius warm thee, reader, stay ;
If merit touch thee, shed a tear ;
Be Vice and Dulness far away—
Great Hogarth's honour'd dust is here."

Beneath the same tomb are interred Mrs. Hogarth, who died at the age of eighty ; and her mother, Lady Thornhill, aged eighty-four ; Hogarth's sister, aged seventy ; and Mary Lewis, spinster, eighty-eight.

On the west side of the tomb are these lines, which accord better with the taste of the last century than the present :—" *Time* will obliterate these inscriptions, and even the pyramid must crumble into dust ; but Hogarth's fame is engraven on tablets which shall have longer duration than monumental marble."

Near to Hogarth's tomb will be found that of De Loutherbourg, R.A., who died in 1812. Here also lie the remains of Kent, whose talents lay in ornamental architecture ; of Sir John Chardin, the traveller, who received the honour of knighthood from Charles II. ; of Ugo Foscolo, the advocate of the independence of Italy, and the contributor of many articles to English literature. Here, likewise, sleeps Charles Holland, the actor, who was in his zenith about 1760. The characters in which he most excelled were lovers, Hotspur, &c. He died on the 7th of December, 1769, at the age of thirty-six ; and among those who surrounded his grave on the day of interment was Foote, the tears of the man of wit being observed trickling down his cheeks.

Crossing the Thames higher up the stream, we alight upon the favourite holiday spot,—

KEW.

Who has not visited this delightful place, so famed for its Gardens? It was about 1730 that the Prince of Wales, father to George III., took a long lease of Kew House, and began to form the pleasure-grounds. Sir Joseph Banks, Sir William Chambers, and other men of note, were subsequently engaged in decorating and completing these grounds, which have now become celebrated in distant parts of the world.

> " So sits, enthroned in vegetable pride,
> Imperial Kew, by Thames's glittering side:
> Obedient sails from realms unfurrow'd bring
> For her the unnamed progeny of spring."

But the lofty plants and choice flowers have beguiled us from our object, so turn we from those elegant gates leading to the Gardens, and cross the Green to the church. It is but a step, and we have already found the object of our visit—the grave of

THOMAS GAINSBOROUGH, R.A.

This painter was born at Sudbury, in Suffolk, in 1727. He received his education at the grammar school of the town; but Nature appears to have volunteered him tuition, for at ten years old he had made some progress in sketching, and before he had reached his twelfth year he had painted several landscapes. Two years later he visited London, and became the pupil of Francis Hayman, who, like himself, was one of the original members of the Royal Academy. At the age of nineteen Gainsborough painted portraits on his own account, first settling at Ipswich, and afterwards at Bath. In 1774 he returned to the metropolis, and eventually reached the highest reputation and social distinction. One of his earliest admirers was Reynolds. Gainsborough offered his " Girl and Pigs " for sale at the price of sixty guineas, but Reynolds took it and paid a hundred. Gainsborough died in London, at Schomberg House, Pall Mall, on the 2nd of August, 1788. Reynolds, in some way or other, had previously offended him; but when Gainsborough was dying he sent expressly for Sir Joshua, who came immediately, and, full of emotion, heard the last words of his friend: " We are all going to heaven, and Vandyck is of the company."

Gainsborough was one of the most pleasing painters of scenes from nature that England has produced. Reynolds said of him: " If ever this nation should produce genius sufficient to acquire us the honourable distinction of an English School, the name of Gainsborough will be transmitted to posterity, in the history of the art, among the very first of that rising name."

In the same churchyard, south of the church, lies a brother Academician,—

JOHNAN ZOFFANIJ,

whose theatrical works are widely known. He was born in Germany, but when young sought his fortune in England. Under the patronage of the Earl of Barrymore, in a short time he acquired much repute. At the invitation of the Grand Duke he visited Florence, in which city he encountered the emperor, who, admiring the works of the painter, inquired his name. Zoffanij told him. "What countryman are you?" "An Englishman," was the reply. "Why your name is German." "True," said Zoffanij, "I was born in Germany—that was accidental: I call my country that where I have been protected." Zoffanij's productions include an able picture of the members of the Royal Academy assembled in their hall on a drawing night, with portraits, among others, of West, Reynolds, Sir William Chambers, Bartolozzi, and Wilson. The last-named painter, familiarly known as "Dick Wilson," was one of the original thirty-six members of the Royal Academy. He was born in 1713, in Montgomeryshire, and closed his career in 1782. He died before his reputation was completely established, though he is now recognised as one of our greatest landscape-painters. His "Niobe," to be found in the National Gallery, is a work of great value. He was frequently in embarrassed circumstances, owing in a great measure to his habits, which were calculated to estrange from him all personal respect. When Zoffanij painted his picture of the Academy, the original sketch exhibited a pot of beer at the elbow of Wilson, an accompaniment which did not redound to the credit of the artist who supplied it. Wilson was made acquainted with the circumstance, and immediately purchased a stout cudgel, making known his intention of placing the same upon the back of his brother of the palette. The infliction, however, was spared Zoffanij, for he speedily withdrew the cause of offence.

In an adjoining grave lies

JEREMIAH MEYER, R.A.,

"Painter in Miniature and Enamel to his Majesty George III." Meyer died June 19th, 1789, in his fifty-fourth year. He was a native of Zubingen, in the Duchy of Wirtemberg; and, coming to England at the age of fourteen, he studied his art with great success under the celebrated Zincke. Upon the north wall of the church is a tablet to the memory of Meyer, surmounted by his medallion bust in white marble. Beneath is the following epitaph written by Hayley:—

> "Meyer! in thy works the world will ever see
> How great the loss of art in losing thee;
> But Love and Sorrow find their words too weak,
> Nature's keen sufferings on thy Death to speak.
> Through all her duties what a Heart was thine!
> In this cold dust what spirit used to shine!
> Fancy and Truth, and Gaiety and Zeal,
> What most we love in life, and losing feel.
> Age after age may not one artist yield
> Equal to Thee in Painting's nicer field;
> And ne'er shall sorrowing Earth to Heav'n commend
> A fonder Parent, or a truer Friend."

Under these lines is sculptured the Goddess of Painting in mournful contemplation.

Leaving Kew, a short but pleasant walk brings us to

RICHMOND,

with its woods and dales, and the rich landscape stretching far beyond:

> "Slow let us trace the matchless vale of Thames
> Far winding up to where the Muses haunt

In Twickenham's bowers, and for their Pope implore
The healing god—to royal Hampton's pile,
To Claremont's terraced height, and Esher's groves.
Enchanting vale! beyond whate'er the Muse
Has of Achaia or Hesperia sung.
O vale of bliss! O softly swelling hills!
On which the power of cultivation lies,
And joys to see the wonders of his toil."

These lines recall us to our present mission, which is to seek the remains of their author, and not to dwell upon the beauties of this Arcadia, which, according to Canova, needs only a few crags to render it perfect. Richmond Church, dedicated to St. Mary Magdalene, abounds with monuments, the most interesting of which, in our present survey, is the plain brass plate against the wall under the west gallery, which informs us that below the tablet lies

JAMES THOMSON.

This favourite poet was born on the 11th of September, 1700, at Ednam, in Roxburghshire, in which beautiful district he passed his boyhood. From a school at Jedburgh he removed to the University of Edinburgh, and then visited London, bringing with him but few worldly possessions. He was, however, rich in hope, for he carried with him his poem of "Winter." Other poets have first entered this metropolis similarly circumstanced. George Crabbe, the "poet of the poor," came here full of manly hopes, but with nothing save poetry in his pockets. James Montgomery had his pockets lined with the same commodity, his heart being equally full of hopes: one bookseller to whom he applied refused his verses, but engaged him as a shopman! Thomas Moore, on his first arrival in London, occupied a front room up two pairs of stairs at 46, George-street, Portman-square, for which he paid six shillings per week. He had then but little money in his purse, but a manuscript translation of Anacreon in his portmanteau.

Thomson, located in London, soon discovered that something more substantial than poetry was required for his support: he soon had his wants, the first which occurred to him being the want of a pair of boots. The "Winter" of our author was published in 1726, the copyright producing him the sum of three pounds. "Summer" followed in the next year, and was succeeded by an edition of the four "Seasons," published by subscription. Thomson likewise wrote for the theatre, and in 1729 presented to the stage his earliest play, *Sophonisba*. A feeble line in this piece, "O, Sophonisba! Sophonisba, O!" gave rise to a waggish parody, and "O, Jemmy Thomson! Jemmy Thomson, O!" was for a time echoed through the town. The later years of Thomson were rendered comfortable by his obtaining a pension of £100 per annum, and likewise the appointment of Surveyor-General of the Leeward Islands, an office which he was allowed to perform by deputy. In his pleasant retreat in Kew Lane he enjoyed a social retirement, and died there in 1748, being removed from thence to his present repose near to his favourite stream :

"Remembrance oft shall haunt the shore
    When Thames in summer wreaths is dress'd,
And oft suspend the dashing oar
    To bid his gentle spirit rest."

With his universal sympathies, Thomson is one of the

most popular of our poets. He was a true lover of Nature, and in the truthful description of her "Seasons" he exhibits the exuberance of his genius. The tablet erected in Richmond Church to his memory can scarcely be deciphered, but the inscription appears to be as follows :—

"In the earth below this Tablet are the remains of

James Thomson,

Author of the beautiful poems entitled 'The Seasons,' 'The Castle of Indolence,' &c., who died at Richmond on the 22nd of August, and was buried there on the 29th, O. S., 1748. The Earl of Buchan, unwilling that so good a man and sweet a poet should be without a memorial, has denoted the place of his interment, for the satisfaction of his admirers, in the year of our Lord 1792.

>Father of light and life! Thou Good Supreme!
>Oh! teach me what is good. Teach me Thyself!
>Save me from folly, vanity, and vice,
>From every low pursuit, and feed my soul
>With knowledge, conscious peace, and virtue pure,
>Sacred, substantial, never-fading bliss!"

Upon the exterior of the church, against the western end, close by the tower, we find a marble slab, with a medallion portrait, erected to the memory of

EDMUND KEAN.

This distinguished actor was born in London about 1787: the precise date of his birth is unknown. His father cared little for him, and his mother equally neglected him, when Miss Tidswell, an actress at the patent theatres, took charge of him, and gave him a sort of theatrical education. At the age of ten years he was an intelligent, merry, reckless boy, with a pair of brilliant eyes and a superb head of jet-black hair. He accompanied

Tablet to Edmund Kean, Richmond Church, Surrey.

Miss Tidswell in her itinerant performances, and proved so clever that once, when at Windsor, he was required to give his recitations before George III. at the Castle, which he did to the great delight of his Majesty, who rewarded him with a handsome present. He subsequently joined several provincial companies, encountering innumerable vicissitudes. In 1808 he married, and for the next six years struggled hard for fame and bread. In 1810 was born, at Waterford, his second son, Charles Kean. The year 1814 brought with it a great change in the condition of Edmund Kean. His fame had already reached the metropolis, and on January 26th was announced, in the playbills of Drury Lane, *The Merchant of Venice*—"Shylock by Mr. Kean, from the Exeter Theatre." There had been no previous puffing, and the house was thinly attended, but the applause was tumultuous. He repeated the character, the house was well filled, and his fame was thenceforth established. The nightly receipts (after the first performance, which amounted to £164) averaged £500. He was now engaged by the Drury Lane Committee at a weekly salary of £20. Not long after they made him a present of £500, for he had saved Drury Lane Theatre from ruin.

Kean's career of success, including a visit to America in 1820, was uninterrupted until 1825, when, in an action brought by the husband of a silly, forward woman, a verdict was pronounced against him. The public were exasperated with the actor, but his friends defended him. By this partisan feeling he was driven from the stage, when he paid a second visit to America, and in two seasons in the United States was very successful, and saved a considerable sum of money. He returned to England;

his former enemies had relinquished their animosity, but it was in vain; his health and spirits were broken. He had placed his son Charles at Eton College. When his father found that he was disposed to become an actor he absurdly quarrelled with him and abandoned him. Charles Kean shortly afterwards appeared at Drury Lane Theatre: he subsequently visited the United States. On his return his father became reconciled to him, and on March 25th, 1833, he was announced to play Othello to his son's Iago at Covent Garden Theatre. Kean struggled through the part as far as the speech, "Villain, be sure," when his head sank on his son's shoulder; he was borne off the stage, and his acting was at an end. The audience, in kindness, immediately left the theatre. Kean lingered on at his residence at Richmond for awhile, and he became reconciled with his wife, who attended him till his death on May 15th, 1833. His remains were interred near the principal entrance to Richmond Church, in the presence of some thousand spectators, who came from far and near with an offering of regret to departed genius.*

The tablet is an unostentatious tribute of filial affection, which is characteristic of an exemplary life commenced under conflicting circumstances. The monument is of white marble—sculptured drapery, a medallion of Kean, and beneath it, "Edmund Kean. Died May, 1833. Aged 46."

* After the ceremony in the church a comedian was with difficulty making his way therefrom. "And this is all we shall ever see of Edmund Kean," he was heard to remark. "Poor fellow!" continued he, wiping the tears from his cheek; "he has drawn a full house, though, to the last." This levity is unredeemed by the conventionality of the remark.

The inscription tablet is placed upon black marble; and the supporting marble, which is slightly veined, bears these words:—" A Memorial erected by his son, Charles John Kean, 1839."

Edmund Kean, who thus descended into the grave before he had reached his forty-sixth year, was an actor of great original genius, possessing vigour, pathos, and sarcasm of the highest order. Stepping forward with a bold spirit and an eagle eye, he elucidated the beauties of Shakspeare, and infused into the prostrate drama the breath of life. By the force of mental energy, he met opposing circumstances, and enthusiasm for his art raised him to the summit of histrionic renown. He was indisputably the greatest tragedian of modern times; perhaps he has not been surpassed at any time. The widow of Garrick admitted that he rivalled her husband in the performance of Richard III.

Of Kean's irregularities in private life much may be said in extenuation, if we consider the blighting circumstances of his early career; and, as regards his later life, if we remember how much easier it is to bear prosperity than adversity. He undoubtedly possessed many excellent and redeeming qualities.

From Richmond we cross the Thames to a group of interesting memorials at

TWICKENHAM.

Horace Walpole gave some importance to this pretty village by his purchase, in 1747, of the villa which, subsequently known as Strawberry Hill, became so celebrated.

Here he collected rich treasures of art; and here, in 1757, he set up a printing-press, at which he printed his own works and some others. Amid his collection, however, there were found no gatherings of his literary contemporaries, for whom he entertained but little love or respect. By him Goldsmith was complimented with the prefix of " Silly," whilst before his charitable sympathy Chatterton will ever stand as a reproach. The treasures of Strawberry Hill, a few years since, were scattered throughout the world; but they have been, in part, re-assembled by the present noble owner of the villa. Twickenham, at one time, was likewise the residence of another celebrated character, Louis Philippe, whose varied fortunes bore almost the stamp of romance—citizen of the Jacobin Club, brigadier of the army on the frontier, the Scandinavian traveller, the American wanderer, the Swiss schoolmaster, the Twickenham ratepayer, the King of the French (with a fortune unmatched in Europe), and the exile at a lowly inn on the Sussex coast. From further thoughts, however, of Horace Walpole and Louis Philippe we turn towards the church at Twickenham, in which repose the ashes of

ALEXANDER POPE,

who was born in Lombard-street, May 21st, 1688. Pope was of a delicate constitution, and much deformed. In his youth he resided in Windsor Forest; and in some early visit to the Castle he may have reflected upon the rival kings of York and Lancaster lying peacefully together, and may then have been impressed with the great distinctions that are levelled in the grave, so beautifully referred to by him in the following lines, not out of place in our present "Visits:"—

"Let softest strains ill-fated Henry mourn,
And palms eternal flourish round his urn;
Here, o'er the martyr king, the marble weeps,
And, fast beside him, once-fear'd Edward sleeps,
Whom not the extended Albion could contain,
From old Bolerium to the German main.
The grave unites, where e'en the great find rest,
And blended lie the oppressor and the oppress'd."

With his schoolmaster, Deane, Pope resided in Marylebone, and subsequently at Hyde Park Corner. Though a mere child, he was occasionally taken to the theatre, and compiled a drama which his schoolfellows performed; and with the assistance of the gardener. He soon, as he himself tells us, "lisp'd in numbers," and his "Ode to Solitude" was written before he was twelve years old. He removed to Chiswick, "under the wing of my Lord Burlington," where his father died in October, 1717. Pope next removed to Twickenham, with which place his remaining life became so intimately connected. He died on the 30th of May, 1744, at the age of fifty-six years and nine days.

Pope and his parents are interred in the church at Twickenham.* To their memory the poet erected a monument; and to his own, but some years after his decease, the awakened gratitude of Bishop Warburton placed a memorial of grey marble, and in the pyramidal form, displaying a medallic bust of the poet; and beneath

* The poet's grave is marked by a stone inscribed with the letter P., in the middle aisle of the church.

are the following lines by the bishop—a reprehensive attempt at smartness :—

"Alexandro Pope,

M. H. Gulielmus Episcopus, Glocestriensis amicitiæ causâ fac. cur.
1761.

Poeta loquitur.
For one who would not be buried in Westminster Abbey.
Heroes and kings, your distance keep;
In peace let one poor poet sleep,
Who never flatter'd folks like you:
Let Horace blush, and Virgil too."

As a poet Pope ranks exceedingly high, no writer having been more successful in correctness of versification or in splendour of diction. As a man he was open to flattery and prone to resentment. He could use ridicule against his rival, but was remarkably sensitive when the same weapon was directed against himself. Cibber, the hero of his celebrated "Dunciad," on some occasions paid back the poet's attacks with interest. "I have heard," says Johnson, "Mr. Richardson state that he attended his father, the painter, on a visit, when one of Cibber's pamphlets came into the hands of Pope, who said, ' These things are my diversion.' They sat by him while he perused it, and saw his features writhing with anguish; and young Richardson said to his father, when they returned, ' that he hoped to be preserved from such diversions as had been the lot of Pope.' "

On our visit to Westminster Abbey we referred to a monument which possessed no body: the remains of the genius thus commemorated are here—those of

SIR GODFREY KNELLER,

who refused to be buried in the Abbey for the reason previously assigned. This painter was born at Lubeck about 1648, and studied mathematics and fortifications at Leyden, with the view of a military career. His taste for painting, however, prevailed, and, after studying under some good masters, in 1674 he came to England,

> "Whose strength is in the altar,
> The cottage, and the throne."

Kneller was much patronised by Charles II. and his two successors. For William III. he painted several portraits, which are to be found in the collection at Hampton Court. He died on the 26th of October, 1723. Sir Godfrey at one time resided in Bow-street, Covent Garden, his studio being often visited by Pope and Gay. Radcliffe, the physician, was his next-door neighbour. " Kneller," says Horace Walpole, " was fond of flowers, and had a fine collection. As there was great intimacy between him and the physician, he permitted the latter to have a door into his garden; but Radcliffe's servants gathering and destroying the flowers, Kneller sent him word he must shut up the door. Radcliffe replied, peevishly, ' Tell him he may do anything with it but paint it.' ' And I,' answered Kneller, ' can take anything from him but his physic.'"

Radcliffe, when a student at Oxford, had so few books that Dr. Bathurst, the President of Trinity, once on a visit to him in his rooms, asked him where his library was. " There, sir," said Radcliffe, pointing to some glass phials, a herbal, and a skeleton, " there, sir, is Radcliffe's library."

This student, at his death, left £40,000 to build a library at Oxford, with other large funds for books, &c. The world is now, from this bequest, in possession of the magnificent Radcliffe Library.

We must not leave the church of Twickenham without calling to mind that it received the remains of

MRS. CLIVE,

or "Kitty Clive," as this once popular actress was playfully called. Born in Herefordshire in 1711, she was engaged at Drury Lane when she had reached her seventeenth year. She continued the delight of the town until 1769, a period exceeding forty years from her first appearance, when she retired from the profession, speaking an epilogue on the occasion written by Horace Walpole. Her remaining days, finally brought to a close on the 6th of December, 1785, were passed in independence and comfort. Mrs. Clive resided for many years at Twickenham, at Marble Hill Cottage, facing the Thames. Her neighbour, Horace Walpole, as well as many other persons of rank and eminence, courted her society. A letter from the "elegant trifler," dated "Strawberry Hill, November 3rd, 1774," has the following passage:—"My chief employ in this part of the world, except surveying my library, which has scarce anything but the painting to finish, is planting at Mrs. Clive's, whither I remove all my superabundancies. I have lately planted the green lane that leads from her garden to the common. 'Well,' said she, 'when it is done what shall we call it?' 'Why,' said I, 'what would you call it but Drury Lane.'"

Mrs. Clive appears to have been a superlative actress,

"fairly opening the book of nature, and pointing out every valuable passage." Churchill says of her,—

> "In spite of outward blemishes she shone,
> For humour famed, and humour all her own.
> Easy, as if at home, the stage she trod,
> Nor sought the critic's praise, nor fear'd his rod."

With her sweet looks and silver tones, "Kitty" was one of Garrick's incessant persecutors, constantly importuning him to patronise some poor actor, or otherwise disturbing the great player's equanimity.

From Twickenham we pass to the adjacent village of

TEDDINGTON,

where we find, in the churchyard, a tablet raised to

MRS. WOFFINGTON.

An Irish girl of great beauty, she was born in Dublin in 1718, and early in life appeared upon the stage to aid a widowed mother. From the theatre of her native city she was transferred to the boards of Covent Garden in November, 1740, one year before Garrick blazed forth to the public at Goodman's Fields. Mrs. Woffington possessed superior beauty and grace, and the industry with which she cultivated her profession, by observing the instructions of Cibber, and paying great attention to Garrick, soon established her as a popular favourite, to which her natural vivacity and elegant form greatly contributed. Mrs. Woffington was suddenly taken ill whilst playing Rosalind; she tottered, and became speechless, and her gay career was ended. She survived some months. The tablet to her memory bears the following inscription :—" Near this monument lies the body of Margaret Woffington, spinster, born October 18th, 1718, who departed this life March 28th, 1760, aged forty-two years." Hogarth's picture of this celebrated actress is at Bowood, in the collection of the Marquis of Lansdowne.

Near to the remains of "captivating Peg" are those of

PAUL WHITEHEAD,

who was born in Holborn in 1710, and was apprenticed to a mercer in the City. As a poet he exhibited more judgment than genius : he wrote strong partisan satires, gained wealthy patrons, and rose to become poet-laureate.

Whitehead died in December, 1774, in Henrietta-street, Covent Garden. Teddington received his remains, with the exception of his heart, which he requested in his will might be taken from his body and inclosed in an urn, to be deposited in a mausoleum at High Wycombe, on the grounds of his patron, the Lord Le Despencer. The urn bears this inscription :—

> "Unhallow'd hands, this urn forbear;
> No gems, nor orient spoil,
> Lie here conceal'd; but, what's more rare,
> A HEART that knows no guile."

Many poets have dedicated the effusions of their brains to their patrons, but few, like Paul, have bequeathed their hearts. He left £50 to defray the expenses of this ceremony.

HIGHGATE.

This village is supposed to owe its origin to the erection of a toll-gate here by a bishop of London some five centuries since. A view of London is gained from this eminence, to which we give a passing glance, and then seek the grave of

SAMUEL TAYLOR COLERIDGE.

To Devonshire was this poet indebted for his birth, on the 21st of October, 1772, at St. Mary Ottery, of which parish his father was vicar. The earlier portion of his education was received at Christ's Hospital, from whence he removed to Cambridge. Prior, however, to the completion of his studies, he had fallen in love, and had been rejected, when, in a fit of despondency, he suddenly hastened to London, and enlisted as a common soldier in the 15th Elliott's Light Dragoons. " Do you think," said the general of the district to him, when inspecting the recruits, "you can run a Frenchman through the body?" " I do not know," replied Coleridge, "as I never tried; but I'll let a Frenchman run me through the body before I'll run away." This was deemed satisfactory, and our future poet was turned into the ranks. He soon discovered, however, that he had mistaken the bent of his genius, and that he was not destined to become a military hero. He was compelled, for instance, to secure the aid of a comrade in order that his horse might be rubbed down with credit; in return for which service he favoured his friend with love stanzas to present to his mistress. Coleridge, it is said, was more-

over an indifferent horseman, and in mounting on one side
of his charger he would occasionally fall over on the other.
This state of affairs continued from December, 1793, to
April, 1794, when the classical acquirements of the young
recruit were accidentally discovered. Explanation followed,
and he was removed from the army by his friends. Coleridge now entered the republic of letters, and among his
many speculations he started a periodical entitled *The
Watchman*. His want of order and punctuality, however,
with his philosophical theories, soon tired out his readers,
and the work was discontinued after the ninth number.
Coleridge himself relates an amusing illustration of the
unsaleable nature of the publication. Happening to rise
one morning at an earlier hour than usual, he observed his
servant girl putting an extravagant quantity of paper into
the grate in order to light the fire, and mildly checked
her for her wastefulness. " La, sir ! " was the reply of
Nanny ; " why it's only Watchmen."

Coleridge was an invaluable friend and companion, and
his conversation was an intellectual treat. He possessed
a powerful imagination and a marvellous spirit, though his
genius was somewhat erratic. Indulging in metaphysical
speculation, some of his prose works are rendered obscure
by the introduction of abstruse discussion. His poetical
compositions display a great command of language, and
the poet consequently stands out in bolder relief than the
philosopher.

We may here appropriately introduce a specimen of
Coleridge's fine poetic talents in the following lines,
written on the occasion of a visit being paid him in the
country by Charles Lamb and his sister. Prevented by

an accident from accompanying his visitors, he thus followed them in thought:—

> "Yes, they wander on
> In gladness all; but thee, methinks, most glad,
> My gentle-hearted Charles; for thou hast pined
> And hunger'd after nature many a year,
> In the great city pent, winning thy way
> With sad, yet patient soul, through evil and pain
> And strange calamity! Ah, slowly sink
> Behind the western ridge, thou glorious sun;
> Shine in the slant beams of the sinking orb,
> Ye purple heath flowers! Richlier beam, ye clouds!
> Live in the yellow light, ye distant groves!
> And kindle, thou blue ocean! so my friend,
> Struck with deep joy, may stand as I have stood,
> Silent with swimming sense; yea, gazing round
> On the wide landscape, gaze till all doth seem
> Less gross than bodily, and of such hues
> As veil the Almighty Spirit when yet he makes
> Spirits perceive his presence."

Coleridge died on the 25th of July, 1834, having previously written for himself the following epitaph, which is striking for its simplicity and humility:—

> "Stop, Christian passer-by! Stop, child of God!
> And read with gentle breast. Beneath this sod
> A poet lies, or that which once seem'd he;
> Oh, lift a thought in prayer for S. T. C.!
> That he who many a year, with toil of breath,
> Found death in life, may here find life in death;
> Mercy for praise—to be forgiven for fame,
> He ask'd and hoped through Christ—do thou the same."

Our next visit is to the grave of one of Coleridge's schoolfellows at

EDMONTON,

a village on the post road from London to Hertford. Here, in the churchyard, lie the remains of

CHARLES LAMB,

the warm-hearted and genial Elia, whose name has ever been dear to us. He was born on February 18th, 1775, in Crown Office Row, Inner Temple ; and at the age of seven, being then in the school of Christ's Hospital, his appearance is thus described:—"Small of stature, delicate of frame, and constitutionally nervous and timid, he would seem unfitted to encounter the discipline of a school formed to restrain some hundreds of lads in the heart of the metropolis, or to fight his way among them. But the uniform sweetness of his disposition won him favour from all." At the age of twenty-one, having then been for three years a clerk in the India House, he began to write verses. There is no "story" to connect with the after-career of Charles Lamb. His life was made up of great affections and deep domestic sorrows ; and if a little frailty was thrown in, there was likewise added a noble-mindedness which shone resplendent over all. He died on the 27th of December, 1834, five months only after the death of his friend and schoolfellow, Coleridge. "However much of him has departed," said poor Thomas Hood, who has since followed, "there is still more of him that cannot die ; for as long as humanity endures, and man holds fellowship with man, his spirit will be extant."

Lamb, it is pretty generally known, stammered in his speech. Some one was mentioning in his presence the cold-heartedness of the Duke of Cumberland, in restraining the duchess from rushing up to the embrace of her son, whom she had not seen for a considerable time, and insisting on her receiving him in state. "How horribly *cold* it was," said the narrator. " Yes," said Lamb, in his stuttering way; " but you know he is the Duke of *Cu-cumber-land.*" This was an instance of stammering wit.

Lamb's gravestone is inscribed with the following lines from the pen of the Rev. H. T. Cary:—

"Farewell, dear friend! that smile, that harmless mirth,
No more shall gladden our domestic hearth;
That rising tear, with pain forbid to flow—
Better than words—no more assuage our woe.
That hand outstretch'd from small but well-earn'd store
Yields succour to the destitute no more.
Yet art thou not all lost: through many an age,
With sterling sense and humour, shall thy page
Win many an English bosom, pleased to see
That old and happier vein revived in thee.
This for our earth; and if with friends we share
Our joys in heaven, we hope to meet thee there."

From one of Lamb's delightful letters, written in November, 1824, we learn that the drudgery of his position in Leadenhall-street began to affect him. Congratulating one of his dearest friends upon his marriage, he thus writes in his own quaint figures of speech:—

" By the way, the deuce a bit of cake has come to hand, which hath an inauspicious look at first; but I comfort myself that that mysterious service hath the property of sacramental bread, which mice cannot nibble, nor time moulder. I am married myself—to a severe stepwife— who keeps me, not at bed and board, but at desk and board, and is jealous of my morning aberrations. I cannot slip out to cóngratulate kinder unions. It is well she leaves me alone o'nights—the accursed Day-hag BUSINESS. She is even now peeping over me to see I am writing no love letters. I come, my dear. Where is the Indigo Sale Book?"

Returning from the grave of "gentle Elia," deeply impressed by thoughts of the sincerity of his affections, we seek the burial-place of one with whom in life Charles Lamb had some converse, and who was the last to quit the board around which so many celebrated men had gathered. For this purpose we wend our way towards another of the suburbs of the wide-spreading metropolis, to

HORNSEY,

in the thirteenth century called Haringhee, and subsequently Haringey, whence is derived its present name.

From time immemorial the manor has belonged to the see of London; and among the rectors of the parish we may mention Lewis Atterbury, brother of the Bishop of Rochester, and likewise William Cole, author of much antiquarian research, preserved in MS. in the British Museum. An episcopal palace was anciently to be found here, and the place has likewise some historic associations. In 1386, for instance, the Duke of Gloucester and other nobles assembled in Hornsey Park to oppose the favourite of Richard II.; and here, likewise, Edward V., after the death of his father, was met by a procession of the citizens of London on his approach to the capital.

Hornsey Church, dedicated to the Virgin Mary, retains little of its pristine character, but groups picturesquely with the trees and meadow scenery. In the church is buried Samuel Buckley, the learned editor of Thuanus,

Tomb of the Poet Rogers, Hornsey Churchyard.

or "De Thou's History of his Own Time," in choice Latin, 1741. As we admire this pleasant locality, we are reminded that it was a favourite haunt of Goldsmith in his suburban rambles; and Goldy's worthy successor, Washington Irving, has embalmed Hornsey in his polished pages. Of the love of another classic mind for this nook of quiet we find more tangible evidence in a monument erected in the churchyard to the memory of the patriarch of English poets,—

SAMUEL ROGERS,

a remarkable man, who outlived two or three generations of men. The village of Newington Green was the place of his birth, in the year 1763. His education, though private, was conducted with great care. He began the study of the world on the Continent, and, after a tour through the principal part of Europe, found himself located in the banking-house of his father, in St. Clement's Lane, Lombard-street. Extreme delicacy marked his early years; and, as he has himself told us, "from his cheek, ere yet the down was there, health fled." Though apparently destined for business, he possessed a love of intellectual pursuits. His taste was gratified by foreign travel, and he gracefully sang of Italy, as seen by him in her milder aspect:

"Nature denied him much,
But gave him at his birth what most he valued,
A passionate love for music, sculpture, painting,
For poetry, the language of the gods,
For all things here or grand or beautiful,
A setting sun, a lake among the mountains,
The light of an ingenious countenance,
And what transcends them all, a noble action."

The poet Bowles is said to have "delighted and inspired" the muse of Coleridge. In like manner the perusal of Beattie's "Minstrel" gave to Samuel Rogers, when but nine years old, a desire to be entered in the tuneful list, and he early aimed at authorship. With his "Ode to Superstition" the world was favoured at a time when Robert Burns began to fling upon the endless stream his rude but enduring verses. In 1792 appeared the "Pleasures of Memory," which succeeded in establishing the reputation of its author. Twenty years later (for our banker-bard wrote sparingly) came "Columbus," succeeded in time by "Jacqueline," "Human Life," and lastly, "Italy." The illustration of this poem is said to have cost ten thousand pounds, Turner and Stothard supplying it with some exquisite designs.

In reference to this slowness of composition Sydney Smith once made merry at Rogers's expense. Being asked whether Rogers had written anything lately, "Only a couplet," was the reply. "*Only* a couplet!" exclaimed the humorist. "Why what would you have? When Rogers produces a couplet he goes to bed, and the knocker is tied, and straw is laid down, and caudle is made, and the answer to inquiries is that Mr. Rogers is as well as can be expected."

For more than half a century Samuel Rogers resided in St. James's Place, in a house familiarly known as "Memory Hall." Here, in the midst of gems of art, were his chief poems written; and here he gathered round him the celebrities of his time. Within those walls have assembled Scott, Byron, Moore, Crabbe, Campbell, Southey, Wordsworth, Chantrey, Flaxman, Wilkie, Stothard—the poets and the painters—who, one by one, finally departed from the feast, leaving the hospitable host alone at the board. More than one generation passed away; but there still sat the poet and the wit, with tender heart and open hand, dispensing countless acts of kindness.

Rogers outlived his critics, and survived those he had an ambition to please. His was a life of intellectual disport. Easy were his fortunes, and his existence, like his verse, was calm and dignified. The fierce struggles of life, with which too many of the children of song are familiar, were to him unknown.

We have engraved the poet's monument in this suburban burial-ground, which we now leave for the last home of one of Rogers's great contemporaries.

CROSTHWAITE, CUMBERLAND,

is a beautiful hamlet, situate near to Keswick, on the banks of the Lake of Derwentwater. The district of the Lakes of Cumberland and Westmoreland is one of peculiar loveliness, and has not inaptly been termed the English Eden. Such a spot could not possibly have escaped the notice, and must consequently have secured the praise, of the poets. Gray was attracted thither nearly a century since, and dwelt in raptures upon the charms of Grasmere, which he described as opening upon "one of the sweetest landscapes that art ever attempted to imitate." Wordsworth subsequently lived and died amongst the lakes; Coleridge, whose grave we have just quitted, passed many years in the midst of what he characterised a "cabinet of beauties;" and in the churchyard of Crosthwaite we encounter the resting-place of another of the "Lakers,"—

were not forsaken by their friends. Hazlitt came to their favourite haunt on a visit, as did Lamb and Scott. Did not the lakes put on their choicest attire to welcome such visitors as Southey, Wordsworth, Coleridge, Hazlitt, Lamb, and Walter Scott?

Southey continued to reside at Greta until his death. Incessantly engaged in study and in composition, he ceased not until the dark shadow surrounded his home, and he looked upon the beauties by which he was environed as upon a gloomy void. The mind had given way to mental darkness, and death ultimately came to him as a blessing:

"How frail a thing is man!
The sunny morn the exhalation rears into a cloud—
At night it falls in tears."

So long previously as 1812 Southey had been impressed by a fear of insanity. In a letter at that time written to a brother poet he observed:—

"Nature gave me an indefatigable activity of mind, and a buoyancy of spirit which has ever enabled me to think little of difficulties, and to live in the light of hope. These gifts, too, were accompanied with an hilarity which has enabled me to retain a boy's heart to the age of eight-and-thirty; but my senses are perilously acute—impressions sink into me too deeply; and at one time ideas had all the vividness and apparent reality of actual impression, to such a degree that I believe a speedy removal to a foreign country, bringing with it a total change of all external objects, saved me from immediate danger."

Southey was a voluminous writer, and from his capacious intellect proceeded works upon almost every subject. To a great extent, however, he failed in attracting human affections, for books were more frequently his study than nature; and hence, though so distinguished as a poet, a scholar, and a critic, he is less popular than some of his gifted associates.

We have referred to a gifted group of visitors to the Lakes, but they have all been gathered into the garners of death. Hazlitt resigned his critical pen in 1830; Scott ceased his minstrelsy in 1832; Coleridge passed away two years later, and in a few weeks was followed by Lamb. The bard of Rydal Mount was the last to quit the scene, on the beauties of which he had so long lingered; but, previously to his witnessing for the last time the departure of the sun behind the hills which bounded his residence, he penned for Southey the following epitaph:—

"Sacred to the Memory of

Robert Southey,

whose mortal remains are interred in the neighbouring churchyard. He was born at Bristol, October 4, 1774, and died, after a residence of nearly forty years, at Greta Hall, in this parish, March 21, 1843.

Ye torrents foaming down the rocky steeps;
Ye lakes wherein the Spirit of Water sleeps;
Ye vales and hills, whose beauty hither drew
The poet's steps, and fix'd him here, on you
His eyes have closed; and ye, loved books, no more
Shall Southey feed upon your precious lore,
To works that ne'er shall forfeit their renown,
Adding immortal labours of his own,
Whether he traced historic truth with zeal,
For the State's guidance, or the Church's weal;

Or Fancy, disciplined by studious Art,
Inform'd his pen, or Wisdom of the heart,
Or judgments sanction'd in the patriot's mind
By reverence for the rights of all mankind.
Large were his aims, yet in no human breast
Could private feelings find a holier nest.
His joys, his griefs, have vanish'd like a cloud
From Skiddaw's top; but he to heaven was vow'd
Through a long life, and calm'd by Christian faith
In his pure soul the fear of change and death."

In Crosthwaite Church is a recumbent effigy of Southey, of white marble, sculptured by Lough; and in Bristol Cathedral is a marble bust of the poet, placed upon a pedestal, within a canopied recess. In addition to these memorials is the tablet, surmounted by the poet's bust, in Westminster Abbey.

RYDAL MOUNT

presents a continuation of the beauties so abundantly scattered over the district in which we left Southey to his repose. This was the mountain-home of Wordsworth, from whence came the calm voice to which the world at first refused to listen. For the tranquil atmosphere of the country he felt an attachment which could not be supplanted:

" Though absent long,
These forms of beauty have not been to me
As is a landscape to a blind man's eye;
But oft in lonely rooms, and 'mid the din
Of towns and cities, I have owed to them,
In hours of weariness, sensations sweet,
Felt in the blood, and felt along the heart,
And passing even into my purer mind
With tranquil restoration—feelings, too,
Of unremember'd pleasure; such, perhaps,

As may have had no trivial influence
On that best portion of a good man's life,
His little, nameless, unremember'd acts
Of kindness and of love."

Such was the bard's impression on revisiting the banks of the Wye, near to Tintern Abbey. But it was amid his native lakes his spirit lived, and for ever associated the name of Rydal Mount with that of

WILLIAM WORDSWORTH.

It was on the 23rd of April, 1616, that William Shakspeare died at Stratford-upon-Avon, surrounded by the rich woodlands with which his boyhood had been familiar; two hundred and thirty-four years later (April 23rd, 1850) William Wordsworth resigned his last sigh amid the lakes and mountains which had charmed his earliest fancy. He was born in April, 1770, at Cockermouth, in Cumberland, his father having been the law agent of the Earl of Lonsdale. The grammar-school at Hawkeshead received him at a befitting age, and before he quitted the same he had penned some chaste lines in praise of the surrounding scenery. Thus in his childhood

"was poetic impulse given
By the green hill and clear blue heaven."

At the age of seventeen Wordsworth was removed to Cambridge, and three years later he made a pedestrian tour through France and Switzerland. His earliest publication was "The Evening Walk" and "Descriptive Sketches." Quitting the university, he proceeded to London, and next to the banks of the Loire, where he resided for two winters. Returning to England, in 1802 he introduced to his beautiful cottage at Grasmere, Mary Hutchinson, cousin as well as wife. There was peace in the midst of his household, but the critics were fiercely assailing him from without. Some portion of his "Lyrical Ballads" had been published, and excited great hostility, the Edinburgh reviewers leading the forces fiercely against him. It was in November, 1802, that the *Edinburgh Review* first appeared, in which number Francis Jeffrey, in a notice of Southey's "Thalaba," assailed the Lake Poets, and subsequently directed against Wordsworth a special review. Byron, too, figured in the ranks of the opposition, as his celebrated satire can testify:—

"Next comes the dull disciple of thy school,
That mild apostate from poetic rule,
The simple Wordsworth, framer of a lay
As soft as evening in his favourite May."

It is known, however, that his lordship subsequently regretted these satiric lines, and in his own copy drew his pen through them. Francis Jeffrey, too, in time relented, and praised the poet against whom he had often made an onslaught.

Wordsworth's great poem, "The Excursion," appeared in 1814, and encountered the same hostility which had beset its predecessors. But the bard of Rydal was not to be deterred from his purpose, and continued to throw poem after poem before his antagonists, who at length, as in the cases cited, began to labour in his behalf. In 1830 Wordsworth revisited Scotland—he had been to the grave of Robert Burns twenty-seven years previously—and took an affectionate farewell of Scott, who had been his guest at Rydal, but who was now fast hurrying down the hill of life.

With the appreciation of Wordsworth's poetry came distinction and honours, and in 1843 he was appointed to the laureateship. His succeeding seven years were passed, as, in fact, the greater portion of his life had been, in the retirement of nature. Looking back upon the road by which he had journeyed, and noting the absence of many who once accompanied him, he plaintively asks,—

"How fast has brother follow'd brother,
From sunshine to the sunless land!
Yet I, whose lids from infant slumbers
Were earlier raised, remain to hear
A timid voice that asks in whispers,
'Who next will drop and disappear?'"

Wordsworth, with his humane philosophy, possessed great excellence, though he failed to reach the highest point in literature, owing in part to the absence of reality in his poetic characters. The earnestness of inspiration is rarely found in his compositions, but in his artless style he has written more than sufficient to win from the world its esteem and gratitude. The object of his earnest study during a long life was Nature, who in return presented to her student the charms in which he delighted, and amid which the poet lies in his grave at Rydal Mount.

STRATFORD-UPON-AVON.

The name of this pleasant old English town is derived from the *street* or road upon which it stands, and the *ford* across the Avon, which, before the days of bridges, had to be crossed in the most primitive manner. It has derived a world-wide reputation from having given birth to William Shakspeare, whose genius secured him the reverence of the intellectual world. Here are preserved relics of his presence, to which the most distinguished men of their time have, generation after generation, tendered homage :

" Think not, Britannia, all the tears are thine
Which flow a tribute to this hallow'd shrine:
Pilgrims from every land shall hither come,
And fondly linger round the poet's tomb."

Stratford is associated with the early hopes and struggles of the bard, and here he returned to close his days. The mansion in which he last lived is gone, together with the mulberry tree which, according to tradition, was planted by his own hand ; but we have still the house in which he was born, as well as the church in which are preserved his ashes. The gentle Avon, too, still intersects the district, though from Davenant we learn that, when the poet quitted the scene,

" The piteous river wept itself away."

The parish church of Stratford is a large and handsome structure, with a central tower surmounted by a spire. Let us pass through its beautiful avenues, and in the well-known chancel seek the bust to which is appended the name of

WILLIAM SHAKSPEARE.

The biography of this poet for all time is confined to his birth, marriage, authorship, and death, little else being accurately known. He was born at Stratford on the 23rd of April, 1564. Such, at least, is the date assigned, but without any direct evidence. The records of the parish church prove that he was baptized on the 26th of April; and the inference is, from the custom then adopted, that he was born two or three days previously. During the same year Stratford suffered a fearful visitation, the plague stalking through its streets, and bearing to their graves one-sixth of the population. The red cross was upon many a door; but the inmates of the lowly house in Henley-street, where the infant Shakspeare slept, was left by the pestilence unscathed, and the gifted one was saved. With him the Spirit of Genius subsequently wandered

> "Over the hills, and far away
> Beyond their utmost purple rim;
> Beyond the night, across the day,
> Through all the world she follow'd him."

As to the business followed by Shakspeare's father there have been endless theories, affirmations, and contradictions; but Mr. Charles Knight shows that he was what would now be termed a "gentleman farmer." In 1571 John Shakspeare was chief alderman of his town, and about the same year it is presumed his son was sent to the Free Grammar School of Stratford. Before the close of 1582 William Shakspeare, being then but eighteen years and a half old, was married to Anne Hathaway. Children came around him, but it is unknown how these new claims upon his industry were met, or what led him from his favourite Avon to the banks of the Thames. We have heard much of deer-stealing propensities, and of a libellous ballad upon Sir Thomas Lucy; but, having no proof of the fact, we must award the delinquent the advantage of the doubt; though the grey-headed men of Stratford informed Betterton, the actor, that in his youth their townsman was a "wild young fellow." Arrived in London, what was his earliest occupation? Did he hold horses for those patrons of the drama who then visited the

P

theatres, and required such aid ? We know not; for the biography of our bard is a blank from 1585, when his twin children were baptized at Stratford, until November, 1589, when his name appears as one of her Majesty's "poor players."

Respecting the first appearance of Shakspeare as a dramatist, doubts exist as to the precise period; and, notwithstanding the labour and talent bestowed upon the subject, little more than conjecture can even now be formed. His introduction to the theatre was doubtless in some humble capacity, and minor characters in the then popular pieces were probably assigned him. Of his merits as a player we have no data on which to found an estimate: had he been eminent as an actor, the world might never have received what now constitutes the noblest efforts of human genius. His merits as a dramatist soon advanced him in the regard of the great and the noble, and secured him the favour of two successive sovereigns. He became important in the management of the theatre, and participated in all the emoluments of the company. Being comparatively opulent, he purchased the most respectable house in his native Stratford, known as "New Place," and to this favoured spot he retired, but, as Mr. Knight shows, continued to write plays for the stage till he was removed by death.

The scenery of the neighbourhood was once more familiar to the bard, who doubtless wandered again through fields which had inspired many of those fancies which delight posterity. It was through their green paths that he was first led by Nature, from whom he received his precious gift:

"'This pencil take,' she said, 'whose colours clear
Richly paint the vernal year;
Thine, too, these golden keys, immortal boy!
This can unlock the gates of joy;
Of horror that, and thrilling fears,
Or ope the sacred source of sympathetic tears.'"

On his return to these haunts, we may feel assured that the fields leading to Shottery, the "prettiest of hamlets," were again trodden, for it was there Anne Hathaway had been wooed and won. It is pleasing to know that those less blessed than himself were not absent from his thoughts. The discovery of the last notice of the bard during his life, and written a few months before his death, assures us that he was then taking part with the poor against the inclosure of the common lands near Stratford.

The closing scene of his own life-drama too speedily followed his return hither, and brought with it a sorrowful day to Stratford. The 23rd of April, 1616, witnessed its mourning, for the " myriad-minded " was then left sleeping in the church which had witnessed his baptism and his marriage.

The town of Stratford has increased considerably of late years; but, with the exception of the places associated with Shakspeare and a half-timbered house-front in one of the streets, there is little to interest the antiquarian visitor. Nevertheless, the name and genius of Shakspeare have invested Stratford with a celebrity outvied by no other such locality in the world; for it is the scene of the *alpha* and *omega*, the beginning and the end, of genius, the exercise of which has done more to humanise, charm, and exalt mankind than has ever been accomplished by any kindred spirit. The houses at Stratford are, for the most part, meanly built; but, as you seek in and about it the localities consecrated by the genius of the great Poet, *you think of Shakspeare alone.* As you enter the town by the old bridge over the Avon, you reflect that across this very structure Shakspeare must often have walked. " Rich and pleasant as is the distant prospect of the town," says one imbued with the love of Shakspeare,* " it takes its crowning glory from the mighty genius whose dust reposes at our feet. It is his genial spirit which pervades and sanctifies the scene ; and every spot on which the eye can rest claims some association with his life. We tread the very ground that he has trod a thousand times, and feel, as he had felt,—

'That the heaven's breath
Smells wooingly here.'

" A little way off to the right we can almost trace the spot where, quiet and sequestered in the fields of Shottery, stands the homestead of his early love. More bosomed, on the other hand, surrounded with majestic elms and antique oaks, we catch a glimpse of Charlecote, the ancient seat of the Lucys. Immediately beneath us is the dwelling of his youth in Henley-street; and near to it stands the chapel of the guild, marking at once the locality of his school and the home of his choice, New Place."

A few paces further still, and the eye rests contemplatively on that " last scene of all "—the venerable church— the tranquil depository of his sacred ashes, till

* Howard Staunton.

"The cloud-capp'd towers, the gorgeous palaces,
The solemn temples, the great globe itself,
Yea, all which it inherit, shall dissolve;
And, like an unsubstantial pageant, faded,
Leave not a rack behind!"

How strikingly picturesque is the church, environed in lofty elms, save where its graceful spire is mirrored upon the peaceful Avon!

"Here the bard divine,
Whose sacred dust yon high-arch'd aisles inclose,
Where the tall windows rise in stately rows
Above the embowering shade."

We approach the church by the overarching lime-tree walk, and enter from the north, through the nave and choir, to the chancel, where is the dust of Shakspeare, the stone covering the poet's grave being inscribed with these extraordinary lines:—

"GOOD FREND! FOR JESUS' SAKE, FORBEARE,
TO DIG THE DUST ENCLOASED HEARE:
BLESTE BE YE MAN YT SPARES THES STONES,
AND CVRST BE HE YT MOVES MY BONES."

" There is something," says Mr. Staunton, " indescribably awful and affecting in the sense of contiguity even with the mouldering dust of Shakspeare; and we found it a relief when a friend, as if responding to our impression, whispered, " I never felt, in all its power, the majesty of Shakspeare's greatness till I stood upon his narrow grave."

On the left of the chancel, almost immediately above the poet's grave, is the far-famed mural monument with a bust, life size, beneath an arch, between two Corinthian columns of black marble. Upon the entablature are the arms of Shakspeare (surmounted by a skull), and two small figures sitting, one holding in his right hand a spade, and the other, whose eyes are closed, having in his left hand an inverted torch, and his right resting upon a skull. This monument was certainly erected before 1623. Originally the bust was coloured to resemble life. The hands and face were of flesh colour, the eyes of bright hazel, and the hair and beard auburn; the doublet or coat was scarlet, over which was a loose black tabard, or coat without sleeves. The upper part of the cushion on which the poet's hand rests was green, the under half crimson, and the tassels were gilt. The monument was repaired in 1748, but in 1793 Mr. Malone had the bust covered with white paint! Upon the tablet beneath is the following inscription:—

"JVDICIO PYLIVM, GENIO SOCRATEM, ARTE MARONEM,
TERRA TEGIT, POPULUS MŒRET, OLYMPVS HABET.
STAY, PASSENGER, WHY GOEST THOV BY SO FAST,
READ, IF THOV CANST, WHOM ENVIOVS DEATH HATH PLAST
WITHIN THIS MONVMENT, SHAKSPEARE, WITH WHOME
QUICK NATURE DIDE; WHOSE NAME DOTH DECK YS TOMBE,
FAR MORE THAN COST; SITH ALL YT HE HATH WRITT
LEAVES LIVING ART BVT PAGE TO SERVE HIS WIT.
OBIIT ANO. DOI. 1616. ÆTATIS 53. DIE 23 AP."

It were idle to dwell upon the genius of Shakspeare. There have been a few brief periods of eclipse since his death; still, these were but preludes to greater brightness. "The twilight has to darken before the day can break;" and, like the sun new risen, the radiance of the poet's fame now illumines the greater portion of the globe. With Emerson we may ask, "What mystery has he not signified his knowledge of? What king has he not taught state? What maiden has not found him finer than her delicacy? What lover has he not outloved? What sage has he not outseen?"

We leave the bard, then, in his sacred chancel:—

"He so sepulchred in such pomp dost lie,
That kings for such a tomb would wish to die."

Shakspeare had his rivals and detractors. One of the most prominent of the former we shall find interred at

DEPTFORD,

in whose dockyard Peter surnamed the Great once worked as a shipwright. John Evelyn likewise dwelt here. It is situate on the river Ravensbourne, at its afflux with the Thames, and here was formerly a deep ford, whence the name Deptford is derived. Here is the grave of

CHRISTOPHER MARLOWE,

the dramatist, who was born at Canterbury, and was baptized at the church of St. George the Martyr on the 26th of February, 1563-4. He was the son of a shoemaker, but received a good education at King's School in his native city, from whence he was removed to Cambridge, where he took the degrees of B.A. and M.A. Quitting his academic pursuits, he became connected with the stage, and was the most celebrated of Shakspeare's predecessors. The plots of his pieces assumed a more regular character than those previously arranged, and he was only eclipsed by his great successor. Marlowe was the author of six tragedies, and joined with Nash and Day in writing two others. He prematurely closed his career in a strange affray. His remains were interred in the church of St. Nicholas, the entry in the records of burials there being as follows :—" 1st June, 1593. Christopher Marlow, slain by Francis Archer." Marlowe is styled by Heywood the "best of poets." No greater writer preceded him, whilst his fiery imagination and strokes of passion communicated a peculiar impulse to those who followed him. In his *Tamberlaine* many passages of poetic beauty occur; for example, the following rhapsody delivered by that hero on the supposed death of his queen :—

> " Now walk the angels on the walls of heaven,
> As sentinels to warn th' immortal souls
> To entertain divine Zenocrate.
> Apollo, Cynthia, and the ceaseless lamps
> That gently look'd upon this loathsome earth,
> Shine downward now no more, but deck the heavens
> To entertain divine Zenocrate.
> The crystal spring, whose taste illuminates
> Refined eyes with an eternal sight,
> Like tried silver, runs through paradise,
> To entertain divine Zenocrate.
> Then let some holy trance convey my thoughts
> Up to the palace of the empyreal heaven,
> That thus my life may be as short to me
> As are the days of sweet Zenocrate."

DOVER.

In this old town are the vestiges of several ancient religious houses. The ecclesiastical annalists have handed down to us traditions of a very early Christian church—some say the first Christian church—having been erected within the original Roman, or earlier than Roman, hill fort in Dover Castle. Little is left of this interesting ruin of probably one of the earliest religious structures in the kingdom. The church of St. Mary-le-Grand is said to have been reared in 696 by Withred, King of Kent.

The burying-ground of this old church—the structure itself having long been in ruins—has often been visited, for resting in the midst of its desolation are the remains of

CHARLES CHURCHILL.

This poet was born in Westminster in 1731, his father being the curate of the parish of St. John's, in that city. Denied admittance at the University of Oxford—from causes differently explained—he obtained a Welsh curacy, yielding the sum of £30 per year, to increase which he is said to have profanely engaged in the sale of cider! The speculation, however, failed, as did several others in which he embarked upon his return to London. In March, 1761, Churchill published his celebrated "Rosciad." This memorable work—which, with much spirit and vivacity, examined the merits and defects of the metropolitan performers—gave to its author considerable reputation. He continued to wield his pen in general satire until the close of his career, which occurred through a fever, at Boulogne, on the 4th of November, 1764, he being then but thirty-three years old. Churchill, with respect to his grave, left behind him the following wish:—

"Let one poor sprig of bay around my head
　Bloom whilst I live, and point me out as dead;
　Let it, may Heaven indulgent grant my prayer,
　Be planted on my grave, nor wither there;
　And when, on travel bound, some rhyming guest
　Roams through the churchyard while his dinner's dress'd,
　Let it hold up this comment to his eyes—
　Life to the last enjoy'd, here Churchill lies!"

About fifty years after his death, the poet's wish was in

part fulfilled, a bay tree having been planted on his grave by a Deal pilot. It was for some time carefully tended by him, but it did not thrive, and has long since disappeared. The bay, however, had been planted, and the "rhyming guest" roamed through the churchyard in the person of Lord Byron, whose impressions he has thus recorded :—

> "I stood beside the grave of him who blazed
>   The comet of a season, and I saw
> The humblest of all sepulchres, and gazed,
>   With not the less of sorrow and of awe,
> On that neglected turf and quiet stone,
>   With names no clearer than the names unknown
> Which lay unread around it; and I ask'd
>   The gardener of that ground why it might be
> That for this plant strangers his memory task'd
>   Through the thick deaths of half a century.
> And thus he answer'd: 'Well, I do not know
> Why frequent travellers turn to pilgrims so.
> He died before my day of sextonship,
>   And I had not the digging of his grave.'
> And is this all? I thought; and do we rip
>   The veil of Immortality, and crave
> I know not what of honour and of light
> Through unborn ages, to endure this blight
>   So soon and so successless?"

BEACONSFIELD,

in Buckinghamshire, is situated upon an eminence, on which a beacon formerly stood: hence its name. In the parish church is resting

EDMUND WALLER.

First cousin to Hampden, and likewise to Cromwell, this poet was born on the 3rd of March, 1605, at Coleshill, in Hertfordshire. Whilst an infant his father died, leaving him a yearly income of more than three thousand pounds —a rare commencement of a poet's career. At Eton he received some portion of his education, which was completed at King's College, Cambridge. Waller entered Parliament before he had reached his twentieth year, and became known at the court of James I. Though rich by inheritance, he had previously to this formed an acquaintance with poetry, his earliest production being "The Prince's Escape at St. Andero." He married at the age of twenty-six, but became a widower, when the Lady Dorothy Sidney attracted his attention. His passion was urged with all the fluency with which poetry could invest it; but his high-born heroine—whom he had so often addressed as "Saccharissa"—gave her hand to the Earl of Sunderland. In her old age she encountered Waller, and inquired when he would again write such verses upon her, receiving in answer, "When you are as young, madam, and as handsome as you were then."

In his political character Waller was one of the commissioners nominated by the Parliament to treat with Charles at Oxford, and was subsequently connected with the engagement known as "Waller's Plot," the discovery of which has been variously related. From these treasonable involvements he escaped by the payment of several thousand pounds, and passed into exile, ultimately obtaining from Cromwell a permission to return to England. He resided for some time, with a diminished fortune, at Hall Barn, near to Beaconsfield. In the Parliament first summoned by the second Charles, Waller sat for Hastings, in Sussex. We are told by Burnet that he was "the delight of the house, and though old, said the liveliest things of any among them." When thus referred to Waller had reached his seventieth year. Even at this age he renewed his claims to poetical distinction, and appears to have lost but little of his earlier ability; and when grown aged, and scarcely able to see, he dictated several divine poems. He died on the 21st of October, 1687, having reached his eighty-second year. He is buried in the churchyard, beneath a marble altar-tomb, with a pyramidal obelisk rising from the centre, and a votive urn at each angle: on the east side is the inscription in Latin.

Waller, with much singularity of character, was weak in resolution and lax in politics. He had a world of faults— could plot rebellion, and then offer slavish adulation to the controlling powers, alike to Cromwell and to Charles. As a poet he is considered to have "added something to our elegance of diction, and something to our propriety of thought." He was the most correct poetical writer that we had before Pope, and his example had considerable effect in regulating the form and refining the manner of our poetry, although it may have also helped somewhat to tame its spirit.

The church of Beaconsfield must not be quitted without a visit of respect being paid to the grave of Edmund Burke, a man of transcendent genius. Literature at one time welcomed his contributions, and the senate was charmed by his oratory. Affixed to his name are many great distinctions, but none stand out more honourably than the circumstance of his having rescued from obscurity the poet Crabbe, and Barry the painter. Honour, then, to the memory of Edmund Burke!

Whilst in the county of Bucks a visit should be paid to the resting-place of a classic poet and man of refined taste, at

STOKE,

the pleasant hamlet situated not far from Eton College, the "antique towers that crown the watery glade." It was at the fine old manor-house of Stoke Pogis, at which Elizabeth was entertained in 1601, that the Lord Chancellor Hatton once resided:

> "Full oft within the spacious walls,
> When he had fifty winters o'er him,
> My grave lord keeper led the brawls—
> The seals and maces danced before him."

From the picturesque remains of this ancient pile we wander into the churchyard, which possesses much poetical interest. The minstrel whose grave we seek has frequently stood in the shadow of this dark tree, contemplating the scattered mounds. It was here that, in all probability, he conceived his universally admired "Elegy," and thought of the unrecognised dead:

> "Perhaps in this neglected spot is laid
> Some heart once pregnant with celestial fire;
> Hands that the rod of empire might have sway'd,
> Or waked to ecstasy the living lyre."

If such, the poet has himself laid down by their side, for this is the grave of

THOMAS GRAY.

This "student of Cambridge" was born on the 26th of December, 1716, in Cornhill, at No. 41, a few doors from Birchin-lane. From his father, who was an Exchange broker, he received little save harshness and restraint; but for this unkindness he received ample compensation in the devotedness of an excellent mother. Separated from her husband, and engaged with her sister in a millinery business, she directed her chief energies to the advancement of her son, who, by her exertions, was sent first to Eton and subsequently to Cambridge. In a later period of his life he looked from a distance upon the college he had first entered, and thought with some degree of sadness upon the change effected by time:

> "Ah, happy hills! ah, pleasing shade!
> Ah, fields beloved in vain!
> Where once my careless childhood stray'd,
>   A stranger yet to pain:
> I feel the gales that from ye blow
> A momentary bliss bestow,
> As, waving fresh their gladsome wing,
>   My weary soul they seem to soothe,
>   And, redolent of joy and youth,
> To breathe a second spring."

At Cambridge Gray continued to reside for many years, labouring with much intensity in the acquirement of classical knowledge, relieving at times his profounder studies by poetical composition. In 1747 he published his "Ode to Eton College," which was followed by his "Elegy Written in a Country Churchyard," and still later his "Pindaric Odes." Upon the death of Cibber, in 1757, he was offered the laureateship, which he declined, and subsequently secured the more lucrative office of Professor of Modern History. His health began to decline shortly after receiving this appointment, and, being suddenly seized with gout in the vital parts of his system, he lingered but a few days longer, finding rest from his sufferings on the 30th of July, 1771, in the fifty-fifth year of his age.

Gray, whilst at Eton, became acquainted with Horace Walpole, with whom he travelled in France and Italy. He was an occasional visitor at Strawberry Hill, and when a printing-press was introduced into that Gothic castle by the acknowledged "emperor of gossips and king of letter-writers," its first use was applied to the printing of Gray's "Bard" and his "Progress of Poesy." Of the first poem Walpole thus wrote to Richard Bentley, the artist:—

"Strawberry Hill, September 18th. Gray has lately been here. He has begun an ode, which, if he finishes equally, will, I think, inspirit all your drawing again. It is founded on an old tradition of Edward I. putting to death the Welsh bards. Nothing but you, or Salvator Rosa and Nicolo Poussin, can paint up to the expressive horror and dignity of it. Don't think I mean to flatter you: all I would say is that, now the two latter are dead, you must of necessity be Gray's painter."

Another of Gray's friends, whom he occasionally met at Strawberry Hill, and who lived to become his literary executor, was William Mason. He also is known to us as a poet, and has his monument in the renowned "Corner." He was born in 1725, and after leaving Cambridge entered into holy orders. His poetry, though boasting of a rich diction, is deficient in the simplicity calculated to render it popular. Mason died in 1797, having survived his friend more than a quarter of a century.

Gray throughout his life was a devoted scholar, a desire for varied knowledge being his ruling passion. He possessed a fastidious taste, and as a man was reserved and even haughty. He wrote but little: he has, notwithstanding, bequeathed us some highly-finished specimens of poetry. There is a discipline perceptible in his muse, over which is thrown a philosophic sadness. Of earnestness and fancy we see but little in his writings, but in their place studied correctness and refined polish. His " Elegy " has been universally read, and is calculated long to preserve the reputation of its author.

When in Westminster Abbey we pointed to the tomb erected there to Gray's memory. We may here give its inscription:—

"𝕿𝖍𝖔𝖒𝖆𝖘 𝕲𝖗𝖆𝖞,
July 30, 1771. Aged 54.

No more the Grecian muse unrivall'd reigns;
To Britain let the nations homage pay:
She felt a Homer's fire in Milton's strains,
A Pindar's rapture in the lyre of Gray."

The poet, however, does not repose in that favoured transept, having himself selected the secluded churchyard of Stoke. His mother and his aunt—from whose industry and warm affection his own education, and the consequent gratification of his life, had been derived—were here consigned, and by his own special desire he sleeps by their side, under a handsome tomb which he had erected to their memory; but he rests here without any monumental inscription. Let us, before leaving a spot so sanctified by affection, copy the simple epitaph supplied by the poet to his excellent mother, and which breathes the quiet sadness so characteristic of his verse:—

"Here Sleep the Remains of
𝔇𝔬𝔯𝔬𝔱𝔥𝔶 𝔊𝔯𝔞𝔶, 𝔚𝔦𝔡𝔬𝔴,
The careful, tender mother of many children,
One of whom alone had the misfortune to survive her."

Gray was at one time ridiculed, but honour is now paid to his name.* A brother poet, Walter Savage Landor, has recently offered to his memory the following tribute:—

GOLDSMITH AND GRAY.

"Sweet odours and bright colours swiftly pass,
Swiftly as breath upon a looking-glass.
Byron, the school girl's pet, has lived his day,
And the tall Maypole scarce remembers May.
Thou, Nature, bloomest in perennial youth:
Two only are eternal—thou and Truth.
Who walks not with thee through the dim churchyard?
Who wanders not with Erin's wandering bard?
Who sits not down with Auburn's pastor mild,
To take upon his knee the shyest child?
These in all hearts will find a kindred place,
And live the last of our poetic race."

WELWYN, HERTS,

has its memorials of a poet, and one, too, who for many years was its rector, and has been for nearly a century resting by the scene of his sacred duties. This was

EDWARD YOUNG, LL.D.

He was born at Upham, near Winchester, in June, 1684, his father being at that time the rector of the parish. Young was placed upon the foundation of Winchester College, where he continued until his eighteenth year, when he

---

* The accomplished Earl of Carlisle, in a lecture replete with poetry and graceful feeling, has commemorated the genius of Gray.

was sent to Oxford. Soon after his entrance into public life he became a courtier, and his performance of that character was marked with servility. His poetical career may be dated from 1713, when he published an epistle on the creation of peers by Queen Anne. During his extended life Young wrote many works, three of which were devoted to the stage. Thus in 1719 he gave to Drury Lane his play of *Busiris;* and two years later brought forward his best-remembered piece, *The Revenge.* On his appointment as chaplain to George III. he withdrew from the theatre his play of *The Brothers,* which had been placed in rehearsal. A quarter of a century later he allowed this piece to be performed, intending to give the profits thereof to the Society for Propagating the Gospel; but, as those profits did not exceed £400, he took the same, and generously presented the society with a thousand guineas.

In 1730 Young was appointed to the rectory of Welwyn, where his subsequent days were passed. In the year 1731 he married a daughter of the Earl of Lichfield, the relict of Colonel Lee. This lady, by her first marriage, had a daughter, whom the doctor, in her fatal illness, attended to the Continent:

"I flew, I snatch'd her from the rigid North,
And bore her nearer to the sun."

His daughter-in-law's death was followed by that of his wife, and these domestic misfortunes led to the work by which Young's name is best known, the "Night Thoughts," and which is esteemed an ornament to our language. The first portion of this work was published in 1742, when the student of Winchester College had reached his fifty-eighth year. Contrasting the gaiety, and even dissipation of his youth, with the ambition of his maturer years, the pastor of Welwyn expressed his gratitude for his retirement :—

"Bless'd be that hand divine which gently laid
My heart at rest beneath this humble shade!
The world's a stately bark on dangerous seas,
With pleasure seen, but boarded at our peril.
Here, on a single plank, thrown safe ashore,
I hear the tumult of the distant throng,
As that of seas remote or dying storms,
And meditate on scenes more silent still;
Pursue my theme, and fight the fear of death.
Here, like a shepherd, gazing from his hut,
Touching his reed, or leaning on his staff,
Eager ambition's fiery chase I see.
I see the circling hunt of noisy men
Burst law's inclosure, leap the mounds of right,
Pursuing and pursued, each other's prey,
As wolves for rapine, as the fox for wiles,
Till death, that mighty hunter, earths them all.
Why all this toil for triumphs of an hour?
What though we wade in wealth, or soar in fame,
Earth's highest station ends in 'here he lies,'
And 'dust to dust' concludes her noblest song."

Dr. Young finally laid down his pious pen in April, 1764, having reached the patriarchal age of eighty-four.

He was strict in the performance of his religious duties, domestic as well as public. His accustomed walk of meditation was among the tombs of his own churchyard, but he does not appear to have been severe or gloomy: he was fond of gardening, and his parishioners were obliged to him for a bowling-green and an assembly-room.

Contemporary with Dr. Young were Cowper, Shenstone, and Collins, whose respective graves we next visit—at East Dereham, Hales Owen, and Chichester.

EAST DEREHAM,

situated nearly in the centre of Norfolk, possesses a church which originally belonged to a nunnery, founded by Withburga, natural daughter of Anna, King of East Anglia, and which was destroyed by the Danes. It was made parochial so long since as 798. Bonner, Bishop of London, was one of the rectors of this parish. Here, in the north transept, were interred, in 1800, the remains of

WILLIAM COWPER.

This popular poet was born in November, 1731, at Great Berkhampstead, of which parish his father was rector, as well as chaplain to George II. His sorrows commenced at the age of six years, when his mother, who was allied to several noble families, was taken from him. Throughout his life was the memory of that parent treasured by him; and the receipt of her portrait in after-years was a gleam of sunshine to him in his clouded melancholy, partly expressed in these lines :—

"Time unrevoked has run
His wonted course, yet what I wish'd is done.
By contemplation's help, not sought in vain,
I seem to have lived my childhood o'er again;
To have renew'd the joys that once were mine,
Without the sin of violating thine.
And, while the wings of fancy still are free,
And I can view this mimic show of thee,
Time has but half succeeded in his theft—
Thyself removed, thy power to soothe me left."

After serving a "seven years' apprenticeship to the classics" at Westminster School, Cowper was articled to an attorney, his fellow-clerk being the future Lord Chancellor Thurlow. In 1754 Cowper was called to the bar, and occupied chambers in the Temple. Considering, however, the road of jurisprudence a thorny one, he wandered therefrom into the more pleasing one of literature, and became a contributor to *The Connoisseur*, a periodical first published in January, 1754, and conducted by two of his Westminster schoolfellows, George Colman, the elder, and Bonnel Thornton.

Cowper was subsequently appointed to the office of clerk of the journals to the House of Lords ; but this he was compelled to resign, owing to the shadows of insanity which began to obscure his prospects. Retiring as it were from the world, he was adopted as one of the family of the Rev. Mr. Unwin, in which he continued until its members were removed from life. In the intervals of the gloom which more or less ever surrounded him, he devoted himself to poetic composition. In 1782 he published a small volume of his effusions, which experienced much hostility from the reviewers. This volume was succeeded, three years subsequently, by a second, in which was included "The Task," which secured to its author unqualified praise. Thus encouraged, a bright spot was seen in Cowper's vision, and he sat down to a still greater undertaking, a translation of Homer, who was one of the lights of the world which appear so seldom. To the distance between such rare but abiding stars Cowper has a beautiful reference :—

"Ages elapsed ere Homer's lamp appear'd,
And ages ere the Mantuan swan was heard ;
To carry nature lengths unknown before—
To give a Milton birth—ask'd ages more.

> Thus genius rose and set at order'd times,
> And shot a dayspring into distant climes,
> Ennobling every region that he chose.
> He sunk in Greece, in Italy he rose;
> And, tedious years of Gothic darkness past,
> Emerged all splendour in our isle at last.
> Thus lovely halcyons dive into the main,
> Then show far off their shining plumes again."

A careful revision of his translation of Homer was one of Cowper's latest efforts. His mental affliction was not diminished by increasing years, and he experienced a terrible shock in the death of Mrs. Unwin, the Mary who had so watched his suffering hours, and who is for ever enshrined in his verse. In like manner Byron has immortalised *his* Mary, of whose pictured self he

> " Through hours, through years, through time, 'twill cheer;
>   My hope in gloomy moments raise;
> In life's last conflict 'twill appear,
>   And meet my fond expiring gaze."

Cowper, in the autumn of 1793, thus poured out his affectionate tribute to the promoter of his happiness:—

> " Thy silver locks, once auburn bright,
> Are still more lovely in my sight
> Than golden beams of orient light,
>   My Mary!
>
> " For could I view nor them nor thee,
> What sight worth seeing could I see?
> The sun would rise in vain for me,
>   My Mary!"

He survived Mrs. Unwin little more than three years, and was himself released from his dread and despondency on the 25th of April, 1800. Cowper was among the most various of our writers, and enjoys a popularity exceeded by no poet of his time. By his descriptive power, his lively fancy, and natural pleasantry, we are led to admire the landscape which was dear to himself, and to form one of the circle he so faithfully portrays. Quitting his tomb, we are impressed by sorrowful regret at the melancholy which so shadowed the happiness of the man, and by sincere reverence for the poet, in whose purity was a warm sympathy for all.

HALES OWEN, SHROPSHIRE,

once boasted of an Abbey of Premonstratensian Canons, built by Peter de Rupibus, Bishop of Winchester, pursuant to a charter granted by King John. Among its present objects of interest is a chapel constructed from the remains of a cell erected by the Saxons, soon after the discovery here of the body of Kenelm, son of Kenulph, King of the Mercians, who died in 819. From the ruins of the old abbey, though full of interest, we pass to the churchyard, in which is sleeping the author of some occasionally-remembered pastorals,—

WILLIAM SHENSTONE.

This poet was born on the 18th of November, 1714, and received the principal part of his school education at Solihul, near Birmingham. In 1732 he was entered a commoner at Pembroke College, Oxford, but appears to have taken no degree in the university, nor secured any academical honours. Born to the small paternal estate of Leasowes, he embellished the same for his amusement; and it was from this circumstance principally that his talents as a writer of pastorals became known. Dr. Johnson is somewhat severe upon the ornamentation of Shenstone's estate, with its ruined priory, Gothic shields, cascades, &c.; but it appears to have attracted much notice in its day. Visited once by William Pitt (Lord Chatham), he observed to the owner that Nature had done everything for him, to which Shenstone replied that he hoped he had done something for Nature in return, by displaying her beauties to the best advantage.

Shenstone's earliest production considered worthy of note was a mock-heroic poem entitled "The Diamond;" and in the year 1737 he printed at Oxford a small collection of his poems, which was only privately circulated. Three years later he paid his first visit to London, and next published his "Judgment of Hercules." Some little portion of fame was awarded this production, which was followed by "The Schoolmistress," in the style of Spenser, which Johnson pronounced the most pleasing of his works. These effusions of Shenstone were published by Robert Dodsley, a man of liberal sentiments, with a benevolent heart. He was at one time footman to the Hon. Mrs. Lowther, and while in service he wrote some verses which were praised by Pope; and later in life he became a bookseller in Pall Mall. To some extent he may be termed the patron of Johnson and Burke, for he gave literary employment to both when such assistance was needed, and thus far aided their subsequent advancement. Dodsley was likewise the publisher of Pope and Gray. He died on the 25th of September, 1764, and lies in the abbey churchyard at Durham.

From the embellishment of his estate Shenstone found

time to pen some elegies and a few odes; but he at length grew sedentary and indolent, though occasionally assisting literary friends in the promotion or correction of their works. He is said, for instance, to have suggested to Percy the publication of his "Relics of Ancient Poetry." He passed the later years of his life in credit and reputation, but was suddenly seized with a fever, which terminated fatally on the 11th of February, 1763.

Inactivity and ill health, with a fondness for amusement, caused Shenstone to lavish upon a few topics whatever talents he may have possessed. As a poet he can only be classed in the second rank. He is thus referred to by Mason, in his "English Garden:"—

> "Nor, Shenstone, thou
> Shalt pass without thy meed, thou son of peace,
> Who knew'st perchance to harmonise thy shades
> Still softer than thy song; yet was that song
> Nor rude nor inharmonious when attuned
> To pastoral plaint, or tale of slighted love."

Shenstone is described by a friend, who wrote in 1788, to have been of a good height, rather of a robust than an elegant form. "His favourite dress was a plain blue coat and a scarlet waistcoat, with a broad gold lace, which he seldom changed either winter or summer." Subsequently to his death several testimonials were raised to his worth. Among others, in Hagley Park, the first Lord Lyttleton, under a natural pavilion of stately oaks, erected an urn with this inscription:—"To the Memory of William Shenstone, Esq., in whose verses were all the natural graces, and in whose manners was all the amiable sim_plicity of pastoral poetry, with the sweet tenderness of the elegiac." At Ermenonville, about thirty miles from Paris, a tribute was likewise raised. This was at the seat of the Marquis de Girardin, where a pyramid was erected sacred to the pastoral poets, Theocritus, Virgil, Gesner, and Thomson. Short inscriptions, in the language of each poet, were added respectively on the four sides of the base, and at the foot of the pyramid lay a stone inscribed, " To the Memory of Shenstone."

The remains of Shenstone, by his own desire, were deposited in the churchyard of Hales Owen. In the church was placed an urn bearing the following inscription :—

> " Whoe'er thou art, with reverence tread
> These sacred mansions of the dead !
> Not that the monumental bust
> Or sumptuous tomb here guards the dust
> Of rich or great: let wealth, rank, birth,
> Sleep undistinguish'd in the earth;
> This simple urn records a name
> Which shines with more exalted fame.
>
>   Reader ! if genius, taste refined,
> A native elegance of mind;
> If virtue, science, manly sense;
> If wit that never gave offence;
> The clearest head, the tenderest heart,
> In thy esteem e'er claim'd a part;
> Ah ! smite thy breast and drop a tear,
> For know thy Shenstone's dust lies here."

CHICHESTER CATHEDRAL

claims from us a visit, for it contains a monument of exquisite beauty, from the chisel of Flaxman, raised to the memory of the poet Collins. The original cathedral was founded towards the close of the eleventh century, and was entirely destroyed in the year 1186. The edifice which arose from its ashes, and which is the nucleus of the existing structure, was consecrated on the 13th of September, 1199. Its architecture is of many periods. The spire, which was raised about the year 1337, is nearly three hundred feet high. The cathedral suffered great devastation from the soldiers of the Commonwealth, who were quartered in the church, and carried on with wild fanaticism the work of destruction. Here is a tomb to the memory of the able defender of Protestantism, William Chillingworth; but we are especially attracted to the monument on which we see inscribed the name of

WILLIAM COLLINS.

The city of Chichester was the birthplace of this poet, thus adding another name to the literary band emanating from the county of Sussex. Among those who have sprung from her rural districts—districts which once celebrated in monkish verse the gallant doings of some of the barons of old—we may adduce Thomas Sackville, subsequently the Earl of Dorset, the author of the induction to the "Mirror for Magistrates," as well as of the principal portion of *Gorboduc*, the earliest extant drama in this country which can be termed a tragedy. The "learned Selden," too, was born in this county, as well as the unfortunate Otway. In more recent days Sussex produced Percy Bysshe Shelley, who was born at Field Place on the 4th of August, 1792, and went down into the waters of Spezia on the 8th of July, 1822. Otway, before entering upon the varied scenes of London, doubtlessly wandered by his native stream, the Arun, to which Collins thus refers in his " Ode to Pity : "—

"But wherefore need I wander wide
To old Ilissus' distant side,
    Deserted streams and mute?
Wild Arun, too, has heard thy strains,
And Echo, midst my native plains,
    Been soothed by Pity's lute.

" There first the wren thy myrtles shed
On gentle Otway's infant head :
    To him thy cell was shown ;
And while he sung the female heart,
With youth's soft notes unspoil'd by art,
    Thy turtles mix'd their own."

The name of Collins was added to the list of Sussex worthies in 1721. In 1733 he was admitted of Winchester College. Standing first in the list of scholars to be received in succession at New College, he experienced the original misfortune of his life, for no vacancy existed at the time. He subsequently, however, became a commoner of Queen's College, Oxford. About 1744 he repaired to London, where he designed many works, but lacked the resolution to accomplish his schemes. A "History of the Revival of Learning," and some tragedies, were thus planned, but never carried out. Doubtful of the means of support, and frequently playing with his creditors the game of concealment, Collins could but seldom bring a mind calculated for the exercise of his genius. A change was at length effected in his fortunes by the death of a relative, and two thousand pounds came into his possession. With added means, however, came increased misfortune. In the words of one who knew him well, "While he studied to live he felt no evil but poverty; but no sooner did he live to study than his life was assailed by more dreadful calamities, disease and insanity." Under a depression of mind he laboured some years, with faculties enchained but not destroyed. With a hope of dispelling the clouds which had gathered round him he visited the continent, without experiencing relief. Withdrawing himself from study, he travelled from place to place, his companion being an English Testament: "I have but one book," said he, "but that is the best."

Collins finally retired to his native city, and there, in June, 1759, resigned a life which had been marked with more than its quota of misfortune.* He wrote little, but his productions are highly finished, imagination being linked with much sweetness in figurative language. Tenderness is likewise one of his characteristics; and in some of his poems will be found a beautiful imagery, tinged with sadness and melancholy. His reputation is chiefly built upon his "Odes" (published in 1746), which, though at first neglected—and their cold reception led their author to indifference and evil habits—were subsequently acknowledged to be equal to any contained in the English language. Robert Burns, when invited to the coronation of the bust of Thomson, thus wrote to Lord Buchan:—" Your lordship hints at an ode for the

* "His name has long since been added to the list of unfortunate men of genius. It is remarkable that Chatterton, with whom Collins has been so long associated on that melancholy roll, and who has been said to have imitated Collins in one of his African Eclogues, more than once mentions the poetry of Collins in terms of contempt."—*From a Memoir of Collins, by W. Moy Thomas, prefixed to the Aldine Edition of the Poems.*

occasion; but who would write after Collins? I read over his verses to the memory of Thomson, and despaired."

The monument to Collins was erected by public subscription, to which Magdalen College subscribed liberally. The sculptor, Flaxman, has represented the poet recovering from a wild fit of frenzy; his lute is thrown aside, and in a calm and reclining posture he is seeking consolation from the Gospel. Figures of Love and Pity are entwined above. The inscription, which was written by the poet Hayley and Mr. John Sargent, is as follows:—

> "Ye who the merits of the dead revere,
> Who hold misfortune sacred, genius dear,
> Regard this tomb, where Collins, hapless name,
> Solicits kindness with a double claim.
> Though nature gave him, and though science taught,
> The fire of fancy and the reach of thought,
> Severely doomed to penury's extreme,
> He pass'd in madd'ning pain life's feverish dream,
> While rays of genius only served to show
> The thick'ning horror, and exalt his woe.
> Ye walls, that echoed to his frantic moan,
> Guard the due records of this grateful stone;
> Strangers to him, enamoured of his lays,
> This fond memorial to his talents raise.
> For this the ashes of a bard require,
> Who touch'd the tend'rest notes of Pity's lyre;
> Who joined pure faith to strong poetic powers;
> Who, in reviving reason's lucid hours,
> Sought on one book his troubled mind to rest,
> And rightly deem'd the book of God the best."

HUCKNALL, NOTTINGHAMSHIRE,

possesses the remains of Byron, and is likewise near to the Abbey of Newstead, the ancestral home of the poet.

This seat of the Byrons was originally a priory, founded by Henry II. It is situated in the district known as Sherwood Forest, in which were celebrated the vagaries of Robin Hood and Little John :—

> "A soul of other stamp hath woke
> His song beneath the outlaw's oak;
> One nobly born and proudly bred
> Hath there the mirth and revel led,
> Whose lofty soul and haughty heart
> Were struck as with a poison'd dart;
> One, like bold Robin, proud and kind,
> Of daring thought and generous mind.
> For wild of life, untamed of mood,
> Was Byron, so was Robin Hood:
> All else unlike as saw to sword,
> Lived Newstead's first and latest lord;
> As frost to fire, as tears to mirth,
> As light to darkness, heaven to earth."

Newstead's latest lord,

GEORGE GORDON BYRON,

was born in Holles-street, London, on the 22nd of January, 1788. His father was Captain John Byron, of the Guards, whose profligacy consumed the fortune brought him by the poet's mother, formerly Miss Gordon, of Aberdeenshire. With an income reduced to little more than one hundred pounds per annum, that lady retired to Scotland with her son, devoting her best efforts to his advancement. The "little lame boy" soon became familiar with the wild and mountainous scenery of his new home, which may have contributed to strengthen the energies of his mind :—

"Ah! there my young footsteps in infancy wander'd;
My cap was the bonnet, my cloak was the plaid;
On chieftains long perish'd my memory ponder'd,
As daily I strode through the pine-cover'd glade.
I sought not my home till the day's dying glory
Gave place to the rays of the bright polar star;
For fancy was cheer'd by traditional story,
Disclosed by the natives of dark Loch na Garr."

In his eleventh year the young explorer of the Highlands succeeded to his title, as the grandson of Admiral Byron, the eldest brother of the preceding lord. From a private school at Dulwich, at which he was placed on his return to England, he was removed to Harrow, where he had for a form-fellow the late Sir Robert Peel.

To Newstead Abbey its youthful owner would occasionally repair, his favourite companion being a Newfoundland dog. In his excursions on the lake, he would fall from his boat as if by accident, to try the sagacity and friendship of his comrade, by whom he was soon seized and dragged to the shore. "Boatswain" died at the Abbey in 1808, when his affection was acknowledged in the verse of his noble owner. Scott, in like manner, was attached to his dogs. They were his companions in his study, as well as when abroad; and when the storm burst over his head they were the first in his remembrance. "Sad hearts, too, at Darnick," wrote he on one unhappy morning, "and in the cottages of Abbotsford. I have half resolved never to see the place again. * * * My dogs will wait for me in vain. It is foolish, but the thoughts of parting from these dumb creatures have moved me more than any of the painful reflections I have put down. Poor things! I must get them kind masters. I feel my dogs' feet on my knees—I hear them whining and seeking me everywhere." On a later day, when Scott went back to Abbotsford to die, those dogs welcomed him at the threshold, and he sobbed over them like a child.

In 1805 Byron entered Trinity College, Cambridge, and two years later published his first volume of poems, "Hours of Idleness," printed at Newark. The severity with which these youthful productions were assailed by the *Edinburgh Review* elicited from their author the bitter satire, "English Bards and Scotch Reviewers." Whilst the Edinburgh critics were recovering their breath the noble poet visited the classic shores of the Mediterranean. In May, 1810, when on his way to Constantinople, the practicability of swimming across the Hellespont was discussed by the officers of the frigate in which he was sailing. Byron, whose earliest amusement had been swimming and boating, made the trial, and accomplished the feat. This circumstance is noted by Rogers in his poem of "Italy." A few years subsequently the poets met at Bologna, but over the more youthful bard had come a change:

"Much had pass'd
Since last we parted; and those five short years—
Much had they told. His clustering locks were turn'd
Grey; nor did aught recall the youth that swam
From Sestos to Abydos."

After an absence of nearly three years Byron returned to England, and from his tour resulted "Childe Harold," in which is resplendent the greatness of his genius. This poem was followed by the "Bride of Abydos" and other eastern tales. Whilst the admiration of the world was being showered upon him, Byron was celebrating his success in heartless pleasures. From his dream he at length awoke and married, but without carrying into the domestic circle much affection or fixed resolve. A year of embarrassment followed, the separation came, and Byron uttered his farewell to his wife and child, and to his country. Switzerland and Italy in turn became his home, from whence proceeded the completion of " Childe Harold." " Don Juan," with other poems and tragedies, followed. His earlier irregularities became a passion which knew no restraint, and genius and strength were alike impaired. In 1823 he set sail for Greece, and devoted himself to the redemption of that classic land. By his influence much good was effected; but his career of usefulness was suddenly checked by his death, which occurred at Missolonghi on the afternoon of the 19th of April, 1824, being only thirty-six years and three months old.

"As a poet of description and passion Byron will always occupy a high place. His style is finished, nervous, and lofty; and he excels in painting the strong and gloomy passions of our nature, contrasted with feminine softness and delicacy. He delights in self-portraiture, and can stir the depths of the human heart. His philosophy of life is false and pernicious; but the splendour of the artist conceals the deformity of his design. Parts are so nobly finished that there is enough for admiration to rest upon without analysing the whole. He conducts his readers through scenes of surpassing beauty and splendour—by haunted streams, and mountains enriched with the glories of ancient poetry and valour; but the same dark shadow is ever by his side—the same scorn and mockery of human hopes and ambition. The sententious force and elevation of his thoughts and language, his eloquent expression of sentiment, and the mournful and solemn melody of his tender and pathetic passages, seem, however, to do more than atone for his want of moral truth and reality. The man and the poet were so intimately blended, and the spectacle presented by both was so touching, mysterious, and lofty, that Byron concentrated a degree of interest and anxiety on his successive public appearances which no author ever before was able to boast.

"The rank, youth, and misfortunes of Byron, his exile from England, the mystery which he loved to throw around his history and feelings, the apparent depth of his sufferings and attachments, and his very misanthropy and scepticism (relieved by bursts of tenderness and pity, and by the incidental expression of high and holy feelings), formed a combination of personal circumstances in aid of the legitimate efforts of his passionate and graceful poetry, which is unparalleled in the history of modern literature." *

The false philosophy of his writings is, however, a dark spot upon his fame. Imagining that wrongs pursued him, he sought out the wildest tracts, and " 'mid the din, the stir, lived as a separate spirit." Notwithstanding his strong and gloomy passions, his scorn and mockery of much that was good, his premature demise was deeply mourned in England as well as in Greece. His remains were brought to England, and after lying in state for two days at No. 25, Great George-street, Westminster, were conveyed to the village church of Hucknall, where, too, is resting, by her father's side, the Ada of his most beautiful song, whose name was the last to escape his lips.

> "O, noble Byron! thou hadst light,
> Pure as yon sun, as warm, as bright;
> But thou hadst darkness deeper far
> Than winter night that knows no star.
> I glory in thee, yet I weep
> For thy stern moods and early sleep.
> Oh! hadst thou writ of brother men,
> With milder mood and soberer pen,

---

* Abridged from "Chambers's Cyclopædia of Literature."

> Nor pour'd thy searching spirit proud
> O'er them like lightning from a cloud,
> I could, beneath thy favourite tree,
> Have bless'd—done all but worshipp'd thee!"

In the vault in Hucknall Church, upon the noble poet's coffin, is placed an urn inscribed as follows:—

"Within this urn are deposited the heart, brain, &c.,
OF THE DECEASED
Lord Byron."

At Newstead, to this day, are shown several memorials of Byron: the chamber, and the coroneted bedstead in which the poet slept; the silver-mounted skull to which he addressed his impassioned lines; and in the Abbey garden, the stone to his favourite dog, Boatswain, with its commemorative inscription.

We are now about to take the reader to

BROMHAM, WILTS,

which is marked by the ancient steeple of its sanctuary, and has at least three incidents in its history deserving of note. Nearly a century since (1767) a discovery was made in its parish of a Roman bath; the parish was the birthplace of Webbers, Bishop of Limerick; thirdly—and more suited to our present thoughts—its churchyard has in sacred keeping the remains of the most musical of poets,—

THOMAS MOORE.

This lyrist was born in Aungier-street, Dublin, on the 28th of May, 1780, his father having been a small but respectable tradesman. Moore evinced considerable mental power at an early age; and at the school of a Mr. Whyte (at one time the teacher of Richard Brinsley Sheridan), in his native city, his youthful abilities were exhibited in some private theatricals. Trinity College subsequently received him, and here he became a proficient in Greek and Latin. When only fourteen years old a sonnet from his pen was inserted in a Dublin magazine; five years later his translation of the " Odes of Anacreon " was completed, when he visited the metropolis, intending to enter himself of the Middle Temple. This was in the year 1799, and consequently prior to his twentieth birthday. Thomas Moore soon found himself petted by the aristocracy, and launched into the great world of London. His "Anacreon" was given to the public, and the Prince Regent, with flattering compliments, accepted the dedication. In his weekly communication to his own " Dublin home," the young poet duly informed his mother of the royal favour: " but," continued he, " it has cost me a new coat, for the introduction was unfortunately deferred till my former one was grown confoundedly shabby." The " Odes " were followed, in 1801, by " Thomas Little's Poems and Songs." These objectionable productions—for which the youth of the writer, and the sensual atmosphere by which he was surrounded, can alone plead in excuse—have since been banished by the healthier tone of society. In maturer years the poet looked back upon them with regret, and in the following lines would seem to tender for them an apology:—

> "Oh ! blame not the bard, if he fly to the bowers
> Where Pleasure lies carelessly smiling at Fame;
> He was born for much more, and in happier hours
> His soul might have burn'd with a holier flame."

Some political trifles next occupied Moore's attention, and then followed poems which secured for his name more lasting celebrity. In 1803 he obtained the appointment of Registrar to the Court of Admiralty at Bermuda ; but through the carelessness or dishonesty of a deputy, he became involved in serious liabilities, and in the following year returned to England. He next paid a fitting tribute to his country's minstrelsy by his "Irish Melodies"— lyrics which possess a graceful tenderness of thought, and are known throughout the world. In May, 1817, was published his "Lalla Rookh," which with its flowing imagery of Oriental splendour, brought the poet something more substantial than the adulation which Fashion previously offered—the sum of three thousand guineas. The details of eastern magnificence given in this poem were conceived and elaborated at Mayfield Cottage, in Derbyshire, amidst the snows of winter. Reference to this inclement season reminds us that it was during a hard frost, which had incrusted every window with the most delicate tracery, that an idler scratched with a bodkin, upon the vanishing medium, Moore's lines :—

> "All that's bright must fade,
> The brightest still the fleetest;
> All that's sweet was made
> But to be lost when sweetest."

An old lady of seventy-nine, on observing the same, said quietly, "Ah! that is rhyme upon rime."

Sunshine followed the appearance of "Lalla Rookh," and increased honours were heaped upon the favoured author. His "Diary" makes us acquainted with two instances of substantial regard :—

"23rd. Received from one of my female correspondents (the lady who loved the Irish giant) a Christmas present, consisting of a goose, a pot of pickles, another of clouted cream, and some apples. This, indeed, is a tribute of admiration more solid than I generally receive from these fair admirers of my poetry. The young Bristol lady, who inclosed me three pounds after reading 'Lalla Rookh,' had also very laudable ideas on the subject; and if every reader of 'Lalla Rookh' had done the same I need never have written again."

Moore's Oriental romance was eagerly sought after. Benson Hill relates, in his "Home Service," that writing down the title, he sent a servant girl for the work to the circulating library at which he subscribed. After a long absence she returned, saying, "Pleaze, zur, Mrs. Routh wunt ha' none till the next ship du come in; and at Merryweather's, awver the Change, it be three shillings a pound." "What d'ye mean, girl?" inquired her master; "I sent you to Rees's." "Iss, zure, zur, and thur I went; but a tould I that were my mistake, and zent I right." "Why, surely, he couldn't understand ——" "Oh! a did though, well anough, zur; thof I'd a lost the peaper, I zed the neame playn out to'n." "What name, child?" "Why, arrowroot, zur." "Fancy 'Lalla Rookh,'" says Hill, "warm with sugar, to be taken at bedtime!"

Moore next, in a continental trip, joined the poet Rogers, and subsequently Lord John Russell. He then took up his residence in Paris—a step rendered necessary by the pecuniary liabilities arising with the official defalcations at Bermuda. In the French capital Moore composed his "Loves of the Angels." Returning to England, he eventually took up his permanent abode in a picturesque cottage at Sloperton, about two miles from Devizes, and here his remaining days were passed. Most of his later productions were in prose, of which "The Epicurean" and his "History of Ireland" are the most careful works. Towards the close of his career he addressed to his neighbour, the noble owner of Bowood, the following invitation, exhibiting much of the playful vivacity which distinguished his more youthful effusions:—

"Some think we bards have nothing real—
    That poets live among the stars, so
Their very dinners are ideal;
    And heaven knows too oft they are so.
For instance, that we have, instead
    Of vulgar chops, and stews, and hashes,
First course—a phœnix at the head,
    Done in its own celestial ashes;
At foot, a cygnet, which kept singing
All the time its neck was wringing.
Side dishes thus—Minerva's owl,
    Or any such-like learned fowl;
Doves such as heaven's poulterer gets
When Cupid shoots his mother's pets;
Larks stew'd in morning's roseate breath,
    Or roasted by a sunbeam's splendour;
And nightingales berhymed to death,
    Like young pigs whipp'd to make them tender.
Such fare may suit those bards who're able
To banquet at Duke Humphrey's table;
But as for me, who've long been taught
    To eat and drink like other people,
And can put up with mutton, bought
    Where Bromham rears its ancient steeple,
If Lansdowne will consent to share
My humble feast, though rude the fare,

Yet, season'd by that salt he brings
From Attica's salinest springs,
'Twill turn to dainties; while the cup,
Beneath his influence brightening up,
Like that of Baucis touch'd by Jove,
Will sparkle fit for gods above."

In his rural retirement at Sloperton, Thomas Moore looked back upon his morning life, passed in the drawing-rooms of the great. The evening found the pageant gone, but the poet had raised his own monument, and the man had secured a character for the due performance of his duties. The children he had reared had passed one by one into the grave, and the aged head was finally bowed down in sorrow. Moore died in February, 1852, leaving behind him a brilliant celebrity. Though deficient in the force and dignity associated with a high poetic order, his lyrics exhibit a uniform elegance, pathetic tenderness, a play of wit, brilliancy of fancy, and a richness of ornament, which are always pleasing.

We must not leave Wiltshire without a visit to

TROWBRIDGE,

which is situate on a rocky eminence near to the river Ware. The church is a spacious structure, with chapels attached; and here we find a monument erected by the parishioners to the memory of their worthy rector,—

GEORGE CRABBE,

who is likewise distinguished as the "Poet of the Poor," his writings having revealed to Wealth much of the misery which it has since sought to ameliorate. He was born at Aldborough, in Suffolk, in December, 1754, and received a good education, although his father was in humble circumstances, and was, moreover, a stern and violent man. At the age of fourteen, young Crabbe was placed with a surgeon in his native village, where subsequently he himself followed the healing art. Thus far he had patiently proceeded : his youth had been passed with those who were rude and uncultivated, but neither their companionship nor parental harshness had disturbed or weakened his cheerful temper. Finding, however, that his medical practice offered no prospect of success, Crabbe quitted the fishing village for London, which he entered with a courageous heart and a stock of poems. Fortune, at first, would not recognise the aspirant who so bravely sought her aid. He failed to win the patronage of the publishers, solicited in vain the assistance of the wealthy, and soon became but too familiar with poverty. Grown desperate, he at length left a note, describing his position, at the house of Edmund Burke, and restlessly paced the bridge of Westminster the entire night. The orator possessed a warm heart, and received Crabbe into his hospitable house. He subsequently entered into holy orders, and returned to Aldborough in the capacity of its rector. At his patron's recommendation, he was appointed chaplain to the Duke of Rutland, who, in 1814, presented him with the living of Trowbridge, which he enjoyed for the succeeding eighteen years of his life.

It was in 1781 that Crabbe's poem of "The Library" was published, shortly after his fortunate introduction to Burke. This was succeeded, two years later, by "The Village," which had been revised by Burke and Johnson, and which at once established the claim of its author to the title of a poet. For twenty years the muse of Crabbe was silent. At length, in 1807, he resumed his acquaintance with the reading public, by whom he was heartily welcomed. In that year the "Parish Register" appeared, and was succeeded by "The Borough" and "Tales in Verse;" and in 1819 came forth the last of his principal works, "Tales of the Hall."

Crabbe is well described by Byron as "Nature's sternest painter, and her best;" and his fidelity to his mistress is his distinguishing feature. He has also been termed the Hogarth of verse. In depicting rustic life, he used nothing of art to heighten the effect of the picture, but sought rather to strip it of its brighter colours. He possessed a benevolent mind, with great simplicity of manners. Upon receiving from Mr. Murray, the eminent publisher, the bills for three thousand pounds for the copyright of his poems, he was recommended to deposit them without delay in some safe hands; but he replied that he must take them with him to Trowbridge, and show them to his son, who would not, he said, believe in his good fortune unless he saw the bills. When surrounded by competence Crabbe's thoughts would occasionally revert to the scenes of his youth; and one fine summer day he felt such an irrepressible desire to behold the sea that he suddenly mounted his horse, and rode more than fifty miles to the nearest coast.

With the character of a poet George Crabbe, like "holy George Herbert," blended that of a pious country clergyman. He died on the 3rd of February, 1832, at the age of seventy-eight, having retained to the last his cheerful disposition and his attachment to rural objects.

He was buried at Trowbridge, where the inhabitants have erected, by subscription, a monument, by E. H. Baily, R.A., which is placed in the church. It consists of a group of figures, one representing the poet regarding the sacred volume, and two other figures of angels waiting to bear the departed spirit to its heavenly home. A simple inscription describes Crabbe's abode as rector of the parish for nineteen years, " discharging his duties as a minister and a magistrate, to acquire the respect and esteem of all his neighbours."

In the church of Crabbe's native village, Aldborough, also has been placed a bust of the poet, upon a stone plinth, sculptured with an unstrung antique lyre. Beneath is the following inscription from the pen of the Rev. J. Mitford :—

"To the Memory of
George Crabbe,
The Poet of Nature and Truth, this Monument is erected,
By those who are desirous to record their admiration of his Genius,
In the place of his birth.
Born December 24th, 1774. Died January 29th, 1832."

The bust is admirably executed, the heavy eyebrows being strongly characteristic of the physiognomy of the poet. The cost of the memorial was defrayed by public subscription. The sculptor was Mr. Thurlow, jun., of Saxmundham, a name which reminds one of Lord Thurlow's coarseness when he presented Crabbe with two small livings in Dorsetshire, the chancellor telling him, as he gave them, with a profane prefix, that he was "as like Parson Adams as twelve to the dozen."

We now propose to extend our journey westward, to the grave of a celebrated player, in

BATH ABBEY CHURCH.

The city ornamented by this structure had its monastic institution in an early age of Christianity, the benefactors to the religious house here founded including Osric the Saxon king, Offa King of Mercia, Athelstan, and Edgar. The monastery was destroyed in the reign of Rufus, but was rebuilt by a monk of Tours, John de Villula, who, in 1106, was styled Bishop of Bath. Varied were the fortunes and vicissitudes of the monastery and church in succeeding centuries. It was during the reign of Henry VII. that the erection of the present edifice was begun, but a much later period marked its completion—so long after as the days of James II. The victor of Bosworth Field preferred to the bishopric his secretary, Oliver King, who shortly after his installation commenced the building, but he left at his death his good work unfinished. The Reformation which followed was not favourable to architectural labours; and the rising edifice, watched over with so much parental care by Bishop King, became dilapidated, though in the reign of Elizabeth a few efforts were made to forward its completion.

In our recent visit to the tomb of Gower, in the church of St. Mary Overy, we recorded the gratifying fact that the poet had assisted in the restoration of the building in which he found his last home. Connected with the history of Bath Abbey Church is another instance of the good offices of a poet having been similarly exercised, or at all events been instrumental in its accomplishment. Sir

John Harington, the godson of Elizabeth, and the first translator of Ariosto into the English language, found this church in ruins, and evinced great anxiety for its restoration. Bishop Montague, on his primary visit to Bath, was suddenly caught in a shower of rain, and was induced, on the invitation of Harington, to seek shelter in the church. Sir John took the ecclesiastic into the north aisle, which was roofless, a circumstance which drew from the bishop the remark that the situation did not shelter him from the rain. "Doth it not, my lord?" said Harington. "Then let me sue your bounty towards covering our poor church, for if it keep not us safe from the waters above, how shall it ever save others from the fire beneath?" The appeal was not made in vain, for Bishop Montague nearly completed the Abbey church, which was raised to its present state in 1606, although it has the aspect of a greater antiquity.

Here is the noble old church, with its imposing tower. As originally designed, the edifice formed a very pleasing example of the latest period of pointed architecture; but the alterations of the present century have diminished much of its beauty. On entering we are attracted by its lofty roof and clustered pillars, and its beautiful western window. We pass by many monuments which seek to detain us, particularly that which perpetuates the memory of the liberal prelate we have just referred to, Richard Montague—a memorial raised by his four brothers—and at the south-west end of the nave discover the one we sought —one raised to a follower of Thespis, and who in his day extended the helping hand to one of England's most favourite poets. This is the tomb—which bears the name of

JAMES QUIN.

When pursuing the object of our present labours in the metropolis we paid befitting respect to the grave of Richard Burbage, the hero of the stage in the days of Shakspeare, and likewise stood by the last home of Betterton and Garrick. The second actor named was succeeded in popularity by Barton Booth, whose monument is to be found in Westminster Abbey. Booth died in 1733, and from that time to the period when Garrick seized upon celebrity (1741), Quin was the only performer of any reputation. Born in King-street, Covent Garden, in 1693, he first appeared upon the stage at Dublin, from which city he was transferred to the boards of Drury Lane, where at first he was intrusted with only trifling characters. Quitting that theatre, he joined the forces of Rich at the Lincoln's Inn Fields Theatre, where he soon obtained much popularity; his Falstaff, in particular, being considered a masterpiece of acting. The new Roscius, however, appeared in the east of London, and for some time he maintained a rivalry with the lately-risen star, and during one season entered the arena with him on the same boards, Richard and other characters being represented alternately by them, whilst they occasionally appeared together in the same play; for instance, as Hotspur and Falstaff in *Henry the Fourth*, and Orestes and Pyrrhus in the *Distrest Mother*. Quin, however, soon discovered that in the contest his own reputation declined as that of Garrick's increased.

Quin was appointed teacher of elocution to the junior branches of the royal family, and officiated as stage-manager in 1749, when Addison's *Cato* was represented by them at Leicester House. The prince—subsequently

George III.—enacted the part of Portius; and when, in after-years, the old actor was informed of the excellent manner in which his pupil, the king, delivered his first speech in Parliament, he exclaimed with honest exultation: "Ay, *I* taught the boy to speak."

Compelled by age and infirmity finally to quit the stage, Quin passed the greater portion of his retirement at Bath, where he died in 1766. He was somewhat haughty and imperious in his manner, and occasionally was coarse and quarrelsome; but he possessed "a hand open as the day to melting charity," and foremost among his good deeds stands the record of his aid to the poet Thomson. By the loss of the Secretaryship of Briefs, on the death of the Lord Chancellor Talbot, the author of the "Seasons" became involved, and was confined for a debt of about seventy pounds. Quin was made acquainted with the circumstances, sought out the poet, and introduced himself. Thomson was much disconcerted at the visit, and his uneasiness was not relieved when the visitor informed him he had come to sup with him. Quin, however, added that, as he had supposed it would have been inconvenient to have a supper dressed in that place, he had taken the liberty of ordering one from an adjoining tavern. Sundry bottles of claret having been introduced as a preliminary, and the supper being over, Quin said, "It is time now, Jemmy Thomson, we should balance accounts." The poet here anticipated that some extra demand was to be made upon him, but his fears were set at rest by the speedy rejoinder of his friend. "Sir," said he, "the pleasure I have had in perusing your works I cannot estimate at less than a hundred pounds, and I insist upon this opportunity of acquitting myself of the debt." So saying, he placed a bank-note upon the table and hastily quitted the place.

We have already given an epitaph supplied by Garrick —that of Hogarth, to be found in the churchyard of Chiswick. Here is another specimen of his skill in that description of composition, which we copy from the tomb of him who at one time was deemed his rival:—

> "That tongue which set the table in a roar,
> And charm'd the public ear, is heard no more.
> Closed are those eyes, the harbingers of wit,
> Which spoke before the tongue what Shakspeare writ.
> Cold are those hands which living were stretch'd forth,
> At friendship's call, to succour modest worth.
> Here lies JAMES QUIN! Deign, reader, to be taught,
> Whate'er thy strength of body, force of thought,
> In Nature's happiest mould however cast,
> To this complexion must thou come at last."

True! And thereby assured that the great Falstaff no longer feigns—as in the mimic world—the sleep of death, we quit his grave with the respect due to his generous nature.

Genius is irrespective of country. We therefore, prior to closing our visits, seek the graves of those whom the sister kingdom delights to honour—Allan Ramsay, Burns, Hogg, and Scott. The tomb of the first-named we find in the churchyard of the

GREYFRIARS, EDINBURGH.

This ancient burial-place was originally the garden belonging to the monastery of Greyfriars, which was situated in the Grass Market at Edinburgh. Here are interred numbers of the martyrs of the Covenant. Here, also, rests

GEORGE BUCHANAN,

the accomplished Latin poet and preceptor of James VI. Buchanan was born in Dumbartonshire in 1506, studied at Paris and St. Andrew's, and afterwards acted as tutor to the Earl of Murray; but, through offence given by him to the clergy by a satirical poem, he was obliged to take refuge on the Continent, and did not return to Scotland till 1560. Though he had embraced the Protestant doctrines, he was favourably received at court by Queen Mary, assisted her in her studies, and was employed to regulate the universities, and became principal of St. Leonard's College in the University of St. Andrew's. He joined, however, the Earl of Murray's party against the queen, and was appointed tutor to James VI., whom he is said to have occasionally whipped. He subsequently offended James by publishing his treatise, *De Jure Reyni*, in 1579. Murray spent in retirement the last few years of his life, writing his well-known " History of Scotland," published in 1582. He died in the same year, so poor that his funeral took place at the public expense. As an historian his style is held to unite the excellences of Livy and Sallust. Buchanan has been styled the Scottish Virgil. His great work is his " Paraphrase of the Psalms;" and it has been usual in Scotland to maintain Buchanan for his elegant Latin verse against all the world. Yet this boasted prince of Scottish literature died in his native country penniless!

In the same ground, not far from the ivy-covered tablet of the Christian martyrs, lies

ALLAN RAMSAY,

who has been styled the Scottish Theocritus. He was born of humble parents, on the high mountains that divide Clydesdale and Annandale: he received but a limited education, and was placed, when about fourteen years of age, with a peruke-maker resident in Edinburgh. Destined, however, to assist in the revival of the rural poetry of his country, he succeeded in obtaining notice, first by his social disposition, and next from the ability displayed by him in the composition of verses in the idiom of his country. Exchanging the shop of the hair-dresser for that of a bookseller, he himself published, in 1721, a volume of poems from his own pen, and subsequently issued collections of Scottish poems and songs, which became familiar to the peasantry of his country. In

CANONGATE, EDINBURGH,

in the churchyard, lies the poet of Scottish city life, or rather the laureate of Edinburgh,—

ROBERT FERGUSSON,

who stood prominent among the many who began to "try a song" after the example set by Allan Ramsay. In his education he was more fortunate than his predecessor, having had the advantage of instruction at the Universities of Edinburgh and St. Andrew's. Fergusson died in 1774, before he had reached his twenty-fourth year. He was the more immediate precursor of Burns, by whom his poetry would seem to have been preferred to that of Allan Ramsay. Meeting with Fergusson's poems, the bard of Ayr " strung his lyre anew with emulating vigour," and subsequently placed a stone over the young poet's grave, with the following inscription :—

"Here lies
Robert Fergusson, Poet.
Born September 5, 1751.
Died October 16, 1774.
No sculptured marble here, nor pompous lay,
'No storied urn, nor animated bust;'
This simple stone directs pale Scotia's way
To pour her sorrows o'er her poet's dust."

Quitting the depository of the sacred dust of the faithful Covenanters, and the grave of Fergusson, our thoughts incline to the greatest of Scotland's minstrels, whose monumental vault we find at

DUMFRIES.

The churchyard of St. Michael's, in this parish, received, on the 26th of July, 1796, the remains of a great but ill-fated genius,—

ROBERT BURNS,

the possessor of one of the largest hearts that ever beat in Scotland. In his grave lie with him innumerable errors; yet has the spot been sought by thousands, attesting the worth of mind, and its power over adverse circumstances :—

"Bid thy thoughts hover o'er that spot,
Boy-minstrel, in thy dreaming hour,
And know, however low his lot,
A poet's pride and power.

"Such graves as his are pilgrim-shrines—
Shrines to no code or creed confined—
The Delphian vales, the Palestines,
The Meccas of the mind."

Mausoleum of Burns, Dumfries.

This peasant-bard was born on the 25th of January, 1759, in a small house within a mile or two of Ayr, at that time tenanted by his father, a farmer of limited means. The poet has himself made us acquainted with some portion of his boyhood. " I was a good deal noted," wrote he in August, 1787, " for a retentive memory, a stubborn, sturdy something in my disposition, and an enthusiastic idiot [idiotic] piety. I say idiot piety, because I was then but a child. Though it cost the schoolmaster some thrashings, I made an excellent English scholar; and by the time I was ten or eleven years of age I was a critic in substantives, verbs, and particles." His intellectual gifts shone forth in him when a boy. With warmth of heart he blended much conversational power; and the father—who possessed a mind superior to what might have been expected from him in his station—was proud of the genius of his son, and gave him what extra cultivation his limited means would permit.

The family of Burns included an ancient lady, remarkable for her credulity and superstition. She was the possessor of a large collection of tales and songs, and this, according to the poet, cultivated within him the latent seeds of poetry. Robert became a dexterous ploughman for his age, and plodded on with a name obscure and a condition humble. The powers of his body were given to the labours of the farm ; but his thoughts, we are told, were elsewhere. The plough, under his guidance, passed through the sward, and the grass was scattered far beneath his scythe; but, rapt in the allusions of fancy, he was humming the songs of his country. In his fifteenth autumn he encountered in the harvest-field " a bonnie, sweet, sonsie lass," a passion for whom first taught him to love and to rhyme.

Upon the failure and subsequent death of his father, Robert Burns entered, with his brother, upon the management of a farm, and likewise became known in his neighbourhood as a maker of rhymes. Resigning at length his share in this farm, which was only nominally his own, he thought of proceeding to Jamaica, but was desirous of leaving behind him some memorial of his offerings to the muses. Three hundred and fifty subscribers were obtained to a small volume of poems, and six hundred copies were printed, which produced the young bard, after the liquidation of all necessary expenses, nearly twenty pounds. This edition was published in 1786, at Kilmarnock. Thither would the peasant-poet daily walk from his home, a distance of ten or twelve miles, to correct his proof-sheets. A piece of oat-cake and a bottle of twopenny ale was his customary dinner, and even this humble fare was at times denied him by his poverty!

The publication of these poems gained Burns many friends; his proposed visit to Jamaica was abandoned, and he was advised to visit Edinburgh, with a view to a second edition of his works. In the Scottish capital he became an acceptable guest in the gayest and most elevated circles. It was during this visit that he was first seen by Scott, who, forty years subsequently, thus recorded his impression of the circumstance:—" I was a lad of fifteen in 1786, when he first came to Edinburgh, but had sense and feeling enough to be much interested in his poetry, and would have given the world to have known him. * * * There was a strong expression of sense and shrewdness in all his lineaments; the eye alone, I think, indicated the poetical character and temperament. It was large, and of a cast which glowed (I say literally glowed) when he spoke with feeling and interest. I never saw such another eye in a human head, though I have seen the most distinguished men of my time."

Robert Burns was now fairly introduced to the world. In April, 1787, appeared the second edition of his poems, embellished with a portrait of himself. Nearly three thousand copies were subscribed for prior to the delivery of the work, and the elated author was not only enabled to throw aside his oat-cake and his twopenny ale, but to partake of the choicest pleasures of Edinburgh, and likewise to mount his horse in search of some of the attractive features of his country. In the course of a second tour he visited the churchyard of Dunfermline, where two broad flagstones marked the grave of Robert Bruce, over which he knelt and kissed the stones in sacred fervour. To Edinburgh he continued to pay occasional visits, entering into its varied society, and sharing, unfortunately, in its dissipation. He sought out, however, in these exciting moments, the unmarked grave of the poet Fergusson, to whose memory, as already stated, he erected a humble monument. Finally, on settling accounts with his publisher, he found himself possessed of nearly £500. A considerable portion of this amount he handed to his brother, who had taken charge of the support of his aged mother. He fulfilled the promise of marriage previously made to the object of his affection; and at Whitsuntide, 1788, entered upon a small farm situate on the banks of the river Nith, about six miles from Dumfries.

The public voice at this time had pronounced its verdict strongly in favour of Robert Burns, and the prejudice arising from his humble birth had been surmounted. Received with welcome wherever he appeared, he was too often allured from his rustic labours. His resolutions, naturally unsteady, were thereby easily thrown aside, and his farm eventually was looked upon with disgust. He entered the Excise, which for years he had conceived would yield him certain support when other means had failed. He still occasionally directed the plough and scattered the grain, but the farm was ultimately abandoned. His office in the Excise at first produced him £50 per annum, subsequently increased to about £70. Gradually the irregularities which occasionally marked his career became habitual. There were still affection and gentleness in his conduct at home, but virtue and passion were striving for a mastery, which the latter unhappily secured. Impaired health followed, and Scotland's poet, surrounded by poverty, and in the thirty-eighth year of his age, yielded to the creditor whose claims no man can resist. His remains were interred with military honours, the "Dead March" following them through the streets of Dumfries, accompanied by the sympathy and sorrow of many thousands.

Robert Burns had a manly form, with a dark and haughty countenance; but he possessed a most liberal spirit, and was exceedingly kind and sincere. In his conversation he had a brilliancy of expression which attracted every one. His virtues and his failings were ever at variance, and his defect of character was fatal to his advancement. Scotland received from him an important addition to her songs, and his poetry will ever be admired as the offspring of original genius, for it was the natural language of the soul, which he turned to poetry as his medium of expression. As one who knew him well remarked, "He was a sort of comet in literature, irregular in its motions, which did not do good proportioned to the blaze of light it displayed."

> "Farewell, high chief of Scottish song!
> That couldst alternately impart
> Wisdom and rapture in thy page,
> And brand each vice with satire strong,
> Whose lines are mottoes of the heart,
> Whose truths electrify the sage.
>
> "Farewell! and ne'er may envy dare
> To wring one baleful poison-drop
> From the crush'd laurels of thy bust;
> But, while the lark sings sweet in air,
> Still may the grateful pilgrim stop
> To bless the spot that holds thy dust."

St. Michael's churchyard, Dumfries, contains an immense number of monuments, from the ponderous mausoleum, in which wealth, rank, and genius lie entombed, down to the simple headstone which rears its unadorned form over the remains of unobtrusive citizenship.* In one of the former structures is deposited the mortal part of Burns, originally buried in a corner of the churchyard, where

* Macdiarmid calculated that, exclusively of the ruinous monuments in St. Michael's churchyard, the whole number could not now be furnished for much less than £100,000. Of the first class of monuments there were, when Macdiarmid wrote, 109; of tombstones on pillars, 712; and, besides the modern and perfect table-stones, there were about 1000 more or less dilapidated.

a widow raised a plain stone to his memory. In September, 1815, by a public subscription (to which George IV. contributed fifty guineas), the remains of the poet were raised from their humble resting-place, and transferred to a handsome mausoleum, erected in a more conspicuous part of the churchyard. This structure was designed by Mr. Thomas F. Hunt, of London; and the group of marble placed in the interior, and representing the genius of Scotland investing Burns with her poetic mantle, was sculptured by the well-known Mr. Turnerelli. This mausoleum, like the poet's house in Burns-street, in Dumfries, is visited by thousands of pilgrims; and the "frequent feet" which visit the stately monument have made a beaten path over all the other graves. "Such circumstances," says Robert Chambers, "are mean-sounding, but not insignificant tests of the veneration in which this unfortunate man of genius is held by his country." Our artist has engraved this celebrated mausoleum. A splendid memorial of Burns has also been erected near Ayr, and a monument at Edinburgh, with a statue of the poet, by Flaxman; but neither of these public tributes exceeds in interest the commemorative temple at Dumfries.

We next take the reader to the hilly pastoral parish of

ETTRICK,

which was formerly covered by Ettrick Forest, of which no traces now remain. Flowing by it is the small river of the same name, a tributary of the Tweed in Selkirkshire. The wild mountains at its head once gave shelter to the Covenanters, when driven by persecution from the haunts of men. In the churchyard of this retired district lies one of the most imaginative of the uneducated poets,—

JAMES HOGG,

more generally known as the "Ettrick Shepherd." A cottage on the banks of the Ettrick was his birthplace, and the 25th of January, 1772, was his natal day. Such, at least, was his own statement; but the point as to the period of the year (which was the birthday of Robert Burns) has been disputed. His entire schooling was limited to about six months; for when a mere child he commenced the toil necessary for his own subsistence, first as an attendant on a few cows, being ultimately promoted to the care of a flock of sheep, an employment to which his predecessors had long been devoted.

Robert Hogg, his father, was a man of peculiar character. The old shepherd would never confess or allow, or even in his own mind suppose, that he could be beat or defeated in anything Being out one wintry day with his poetic son on a hill, looking after the safety of the sheep, an incident occurred which drew from him an emanation of this self-esteem. A snow-storm was raging at the time, and the old man, inadvertently going too near the brow, the snow gave way, and he was precipitated to the bottom. The younger shepherd, alarmed for the safety of his father, looked down the side of the hill, and not only saw him standing on his feet seemingly unhurt, but heard him crying out at the top of his voice, "Jamie, ma man, ye were aye fond of a slide a' yere days; let me see ye do that."

At fourteen years of age his industry had placed in Hogg's possession the sum of—five shillings, with which he purchased an old violin, which for many succeeding years was to him a source of amusement. "I had commonly no spare time from labour during the day," he once observed; "but when I was not over-fatigued I generally spent an hour or two every night in sawing over my favourite old Scottish tunes, and my bed being always in stables and cowhouses, I disturbed nobody but myself and my associate quadrupeds, whom I believed to be greatly delighted with my strains. At all events, they never complained, which the biped part of my neighbours did frequently, to my pity and utter indignation." From his infancy the young shepherd possessed a fancy for versification, which was noticed and encouraged by his mother— a self-taught genius of an imaginative mind—who would occasionally say to him, "Jamie, my man, gang ben the house, and mak me a sang." In later days the poet thus alluded to his earlier effusions :—

"For several years my compositions consisted wholly of songs and ballads, made up for the lasses to sing in chorus; and a proud man I was when I first heard the rosy nymphs chanting my uncouth strains, and jeering me by the still dearer appellation of 'Jamie the poeter.'"

The "unspoiled pupil of nature" could indite songs, but he experienced a difficulty in committing them to paper; for ".Jamie," be it remembered, had made but little acquaintance with pen and ink. A helping hand was at length given him by William Laidlaw, the son of one of his employers, who discovered beneath his simple garb the genius there concealed. Cheering him in his poetical attempts, he strove to make his verses known, and ultimately introduced him to Walter Scott, by whom likewise he was patronised. In his most celebrated poem, "The

Queen's Wake," Hogg thus alludes to his amiable and gifted patron :—

> " The land was charm'd to list his lays;
> It knew the harp of ancient days.
> The border chiefs that long had been
> In sepulchres unhearsed and green,
> Pass'd from their mouldy vaults away
> In armour red and stern array,
> And by their moonlight halls were seen
> In visor, helm, and habergeon.
> Even fairies sought our land again,
> So powerful was the magic strain.
>   Bless'd be his generous heart for aye!
> He told me where the relic lay;
> Pointed my way with ready will
> Afar on Ettrick's wildest hill;
> Watch'd my first notes with curious eye,
> And wonder'd at my minstrelsy.
> He little ween'd a parent's tongue
> Such strains had o'er my cradle sung."

In 1801 Hogg attended the Edinburgh market with some sheep for sale; and having to wait until a second market-day, he employed the interim in writing a poem or two from memory, and getting them printed. In the same year a volume of pieces in the old ballad style, entitled " The Mountain Bard," was published for him in the same city without exciting much attention. The shepherd-poet, however, realised by the publication nearly three hundred pounds, which, according to his own statement, drove him " perfectly mad." With this sum he entered into the business of sheep-farming, and lost the entire, being subsequently unable to obtain employment in his own humble calling. In February, 1810, grown desperate by having passed a winter in idleness, he threw his plaid about his shoulders and marched to Edinburgh, determined to push his fortunes as an author. Little encouragement, however, awaited him : in his native hills he could not get employment as a shepherd, and Edinburgh cared but little for his poetry. He started a literary paper called *The Spy*, which was published weekly at fourpence : this step increased his reputation, but did little in filling his purse. In 1813 he published his " Queen's Wake," and the shepherd of Ettrick received from the world its acknowledgment of his genius. Other poetical works followed, and Hogg likewise became one of the first contributors upon the establishment of *Blackwood's Magazine*, which connected him in friendship with its editor, Professor Wilson. In its pages were exhibited Hogg's poetic genius, as well as his broad humour—the latter in the " Noctes," with the blended wit and pathos of Christopher North. Wilson died on the 3rd of April, 1854.

Sir Walter Scott one day visited Hogg while the Waverley authorship was still a mystery. Looking at his friend's library, he discovered that his own prose works formed a conspicuous feature, with the back title, " SCOTT'S NOVELS." " What a stupid fellow of a binder you must have got, Jamie," exclaimed Sir Walter, " to spell Scot's with two *t's!*"

Hogg resided in Edinburgh from 1809 to 1814, when the small farm of Altrive Lake, in the wilds of Yarrow, was presented to him, at a nominal rent, by the late Charles Duke of Buccleuch. The shepherd now seemed on the high road to prosperity. He built a handsome cottage on the farm, and in 1820 tenanted it with a wife. In an evil hour, however, he determined upon farming on a larger scale. His publishing accounts, when settled, produced him about a thousand pounds, and he took a lease for nine years of an adjoining farm. Foresight and calculation were not included in the virtues of Hogg, to whom this speculation proved unfortunate; and at the age of sixty he found himself without a sixpence. He retired to his little farm at Altrive, intending to devote himself to its culture, and to continue his contributions to literature. The latter, though irregular in its aid, secured him many of the comforts of life. In 1831 he visited London, with a view to the issue of a cheap edition of his works. In the metropolis he was entertained at a public dinner, and experienced such marked attention that the visit was considered by him as the great era of his life. He continued to write, chiefly for periodicals, until the close of his career, which occurred on the 21st of November, 1835.

James Hogg has left behind him a fame that will long endure. In taste he was defective, and he possessed but little skill in arranging incidents; but in the wide range of fancy he pictured scenes of surpassing beauty. He had a more playful and discursive fancy than Burns, by whom he was exceeded in the strength of passion and the grasp of intellect. With an utter want of education, he roamed through his native valleys and the wild mountains of the district, and there communed with Nature, from whom he received those gifts of poetical fancy which poverty and early neglect could not wrest from him. With many personal foibles, he was generous and kind-hearted, and his death was deeply mourned in the vale of the Ettrick, the majestic scenery of which first taught him his legendary ballads :

> " I learn'd them in the lonely glen,
> The last abodes of living men,
> Where never stranger came our way
> By summer night or winter day;
> Where neighbouring hind or cot was none—
> Our converse was with heaven alone—
> With voices through the cloud that sung,
> And brooding storms that round us hung."

In the vicinity of these scenes, by the margin of the peaceful Ettrick, we leave the "Shepherd" to his unbroken slumber.

The last Scottish grave we visit is to be found amid the old abbey ruins of

DRYBURGH,

whose ivied walls are stored with poetic associations. Here is the burial-place of Walter Scott. That grave alone is sufficient to invest the spot with an abiding interest, whilst scattered around are innumerable memories of the high priest of literature. With these ruins was Scott charmed in his earliest infancy; in maturer years he once more communed with the old walls, with each surrounding crag and wimpling burn; whilst his latest hour was soothed by the murmur of the river which glides so gently by. From the banks of that favourite stream, the clear, rippling Tweed, it is but a short walk; and not far distant is Abbotsford, the noble home reared by the wizard, in the noontide of his fame, into a castle—" a romance in stone and lime." Dryburgh was originally a house of

Tomb of Sir Walter Scott, Dryburgh Abbey.

Premonstratensian canons, and was founded in the reign of David I., the contemporary of our first Henry. Some seventy years since it became the property of the Earl of Buchan, having for some time previously belonged to Scott's own family—the sepulchre of his ancestors. The abbey presents some rich memorials of the past, surrounded by pines and other trees of luxuriant thickness. Standing by itself, as if defiant of decay, is a picturesque ruin, with unique windows and pointed arches, which are known as St. Mary's Aisle. Beneath the pavement of this Gothic relic—the stones of which press too heavily upon a heart once so warm and genial—lies the minstrel, with his harp unstrung. His wife, who long shared the happiness which so suddenly fleeted from him, for six years slept alone in this cold retreat. He is, however, once more by her side, enjoying the slumber that knows no waking. Beautiful Dryburgh! thou wilt long survive thy companions in decay; for Time, who has scattered them unsparingly around, has clothed thee in a mantle which seems perpetual. The Destroyer loves thee,—

> "He, gentlest among the thralls
> Of Destiny, upon these wounds hath laid
> His lenient touches."

Among the arches of this picturesque fragment creep the ivy and the harebell, green and fresh, above the cold flagstones imprisoned within the iron work, which admits not the flowerets that should decorate a poet's tomb.

Here we may remark that above the first grave we visited in search of the "Relics of Genius"—that of old Chaucer in the Abbey of Westminster—are seen the lofty column and the fretted roof, lit with gorgeous tints from stained windows. Here, in our closing visit, at the Abbey of Dryburgh, we have still greater magnificence, and that in which the sleeper beneath us most delighted: there is above his tomb a beauteous and lofty arch, whilst around him are the scenes which in life his spirit loved. By those scenes he sat and counted out the treasures of antiquity, first unfolded to him in his infancy, when "lame Wattie" was located at Sandy Knowe. Here he summoned up many of those visions upon which the world delighted to look—creations which he clothed with such rich and varied colours; and here, finally, rests the wizard, the spell dissolved, the wand broken.

Silent now is the Abbey of Dryburgh, save when the wind comes sighing through the old ruins, from whence the sound of human voices once issued. The bells ring no more, neither do the white monks sing. Though cold and desolate be these aisles, this is a hallowed spot, in which poetic fancies mingle with the beauties of nature and art, whilst "the blue sky bends over all." Dryburgh, then, is a shrine consecrated to genius—a fitting grave for

SIR WALTER SCOTT.

The gifted writer here entombed was born in Edinburgh on the 15th of August, 1771; and, according to the account given by his nurse, he was "as fine sonsy a bairn as ever a woman held in her arms." When twenty-two months old, he was seized with a lameness which affected him throughout his life. To benefit his health he was placed with his paternal grandfather, whose residence was in a romantic spot, looking over the course of the Tweed; and thus almost before he could walk, as Washington Irving remarks, "he was made familiar with the scenes of his future stories; they were seen as through a magic medium, and took that tinge of romance which they ever after retained in his imagination." At the High School of his native city he was considered a very backward boy; but before he had reached his fifteenth year he had paid court to the Muses, though it was ten years later before he produced verses worthy of his name. He studied the law, and in 1792 was called to the Scottish bar. In 1796 he published some German translations, which created but little interest. Not discouraged, however, he still proceeded, and some ballads gained him the attention of many eminent persons. Appointed Sheriff of Selkirk, and subsequently made one of the Clerks of Sessions, Scott finally relinquished the law, for which he had entertained but little regard, and his remaining life was devoted to literature.

Selkirk has perpetuated the fact of his shrievalty in a tablet bearing the following inscription :—

"Erected in August, 1839,
In Proud and Affectionate Remembrance
OF
Sir Walter Scott, Baronet,
Sheriff of this County
From 1800 to 1832.
By Yarrow's stream still let me stray,
Though none should guide my feeble way;
Still feel the breeze down Ettrick break,
Although it chill my wither'd cheek."

One of the happiest periods of Scott's life was during his residence at Ashestiel, on the Tweed, where he established himself on account of his duties as sheriff. In the enjoyment of full vigour of body and mind, his household enlivened by happy children, he enjoyed far greater pleasure than when reputation had brought dignities and honours. Wandering by the banks of the beautiful river with his favourite dog, he would sit beneath an aged tree, and there were meditated some of the finest verses of " Marmion." This poem was published in 1808, prior to which had appeared the " Minstrelsy of the Scottish Border" (1802), and the " Lay of the Last Minstrel " (1805). The " Lady of the Lake " followed in 1810 ; but the industry and versatility of the writer prevent us from giving even the titles of his works, so rapidly did he fling them before the public. His astonishing mental power is evidenced in the fact that more than one hundred and thirty volumes were issued by him from the press ! It was in 1814 that " Waverley," the first of his celebrated fictions, was published. This work had been commenced nine years previously, but was thrown aside in consequence of the faint approval of those to whom it had been submitted. Its great success, however, when the work was published, induced its author to abandon poetry, and to labour with avidity in his new walk. " Guy Mannering " first charmed its readers in 1815 ; " The Antiquary " and the first series of " Tales of a Grandfather " followed in 1816, and were succeeded, in the two following years, by " Harold the Dauntless " and " Rob Roy." It need scarcely be remarked that the authorship of these works was for years a mystery, and the secret of the " Great Unknown " was confided to but few. It was at length unfolded to the many at the celebration of the Edinburgh Theatrical Fund, February

23rd, 1827. Sir Walter Scott—he had been created a baronet seven years previously—in returning thanks for the respect shown him in drinking his health upon that occasion, observed :—

"It has previously been communicated to about twenty people, and the secret has been remarkably well kept. I have now to say, however, that the merit of those works, if they have any, and their faults, are entirely imputable to myself. I mean, when I say that I am the author, that I am the total and undivided author. I have thus far unbosomed myself, and I know it will be reported to the world. The wand is now broken, and the rod buried."

Scott derived many of the traditionary stories and anecdotes wrought up in his novels from Mrs. Murray Keith, a venerable Scotch lady, who one day taxed him with the authorship in question, which, as usual, was stoutly denied. "What!" exclaimed the old lady, "d'ye think I dinna ken my ain groats among other folks' kail?"

Prior, however to the mask being thrown aside by Scott, shadows had surrounded his prospects. During the commercial excitement of 1825 the discovery was made that the popular author had been for some years in partnership with his printer and early schoolfellow, James Ballantyne, and various circumstances combined placed the firm in the list of bankrupts. The sympathy of the public was awakened on behalf of Scott, and pecuniary assistance was tendered; but with a nobleness of purpose he preferred liquidating his liabilities by his pen. "God grant me health and strength," said he, "and I will pay every man his due." He had now reached the age of fifty-five, and, assigning to trustees the whole of his property, he quitted

Abbotsford — the hall he had himself created — and sat down in a humble lodging in Edinburgh, with a debt before him of £117,000! The pen was now at work, and from its magic point flowed "Woodstock," the first volume of which was written between the third and fifteenth days after the Bankruptcy. The "Life of Napoleon Bonaparte," "Tales of a Grandfather," &c., followed. Before the Christmas of 1830 the startling sum just named was reduced to £54,000, and this was ultimately paid by the labour of Scott's brain; but before the receipt was given the life of the noble-hearted writer had been sacrificed.

Such unexampled efforts materially impaired Scott's health, and a change of climate was recommended. Quitting London in October, 1831, he visited Malta, Naples, Rome, and Venice. Coming down the Rhine he was attacked with apoplexy and paralysis, and with difficulty reached London and Abbotsford. Seated in his chair, he visited every spot of his grounds, so endeared to him by associations. He then insisted on being placed at the desk; but the magic pen had lost its charm — the spell of the wizard was broken. A few days prior to his death he desired to be drawn in his wheeled chair to the library window looking over the Tweed, which he delighted once more to gaze upon. "Here," says Mr. Lockhart, "he expressed a wish that I should read to him, and when I asked from what book, he said, 'Need you ask? There is but one.'" On the 21st of September, 1832, the mighty spirit was gone!

> "Then was the lofty column broke,
> The beacon light was sunk in smoke;
> The trumpet's silvery sound was still,
> The warder silent on the hill."

At his death it was said, in eloquent lamentation, "The gap which he leaves in the world is the token of the space he filled in the homage of his times." Thus died Sir Walter Scott, in the sixty-second year of his age. As remarked by Johnson of Goldsmith, he left no species of writing untouched or unadorned by his pen. There was a genial magnanimity in his character, a kind simplicity in his manners, which exaltation or reverses never disturbed. He possessed a heart open to every one, and passed from those whom he had delighted and instructed with bright aspirations for the future. His honoured remains, by his own desire, were consigned to Dryburgh Abbey. Mr. Lockhart, his son-in-law and biographer, and who now sleeps by the side of his gifted relative, says:—

"The courtyard and all the precincts of Abbotsford were crowded with uncovered spectators as the procession was arranged; and, as it advanced through Dornick, and Melrose, and the adjacent villages, the whole population appeared at their doors in like manner, almost all in black. The train of carriages extended, I understand, over more than a mile; the yeomanry followed in great numbers on horseback, and it was late in the day ere we reached Dryburgh. Some accident, it was observed, had caused the hearse to halt for several minutes on the summit of the hill at Bemerside, exactly where a prospect of remarkable richness opens, and where Sir Walter had always been accustomed to rein up his horse. The day was dark and lowering, and the wind high. The wide inclosure at the Abbey of Dryburgh was thronged with old and young, and when the coffin was taken from the hearse, and again laid on the shoulders of the afflicted serving-men, one deep sob burst from a thousand lips. Mr. Archdeacon Williams read the Burial Service of the Church of England ; and thus, about half-past five o'clock in the evening of Wednesday, the 26th of September, 1832, the remains of Sir Walter Scott were laid by the side of his wife, in the sepulchre of his ancestors, 'in sure and certain hope of the resurrection to eternal life.' "

A beautifully embellished memorial to Scott, in the style of the best period of Gothic architecture, has been erected in Edinburgh ; yet, finely massive though the structure be, in picturesqueness and characteristic solemnity it must yield to the memorial at Dryburgh.

The poet's remains, we have said, rest in St. Mary's Aisle, which is by far the most beautiful part of the abbey. Nature has been most profuse in her decorations of the Gothic walls which form the minstrel's grave, and are almost completely overgrown with foliage, while a number of fine trees have sprung up among the ruins.

" Call it not vain : they do not err
　Who say that, when the poet dies,
Mute Nature mourns her worshipper,
　And celebrates his obsequies ;
Who say tall cliff and cavern lone
For the departed bard make moan;
That mountains weep in crystal rill ;
That flowers in tears of balm distil ;
Through his loved groves that breezes sigh,
And oaks in deeper groans reply ;
And rivers teach their rushing wave
To murmur dirges round his grave."

Lay of the Last Minstrel.

ADDENDA.

ST. JAMES'S CHAPEL, HAMPSTEAD ROAD.

In the burial-ground of this Chapel of Ease to St. James's, Westminster, lie two painters of eminence in opposite walks of art. In the middle of the small square plot, as you enter the gates from the Hampstead Road, on the left hand, is the grave of

GEORGE MORLAND,

whose pictures of coast scenery and animal life are familiar to every one. He was the son of a respectable crayon-painter, was born in 1764, and he received his first instructions in painting from his father, whom he very soon surpassed. When a youth he was introduced to Sir Joshua Reynolds, and obtained permission to copy some of his works. Morland was soon noticed as an artist of no common promise, but he began early to indulge in foppishness of dress, and love of drinking in low company. He was, nevertheless, diligent. He first painted landscapes and coast scenery and conversation pieces; his favourite subjects, however, were domestic animals, horses, dogs, pigs, &c., which he executed in a masterly manner. His masterpiece is thought to be the interior of a stable, with horses, draymen, &c., which he exhibited at the Royal Academy in 1791. He had studied little; indeed, he is stated to have drawn at the Academy only three nights. He afterwards succeeded best in those animals that require least correctness of drawing, such as pigs, guinea-pigs, sheep, asses, &c. In these he is often extremely happy, for no artist ever painted such subjects with greater feeling. He avoided the delicate proportions of the horse by selecting such animals as were old, rough, and clumsy. A white horse was his favourite object, but he succeeded still better in the pig: his touch is well adapted to the representation of its bristly hide, and he seldom fails faithfully to depict the gluttonous and lazy character of the animal. The innocence of the sheep he also portrays very successfully.

In genius Morland has been considered equal to Gainsborough, but the latter best cultivated his talents. In each artist a great sameness of colouring and chiaroscuro is observable, and both are incorrect in drawing and loose in execution. Gainsborough displays refined feeling and an elegant mind in his representations of rustic innocence; while the taste of Morland was of a lower kind, though he delineated the characters he selected with equal success. Morland, with a correct eye for effect, observed and executed with equal rapidity. He is said to have produced in six years the pictures that have established his reputation. His later works, through his unceasing dissipation, fell to vapid imitations of his former excellence, and were poor, meagre, and monotonous; and " these feeble glimmerings of expiring genius show, according to their dates, a regular decay." It is commonly said that he painted upwards of four thousand pictures, but it should be stated that he allowed his companions and picture-dealers to place his name or initials upon worthless productions; and no modern artist's pictures have been so surreptitiously multiplied as those of George Morland. Fine pictures by him are still in request, and obtain larger prices than during his lifetime.

Morland's early days were passed at Kensall Green, on the road to Harrow, where his constant associate was Ward, the painter, whose example of moral steadiness was exhibited to him in vain. Here he married the sister of Ward, who, to make the family union stronger, married Morland's sister. The two painters and their wives then removed to Marylebone, where Morland got rid of his evil companions, and grew sober. But discord arose between the painters' wives, the couples separated, Morland returned to his old habits, and the postboy, the pawnbroker, and the pugilist were summoned again to his side, no more to be separated. "His pictures," says Cunningham, "were mostly produced under the influence of intoxication, and the strong stimulant of immediate payment; they were painted in the terror of want, and in the presence of the sordid purchaser, who risked five guineas in a venture for twenty."

The annals of genius record not a more deplorable story than Morland's. He died at the early age of forty, and was buried in St. James's Chapel ground. His wife, from whom he had been separated for some time, survived him but a few days, and lies interred by his side.

William Collins, R.A., the painter, then a young man, and unknown, attended Morland's funeral. "When all the attendants were gone away, he put his stick into the wet earth as far as it would go, carried it carefully home, and varnished it."—(*Collins's Life, by his Son.*)

The second artist interred here is

JOHN HOPPNER, R.A.,

the celebrated portrait-painter. He was born in London in 1759, and, when young, was one of the choristers in the Chapel Royal, St. James's. He studied afterwards at the Royal Academy; and, founding his style upon a careful study of the works of Sir Joshua Reynolds, Hoppner rose so rapidly in fame that he soon distanced Opie and Owen, and for eighteen years Lawrence was his only rival. Lawrence was patronised by the king, while the Prince of Wales and his party supported Hoppner. He, however, most delighted in painting landscape, in which he displayed a knowledge and comprehension which would do honour to Gainsborough; while, in portrait, Hoppner was his superior. The distinguishing character of his style is easy and unaffected elegance; his colouring is natural, chaste, and powerful, and his tones are mellow and deep; his pencilling is rich and full, and his carnations are fresh and transparent. He is more successful in his portraits of women than in his male sitters; and he is peculiarly fortunate in infantine character, and the playful grace of children.

Hoppner died of dropsy in 1810, having, in the previous year, been elected a member of the Royal Academy, to which he then presented his portrait.

ST. JAMES'S CHURCH, PICCADILLY.

In our notices of the distinguished persons interred in this church (see page 130), we omitted to record that under the altar is buried

GEORGE HENRY HARLOWE,

the historical painter. He was born in London in 1787, and studied first under De Cort, the landscape painter, and next under Drummond. He was then, by the recommendation of the beautiful Duchess of Devonshire, placed under the care of Lawrence, to whom was to be paid one hundred guineas as a pupil, with leave to copy Lawrence's pictures, but without receiving instruction of any kind. Nevertheless, Lawrence employed Harlowe to forward his portraits, and he entered largely into the style and character of his master's performances. He soon quarrelled with Lawrence,* and, as a consequence, when Harlowe offered himself as a candidate as an Associate in the Royal Academy, he was rejected, Fuseli being the only member who voted in his favour. Harlowe commenced with painting history, but was more successful in portraits, and soon obtained many sitters. He then painted "Hubert and Prince Arthur," which proving very attractive, he attempted to blend the two styles, historical and portrait, in one subject, and painted "The Trial of Queen Katherine," or, more

* About this time Harlowe, on a visit to Epsom, painted for the landlord of the Queen's Head public-house there a signboard in a dashing *caricatura* style, and at one corner he placed " *T. Lawrence pinxit.*"

properly, "The Kemble Family," each character being a portrait. Its popularity was very great, and the fine print which was engraved from it by Clint has had an extensive sale both in England and on the Continent.

In 1818 Harlowe went to Italy, and there astonished the Italian artists by the rapidity with which he copied the "Transfiguration" of Raphael in eighteen days, when Canova complimented him by saying that "it rather seemed the work of eighteen years." He was introduced to the pope by Canova, and was elected a member of the Academy of St. Luke, to which he gave his picture of "The Presentation of the Cardinal's Hat to Wolsey in Westminster Hall."

Harlowe returned to London in 1819, and shortly after died of a severe disease, in his thirty-second year, at No. 33, Dean-street, Soho.

ST. JOHN'S WOOD CHAPEL, MARYLEBONE.

This chapel, erected in 1814, is remarkable for its great number of monumental tablets, some of which are fine specimens of sculpture, and are by Chantrey, Behnes, Wyatt, Hardenburg, and Blore. In the vault beneath the chapel are deposited the remains of the wife of Benjamin West, P.R.A., who promised, a short time before his death, to paint an altar-piece, for presentation to the chapel, but died before he could carry this kind intention into effect.

The adjoining burial-ground was one of the first in the metropolis planted with evergreens and flowers, and here rest a player and a painter of note. The first is

DANIEL TERRY,

a comedian of sterling merit, and the friend of Sir Walter Scott, whom he greatly assisted in the fitting-up of Abbotsford. Terry was born at Bath in 1780, and bred to the profession of an architect under Samuel Wyatt. He, however, relinquished this study, and adopted the stage: after performing in the provinces, in 1809 he appeared at Edinburgh, and while there secured the friendship of Walter Scott. In 1812 Terry first appeared in London as Lord Ogilby, in the *Clandestine Marriage*, with great success, at the Haymarket Theatre, and continued to perform at the patent houses until 1825, when, in conjunction with Mr. Yates, he purchased the Adelphi Theatre, from which, however, he soon withdrew to the Continent, in consequence of his embarrassments. He returned to England in 1828, but with broken health and spirits, to re-appear at Drury Lane. He played but one night: shortly after his whole frame was struck with paralysis, and in four days he died, in his forty-seventh year. He was a very able actor in comedy: his style of playing old gentlemen and testy bachelors was very original. He was also a man of classical attainments, and he adapted for the stage—or, as Scott termed it, *terrified*—two of Sir Walter's novels. Terry was twice married, his second wife being the daughter of Alexander Nasmyth, the celebrated painter, and herself a landscape-painter of merit.

In the chapel is a mural tablet to the memory of

JOHN JACKSON, R.A.,

whose remains rest here. He was born at Lastingham, in

Yorkshire, in 1778. From his childhood he delighted in drawing, and at the age of nineteen began to paint portraits at York, patronised by Lord Mulgrave and the Earl of Carlisle. At Castle Howard he copied, with much success, Caracci's picture of the "Three Marys." Under the auspices of Sir George Beaumont, Jackson came to London, and in 1805 became a student at the Royal Academy. In 1807 he established himself as a portrait-painter. In 1818 he was elected R.A. Next year, accompanied by Chantrey, Jackson visited Italy, and was there elected a member of the Academy of St. Luke, and Canova sat to him for his portrait. His style of painting is masculine, true without flattery; his colouring is clear and splendid, and he resembles Reynolds more than any artist since his day. He presented to the church at Lastingham, the place of his birth, a copy, made by him, of the famous "Correggio," in the possession of the Duke of Wellington. Jackson died at his house in St. John's Wood, June 1st, 1831.

Jackson was, in all his works, extraordinarily rapid and sure. A story is related that he commenced and finished, in a single summer's day, as a wager, the portraits of five gentlemen. He received twenty-five guineas for each of them—one hundred and twenty-five guineas in one day: probably no painter ever earned as much by his own labour before. The story is told by Passavant.

Jackson's best works are the portraits of Lady Dover, of Flaxman, and of himself, and the portrait already mentioned of Canova. He painted in all the portraits of thirteen of his fellow Academicians; but that of Flaxman is, in all respects, the best.

KENSALL GREEN CEMETERY.

In the year 1856 were gathered to the tomb two of the most distinguished ornaments of the stage in our time— John Braham and Madame Vestris, who are interred in the cemetery at Kensall Green.

JOHN BRAHAM

was born in London, and when nine or ten years old appeared as a singer at the Royalty Theatre, near Tower Hill. His first teacher was Leoni, the eminent tenor singer; he next became the pupil of Ramuzzini, from whom Braham obtained a pure Italian style. After singing at the Bath concerts, he was engaged at the Italian Opera in 1796, and in the same year at the Oratorios, when he astonished the public by the power and beauty with which, at that early age, he sang the music of Handel. Braham next went to Italy, and remained there several years, singing with great *éclat* at the principal theatres, frequently with Mrs. Billington. In 1801 Braham appeared at Covent Garden Theatre, and thus began his long and splendid career as an English dramatic singer, in the operas of Arne and other old composers, and in the modern pieces of Storace and Braham's own composition; of the latter, *The Cabinet* being popular season after season. Braham's career continued with undiminished lustre for nearly thirty years as the English singer of the age, and the greatest oratorio-singer that the world had ever seen. As a singer of Handel he has no successor.

Braham was prosperous until late in life, when he built

the St. James's Theatre, and purchased the Colosseum, by which speculations he lost a fortune. He then went to America, where he remained several years. After his return he sang at concerts until his failing powers compelled him to retire; but his latter years were rendered easy and comfortable by the filial affection of his children. He continued to enjoy excellent health, through moderation, a cheerful temper, and active habits, until, after a few days' illness, he died, February 17th, 1856, in his eighty-second year. To the last he enjoyed the pleasures of his art, and retained his kindly nature; and he left troops of friends to cherish his memory.

On the 8th of August, in the same year, died

MADAME VESTRIS.

This accomplished actress and singer was born in Dean-street, Soho, London, on the 2nd of March, 1796. She was the grand-daughter of Bartolozzi, the admirable engraver. In 1813 Miss Bartolozzi was married to the celebrated Vestris: he died in 1823, and fifteen years later Madame Vestris married Mr. Charles Mathews.

Madame Vestris appeared at the Italian Opera House on July 20th, 1815, after which she visited Paris, and sang at the Opera, and played at other theatres in that capital.

She first appeared on the London stage as Lilla, in the *Siege of Belgrade*, at Drury Lane Theatre, in 1819, where she continued to perform several seasons. Her career of management commenced at the Olympic Theatre. She next visited America; and, soon after her return, engaged Covent Garden Theatre, the latter with unprosperous results. Her next scene of management was the Lyceum Theatre, where she continued until 1854, when she quitted the stage through an illness which terminated her life.

Madame Vestris was an admirable actress and a charming singer. Her voice was a *mezzo-soprano* of more than usual compass, and her style was full of expression and simplicity. In her several managements she effected more to reform the conventionalities of the stage than either of her predecessors; and her artistic judgment, her taste in costume, and her extensive acquaintance with the accessories of her art, enabled her to raise the realities of the drama to a high standard, for which she will ever be gratefully remembered by her profession and the public.

MADAME SOYER.

At the entrance to the Kensall Green Cemetery is the colossal tomb of Madame Soyer, who was a Miss Jones, the adopted daughter of M. Simoneau, a Belgian artist of some reputation. Madame Soyer was herself a painter, and produced some admirable works, several of which are at Stafford House. Her portraits are faithful as to likeness, and surprisingly vigorous as to execution.

The monument is a pedestal, with an heroic figure of Faith bearing a cross, the whole twenty feet in height. On the pedestal are two cherubim, one holding a crown over the head of a life-size medallic portrait of Madame Soyer, sculptured in marble; beneath are suspended the implements of painting, with laurels. At the back of the pedestal is the palette of the artist, in a glass case; and by her side, in the autumn of 1858, were laid the remains of her husband, Alexis Soyer, the famous *cuisinier*, by whom the above monument was designed.

SOUTHWICK, NEAR BRIGHTON.

Should the visitor to this stately succession of squares, terraces, and crescents become tired of its splendour, and, in quest of rural quiet, wend his way westward of Brighton, the view soon opens into the interior of the country, and commands the ruins of Aldrington Church; further inland the pleasant village of Portslade, with its grey church on a hill, embosomed in foliage; and on the right of the railway, still further inland, the neat village of Southwick, finely situated, and beautifully interspersed with trees. It has an ancient church, with a three-storied tower with Saxon windows and early pointed arches, surmounted by a low spire. The walls of the nave and chancel are also Saxon, the rest of the edifice being of later date. At its north-east angle, in the churchyard, is the grave marked by a stone with a circular tablet, of especial interest to the reader; for here lies one of the most eminent tragedians of our time,—

CHARLES MAYNE YOUNG.

Mr. Young was the son of a surgeon of Fenchurch-street, where he was born in 1777. He was educated at Merchant Taylors' School and at Eton, and studied medicine under a Danish physician in Copenhagen. Preferring the stage, he made his *début* at the theatre in Tottenham-street, and in 1798 he appeared at the Liverpool Theatre as Douglas. Hence he proceeded to Manchester and Glasgow. In 1807 he appeared at the Haymarket Theatre as

Hamlet with great success. In 1810 he joined the Covent Garden company as second to John Kemble, and as chief during his absence. Mr. Young had formed his style on that of Kemble, and acquired a high position in his favourite school. His impersonations of Hamlet, Daran, Octavian, Cassius, Macbeth, and Sir Pertinax Macsycophant, were masterpieces of his art. He possessed a sound judgment and an exquisitely musical voice, which were the elements of his success. He retired from the stage as Hamlet, at Covent Garden Theatre, in 1832, with a handsome competence. He died on June 29th, 1856, in his eightieth year, at Brighton, where he had resided for many years. His urbanity and gentlemanly taste endeared him to a large circle of the best society. He was much attached to hunting, which sport he enjoyed till within a short period of his decease.

ST. LEONARD'S-ON-SEA.

Our next visit is to the grave of a player, whose chequered career adds to the vicissitudes which appear generally to have attended "marriages from the stage."

In the above delightful extension of Hastings, upon one of the most picturesque portions of the Sussex coast, the visitor will find in the churchyard the resting-place of Lady Boothby, who, as

MRS. NISBETT,

but a few years since, was a brilliant actress of some of the best comic characters in our later drama. This lady was the daughter of Frederick Hayes Macnamara, who held a commission in the 57th Regiment during the

Peninsular War. Her histrionic tastes were early developed, and, under the name of Louisa Mordaunt, she flourished as a juvenile theatrical wonder. She grew into a handsome woman and agreeable actress, and first appeared at Drury Lane Theatre as the Widow Cheerly, in 1829, with success; and maintained a good position at the metropolitan theatres until 1831, when she quitted the stage for a time to become the wife of Captain Nisbett, of the 1st Life Guards, of Brettenham Hall, Norfolk. The marriage was one of unbroken happiness, but for seven short months, when Mrs. Nisbett was widowed by an accident in which her husband was killed. Left without fortune, she had no alternative but to return to the stage, which she did in October, 1832, when she re-appeared at Drury Lane. Her greatest dramatic success was achieved at the Haymarket Theatre, as Constance, in Sheridan Knowles's play of the *Love Chase*, which was performed for nearly one hundred successive nights. Another of her comedy triumphs was Lady Gay Spanker, in *London Assurance;* and in neither of these characters has she been approached by any successor. She retained her hold as a public favourite until she again retired from the stage to become wedded to Sir William Boothby. This marriage did not prove so congenial as was her former union. Sir William died in about two years, leaving his widow but scantily provided for. Again she returned to the stage, but the charm of her acting was gone; her joyous high spirits and hearty laugh rang less clear, her brilliant eyes had lost some of their lustre, and her greatest admirers are willing to forget her latest performances. She then retired to St. Leonard's, where she died on

January 15th, 1858, after a short illness, brought on by anxiety and domestic affliction, having lost within eighteen months her brother, her mother, and her sister. Mrs. Nisbett was a genial and kind-hearted woman; and, while the "heart-easing mirth" which she so largely contributed to the public presents a painful contrast with the sorrows and vicissitudes of her private life, she will live affectionately in the grateful memory of playgoers. Her remains rest in St. Leonard's churchyard by the side of her brother, Mr. Macnamara.

ALL SAINTS' CHURCH, CAMBRIDGE.

As the reflective visitor strolls through "Granta's bowers," and admires the magnificence of the buildings of St. John's College, he can scarcely fail to remember the brief span of the life of its amiable and gifted sizar,—

HENRY KIRKE WHITE,

whose ardour in the pursuit of knowledge brought him, in his twenty-second year, to a resting-place in the church of All Saints.

Henry Kirke White was born at Nottingham in 1785, where his father followed the business of a butcher. He was sent to school at three years of age, and early showed a passion for reading. When seven years old he attempted composition in a prose tale. At eleven, in addition to reading and writing, he outstripped his schoolfellows in arithmetic and French; and at the age of thirteen he composed a short poem. He had hitherto assisted his father in his business, but, disliking this occupation, at the age of fourteen he was apprenticed to a stocking-weaver. Still, to use his own words, he "wanted something to occupy his brain," and his mother, moved by his wretchedness at the loom, prevailed upon his father to place him in an attorney's office at Nottingham, where he applied his leisure in studying the Greek and Latin languages, Italian, Spanish, and Portuguese; chemistry, electricity, and astronomy; and drawing, music, and practical mechanics. In his fifteenth year he communicated to a periodical work a translation from Horace, for which he received a silver medal. In 1803 he published a volume of verses, which was harshly treated by the reviewers, but which Mr. Southey considered "to discover strong marks of genius."

A great change had already been wrought in Henry Kirke White's opinions, and his whole intellectual being, by his conversion from his indifference to religion and a tendency towards infidelity, to a deep and passionate conviction of the truth of Christianity. He now bent his whole soul to follow a young friend, under similar influences, to Cambridge, and get himself educated for the church. After much discouragement the Rev. Mr. Simeon, of King's College, procured for White a sizarship at St. John's, with additional pecuniary assistance; but, says Mr. Southey, "the seeds of death were in him, and the place which he had so long looked on with hope served, unhappily, as a hothouse to ripen them." He studied severely for a scholarship, but through ill health could not come forward. He then passed the general college examination, and was declared the first man of his year. At the end of the term he was again pronounced first man. The college now offered him a private tutor in mathematics during the long vacation; but relaxation, not stimulus, was what was wanted. He went to London to recruit his shattered nerves and spirits, but he got no better. He returned to the University worn out in body and mind, and died, after an attack of delirium, on Sunday, October 19th, 1806, when he had just passed the middle of his twenty-second year. Mr. Southey continued his regard for White after his untimely death, by writing a sketch of his career, and editing his " Remains," which passed through several editions.

A tablet to White's memory, with a medallion by Chantrey, was placed in the west end of All Saints' Church by a young American gentleman, Mr. Francis Boot, of Boston. It bears the following inscription by Professor Smythe:—

> " Warm with fond hope and learning's sacred flame,
> To Granta's bowers the youthful poet came.
> Unconquer'd powers the immortal mind display'd,
> But, worn with anxious thought, the frame decay'd.
> Pale o'er his lamp, and in his cell retired,
> The martyr student faded and expired.
> O genius, taste, and piety sincere,
> Too early lost 'midst studies too severe!
> Foremost to mourn was generous Southey seen—
> He told the tale, and show'd what White had been;
> Nor told in vain. Far o'er the Atlantic wave
> A wanderer came, and sought the poet's grave.
> On yon low stone he saw his lonely name,
> And raised this fond memorial to his fame."

Henry Kirke White's verse is fluent and correct, plaintive and reflective, and rich in fancy and description; and he affords a fine example of youthful ardour devoted to the purest and noblest objects.

THE CONCLUSION AND THE FAREWELL.

Here, courteous Reader, our pilgrimage to the shrines of genius must end. In our visits to these last homes of many whom the world has variously regarded in life and death, how chequered have been the reflections which these visits have called up! We have lingered together by many a grave over which tears have fallen, but not despairingly. We would not, if we could, arouse from their slumber those we have found sleeping : they have but retired into another chamber. We are like those who have overslept the hour—when we rejoin our friends " there is only the more joyance and congratulation." We have been impressed by the solemn stillness of these resting-places, and have in fancy seen the shades of the departed hovering over and around them. First came the Poets—"the men of the million, born from out the crowd"—who have been described as torch-bearers, guiding us through the track of life. It is mental power and worthy acts that outlive the fleeting years; and these pupils of wisdom have a claim upon the remembrance of posterity. They battled for human rights, and their inspirations have impressed us with the infinite beauty of Truth and Virtue. By listening to their voices man has been awakened to a sense of his own lofty nature, and humanity has gained new forces in its righteous cause.

The Painter, too, tells us of the beautiful. His

pictured thoughts can elevate the mind, and bid us think kindly of human nature. Paintings have been produced in poverty, and speak to us now of triumph and success—the footprints left upon the sand, which hereafter some struggling artist "seeing may take heart again." Pictures have possessed more than human power: one, we are told, was being painted when the blood of war was flowing in the streets. The soldiers entered the studio, but stayed upon the threshold to gaze upon the ideal art, and finally set a watch that no unholy foot should approach to injure the "created beauty."

The "poor Player" has not been forgotten in our rambles. He needs, more than the Poet and the Painter, to be occasionally brought into remembrance; for how fugitive is the bloom of the histrionic laurel! Harmonious elocution cannot, like poetry, be its own record; and animated graces glimmer faintly only through the memory of a few surviving spectators, who themselves are journeying to where the voice of the children of song is hushed.

The graves we have visited have taught us that pride, and pomp, and power are nothing there—we must look beyond!

"Though fade the laurel leaf by leaf away,
The soul has prescience of a fadeless day;
And God's eternal promise, like a star,
From faded hopes, still points to hopes afar,
Where weary hearts for consolation trust,
And bliss immortal quickens from the dust.
On this Great Hope, the painter, actor, bard,
And all who ever strove for Fame's reward,
Must rest at last—and all that earth have trod
Still need the grace of a FORGIVING GOD."

INDEX OF NAMES AND PLACES.

Adam, the architect, 32
Addison, Joseph, 18
Akenside, Mark, 130
All Saints, Cambridge, 295
Alleyn, Edward, 169
Allhallows Barking, 64
Andrew, St. Undershaft, 64
Andrew's, St., Holborn, 91

Baddely, Robert, 120
Baker, Sir R., 89
Bannister, Charles, 126
Bannister, John, 127
Barnes, Thomas, 159
Barry, James, 82
Barry, Mrs., 41
Barry, Spranger, 41
Bath Abbey Church, 253
Beaconsfield Churchyard, 218
Beaumont, Francis, 8
Behn, Mrs., 38
Betterton, Thomas, 34
Bishop, Sir H. R., 154
Blair, D., 48
Blake, William, 157
Bland, Mrs., 56

Bracegirdle, Mrs., 36
Braham, John, 289
Bride's, St., Fleet-street, 89
Bromham, Wilts, 244
Buchanan, George, 258
Bunhill Fields, 155
Bunyan, John, 156
Burbage, Richard, 138
Burke, Edmund, 220
Burns, Robert, 49, 260
Butler, Samuel, 46, 112
Byron, Lord, 239

Calcott, Sir A., 161
CamdenTownBurial-ground,151
Campbell, Thomas, 29
Canongate, Edinburgh, 259
Catharine Cree, St., 64
Caxton, William, 50
Centlivre, Mrs., 125
Chambers, Sir W., 31
Chapman, George, 133
Chardin, Sir John, 173
Chatterton, Thomas, 93
Chaucer, Geoffrey, 4
Chichester Cathedral, 234

INDEX. 301

Chiswick, 171
Churchill, Charles, 217
Cibber, Mrs., 38
Clement, St., Danes, 104
Clive, Mrs., 188
Coleridge, S. T., 191
Collins, William, 148
Collins, William, 48, 235
Colman, George, the Elder, 143
Colman, George, the Younger, 144
Congreve, William, 32
Cooke, Thomas, 162
Cooper, Samuel, 153
Cowley, Abraham, 12
Cowper, William, 48, 228
Crabbe, George, 48, 249
Crosthwaite Church, Cumberland, 199
Cumberland, Richard, 31
Cunningham, Allan, 160

Daniell, W. R., 161
Davenant, Sir W., 22
Davenport, Mrs., 121
Davidge, G. B., 105
Defoe, Daniel, 156
Denham, Sir John, 15
Deptford, St. Paul's, 215
Dereham, East, 228
Dibdin, Charles, 151
Distant Graves, 108
Donne, Dr., 73
Dover Churchyard, 216
Drayton, Michael, 9
Dryburgh, 272
Dryden, John, 13

Ducrow, Andrew, 161
Dulwich, 169
Dumfries Churchyard, 260
D'Urfey, Tom, 131
Dyer, George, 161

Edmonton Churchyard, 194
Edwin, John, 116
Elliston, R. W., 150
Emery, John, 95
Ettrick, 260

Farquhar, George, 125
Farren, William, 120
Fergusson, Robert, 259
Fitzwilliam, Mrs., 162
Flatman, Thomas, 90
Flaxman, John, 137
Fletcher, John, 61
Foote, Samuel, 42
Fox, John, 66
Fuseli, Henry, 85

Gainsborough, Thomas, 174
Garrick, David, 25
Gay, John, 21
George's, St., Bloomsbury, 149
Gibbons, Grinling, 122
Gifford, William, 31
Giles, St., Cripplegate, 65
Giles, St., in the Fields, 133
Glover, Mrs., 149
Goldsmith, Oliver, 48, 101
Gower, John, 60
Gray, Thomas, 48, 221
Greyfriars, Edinburgh, 257
Grimaldi, Joseph, 151

Gwynne, Nell, 123
Haines, Joe, 119
Hales Owen, 231
Handel, G. F., 31
Harley, J. P., 104
Harlowe, H. G., 285
Haydon, B. R., 147
Henderson, John, 26
Highgate Church, 191
Hogarth, William, 171
Hogg, James, 49, 267
Holbein, the painter, 64
Holland, Charles, 173
Holy Trinity, Brompton, 141
Hood, Thomas, 162
Hoppner, John, 284
Hornsey Churchyard, 190
Hucknall Church, 238
Hull, Thomas, 55

Inchbald, Mrs., 145

Jackson, John, 287
James, St., Hampstead-road, 281
James, St., Pentonville, 151
James, St., Piccadilly, 130, 285
Jerrold, Douglas, 167
John's, St., Waterloo-road, 150
John's, St., Wood Chapel, 286
Johnson, Samuel, 23
Jones, Richard, 132
Jonson, Ben, 10

Kean, Edmund, 180
Keats, John, 49
Kelly, Michael, 121

Kemble, Charles, 163
Kemble, John, 47
Kensall Green Cemetery, 158, 289
Kensington Church, 143
Kent, William, 173
Kew Church, 174
King, Thomas, 120
Kitchiner, Dr., 109
Kneller, Sir G., 48, 187
Kynaston, Edward, 122

Lamb, Charles, 194
Lawrence, Sir T., 85
Lee, Nathaniel, 107
Lely, Sir P., 115
Leonard's, St., on Sea, 293
Leonard's, St., Shoreditch, 138
Liston, John, 163
Loutherbourg, De, 173
Lovelace, Richard, 89
Lowen, John, 105
Luke's, St., Chelsea, 139

Macklin, Charles, 115
Macpherson, James, 17
Margaret's, St., Westminster, 49
Marlowe, Christopher, 215
Martin's, St., in the Fields, 123
Marvell, Andrew, 135
Mary, St. Overie, 57
Mary, St., Paddington, 145
Marylebone Cemetery, 154
Mason, William, 48, 223
Massinger, Philip, 63
May, Thomas, 54
Meyer, Jeremiah, 177.
Miller, Joe, 97

Milton, John, 66
Moore, Thomas, 244
More, Sir Thomas, 139
Morland, George, 281
Mossop, Henry, 141
Mountain, Mrs., 162

Neele, Henry, 92
Newton, Sir Isaac, 47
Nisbett, Mrs., 293
Norwood Cemetery, 165

Ogilby, John, 90
Oldfield, Mrs., 35
Opie, John, 83
Osbaldiston, 165
Otway, Thomas, 105
Oxberry, William, 109

Palmer, Robert, 128
Pancras, St., Old, 152
Parnell, Thomas, 48
Parr, Old, 32
Paul's, St., Cathedral, 69
Paul's, St., Covent Garden, 111
Peter's, St., Pimlico, 132
Pope, Alexander, 48, 184
Pope, Mrs., 44
Portugal-street Burial-ground, 97
Praed, W. M., 161
Prior, Matthew, 19
Purcell, Henry, 47

Quin, James, 255

Rae, Alexander, 121

Raleigh, Sir Walter, 51
Ramsay, Allan, 49, 259
Reeve, John, 141
Reynolds, Sir Joshua, 79
Richardson, Samuel, 90
Richmond Church, 177
Rogers, Samuel, 197
Roscommon, Earl of, 16
Ross, David, 132
Roubiliac, L. F., 129
Rowe, Nicholas, 17
Rydal Mount, 204

Sackville, Earl of Dorset, 89
Scott, Sir Walter, 49, 274
Shadwell, Thomas, 141
Shakspeare, Edmund, 62
Shakspeare, William, 47, 208
Shelley, P. B., 49
Shenstone, William, 231
Sheridan, R. B., 27
Shirley, James, 134
Shuter, Edward, 110
Siddons, Mrs., 47, 145
Skelton, John, 53
Smith, Sydney, 159
Southern, Thomas, 114
Southey, Robert, 48, 200
Southwick, near Brighton, 292
Soyer, Madame, 291
Speed, John, 66
Spenser, Edmund, 7
Stoke Churchyard, 221
Stothard, Thomas, 157
Stow, the chronicler, 64
Stratford-upon-Avon, 207
Suett, Richard, 88

Surrey, Earl of, the poet, 64
Swift, Dean, 48
Sydney, Sir Philip, 72

Talfourd, Sir T. N., 166
Tarlton, Richard, 139
Teddington Church, 189
Temple Church, 99
Terry, Daniel, 287
Thomson, James, 48, 178
Trowbridge Church, 249
Turner, J. M. W., 86
Twickenham Church, 183

Ugo Foscolo, 173

Valpy, Dr., 161
Vandyck, Sir A., 76
Vestris, Madame, 290

Waller, Edmund, 48, 218

Watts, Dr., 47, 155
Webster, John, 92
Welwyn Church, 225
West, Benjamin, 80
Westminster Abbey, 2
White, H. Kirke, 295
Whitehead, Paul, 190
Wilkes, Robert, 119
Woffington, Mrs., 189
Wolcot, John, 117
Wordsworth, W., 48, 205
Wroughton, Richard, 149
Wycherley, William, 114
Wynkyn de Worde, 89

Young, Charles Mayne, 292
Young, Dr., 48, 225

Zoffanij, Johnan, 175

THE END.

www.ingramcontent.com/pod-product-compliance
Lightning Source LLC
Chambersburg PA
CBHW030747230426
43667CB00007B/872